Society and Nature

STUDIES IN SOCIOLOGY

Series Editor: Professor W. M. Williams, University College of Swansea

The aim of this series is to provide essential surveys of key concepts in sociology. Each book reviews the present state of the art, identifies major issues and problems, and examines possible solutions and future avenues of research.

Other titles in the series include:

Friendship: Developing a Sociological Perspective
Graham Allan

Sociology and Development: Theories, Policies and Practices
David Hulme and Mark Turner

Urban Sociology: Society, Locality and Human Nature
Peter Dickens

The Sociology of Labour Markets
Ralph Fevre

Organizations: A Sociological Analysis
Mike Reed

————————————————

By the same author:

Housing States and Localities
(with Simon Duncan, Mark Goodwin and Fred Gray),
Methuen, London, 1985

One Nation? Social Change and the Politics of Locality,
Pluto, London, 1988

Property, Bureaucracy and Culture: The Anatomy of the Middle Classes in Britain
(with Mike Savage, James Barlow and Tony Fielding),
Routledge, London, 1992

Society and Nature
TOWARDS A GREEN
SOCIAL THEORY

PETER DICKENS

TEMPLE UNIVERSITY PRESS
Philadelphia

Temple University Press, Philadelphia 19122

Printed and bound in Great Britain

ISBN 0–87722–968–6 (cloth)
ISBN 0–87722–969–4 (paper)

CIP data available from the Library of Congress

How can you buy or sell the
sky, the warmth of the land?
The idea is strange to us.

If we do not own the freshness
of the air and the sparkle of
the water, how can you buy them?

Every part of this earth is
sacred to my people. Every
shining pine needle, every
sandy shore, every mist in
the dark woods, every clearing
and humming insect is holy in
the memory and experience of
my people. The sap which courses
through the trees carries the
memories of the red man.

The white man's dead forget
the country of their birth
when they go to walk among
the stars. Our dead never forget
this beautiful earth, for
it is the mother of the red man.
We are part of the earth and it
is part of us.

Part of the *Testimony of Chief Sealth* to white
settlers arriving in Duwanish (now Washington
State), 1854 (reproduced from R. Moody (ed.)
(1988), *The Indigenous Voice*, vol.1, Zed Books:
London and New Jersey)

In the government's view, market mechanisms offer the prospect of a more efficient and flexible response to environmental issues, both old and new ... *Privatisation is an important force serving to promote market transparency.*

UK Government (1990), *Our Common Inheritance, Britain's Environmental Strategy*, HMSO: London (Government's emphasis)

CONTENTS

ACKNOWLEDGEMENTS

I am happy to acknowledge assistance from Anna Dickens, Simon Duncan, Tony Giddens, Brian Goodwin, Roger Goodwin, Tim Ingold, Linda Merricks, John Maynard-Smith, Pete Saunders, Andrew Sayer, Marilyn Strathern and Gerry Webster. Ted Benton and John Urry made a number of very helpful comments on the whole manuscript and I am especially grateful to them. Thanks too to the University of Sussex for providing me with a term's paid leave to complete this book. Finally, I must acknowledge the assistance of the Mass Observation volunteers. Their contributions to the Archive resulted in a substantial contribution to this study.

The author and publishers also acknowledge the following: Figure 3.1 from *Motives and Mechanisms* by Harré *et al.*, by courtesy of Methuen; Figure 4.1 from *The Search for Society* by R. Fox, 1989, by courtesy of Rutgers University, New Brunswick, NJ; Figure 6.1 from *Changing the Face of the Earth* by I. Simmons, by courtesy of Basil Blackwell, Oxford. M.O. extracts are reproduced by permission of the Trustees of the Mass Observation Archive and Curtis Brown, London. While every attempt has been made where appropriate to trace the copyright holders of the illustrations used in this book, the author and publishers would be pleased to hear from any interested parties.

INTRODUCTION

A useful if provocative starting-point here is Catton and Dunlap's plea for 'a new ecological paradigm for a post exuberant sociology'.[1] They argued in the early 1980s that sociology developed in an era 'when humans seemed exempt from ecological constraints'. Now, as changing ecological conditions are threatening human societies, the time is right, they argued, to reassess sociological theory as it has come down to us since the nineteenth century. And the disciplinary traditions carved out in the nineteenth century (one for sociology, others for biology and ecology) are not only militating against a solution to ecological problems, they are actually impeding an understanding of their social importance.

What has happened, according to Catton and Dunlap, is that a 'dominant Western worldview' has been well established, one which builds on ancient assumptions that people are superior to other species. This assumption was further reinforced during the creation of the social and natural sciences in the nineteenth century. It was reinforced by one set of disciplines being directly associated with 'man' (the social sciences) and another set with 'nature' (the natural sciences). According to Catton and Dunlap this dominant Western worldview has the following four main features:

1. People are seen as fundamentally distinct from all other creatures on earth. Furthermore, they have dominion over these other species.
2. People are masters of their own destiny. They can choose their goals and learn to do whatever is necessary to achieve them.

3. The world and its resources is vast. This provides unlimited opportunities for humans.
4. The history of humanity is one of progress. For every perceived problem there is a solution. Such progress will never cease.

The basis to Catton and Dunlap's argument is that all these assumptions are 'fundamentally unecological'. But such views are now being challenged by changing experiences and conditions of social and natural life. One of the main challenges is to the foundations of social theory. In particular, these authors argue, sociology is founded on the uniqueness of its subject matter. Durkheim, for example, asserted 'the objective reality of social facts' (norms, associations, institutions) and the irreducibility of such facts to the psychological properties of the individuals involved.

The next step, Catton and Dunlap suggest, should be the construction of a 'New Ecological Paradigm' (NEP). This would rectify the old form of sociology. Human beings would certainly be regarded as having special characteristics but they would be linked to other species with which they are competing for food, space, water and so forth. Again, humans would still be seen as influenced by social or cultural forces and relations but they would also be envisaged as affected by the biophysical environment; pollution, changing climate and so on.

Finally, the 'New Ecological Paradigm' would recognise that certain physical laws cannot be overridden. Especially important here are the First and Second Laws of Thermodynamics. The first states that energy may be transformed from one form (e.g. light) into another (e.g. food) but it can never be created or destroyed. The second states that no process involving energy transformation will occur unless there is a degradation of energy from a concentrated form (such as food or petrol) into a dispersed form (such as heat). The Second Law says that although energy is neither created nor destroyed during transformation some of it is degraded into an unavailable or at least less unavailable form. Energy, in short, cannot be used over and over again without loss of utility.

Catton and Dunlap are also taking issue with many of the more traditional divisions in sociological theory; those between, for example, functionalism and Marxism. They are arguing that 'The

Human Exemptionalist Paradigm' and the 'New Ecological Paradigm' (NEP) cross-cut these more widely discussed divisions. Both these paradigms, they suggest, were founded in old nineteenth-century sociological thinking and both of them need major adaptation as they become grounded within a new NEP paradigm. Unfortunately, however, Catton and Dunlap did not provide a clear picture of what this paradigm might look like. And it is probably true to say that, despite increasing concern with environmental and ecological issues, social theory has still not adequately responded to Catton and Dunlap's challenge.

Chapter 1 of this book largely confirms Catton and Dunlap's conclusions. In doing so it raises an uncomfortable issue for social theory. Can sociology respond to contemporary environmental problems in its present state? As Catton and Dunlap point out, sociology is based on a fundamental division of labour, that between science and social science. The first is broadly for 'nature', the second for 'people'. Sociology cannot therefore adequately respond on the basis of this dualism and dichotomy. It will have to relax its boundaries, as indeed will the sciences: biology, physics and the like. Secondly, the social sciences are themselves quite diverse. Sociologists, Chapter 1 argues, could still afford to become much more open to one another. In particular, critical theory could learn some lessons (including that of being more open to science) from neo-liberals.

Chapter 2 suggests that, rather paradoxically, one of the major reasons why a paradigm of the kind Catton and Dunlap suggest has not been created is that early sociology modelled many of its concepts on biological science. Society has been variously envisaged as a super-organism, or as composed of competing individuals struggling for survival or slowly evolving towards some perfect state. Analogies are not necessarily the problem here. Much, some anthropologists would say all, conceptualisation consists of analogies. These have long been a way in which human beings have made sense of the world and their place in it. But at a certain point they are obstructing our understanding and creating unnecessary problems. In the case of sociology, biological metaphors often resulted in a neglect of the relations between people and nature or the fact that people are themselves subject to biologically inherited forms of behaviour. In the case of neo-liberal theory, on the other hand, the opposite problem persists.

The development of societies is seen as entirely the product of individuals seeking to survive and procreate, and using their environments to this end. Some conceptual framework is needed which is open to contributions from both such understandings.

Chapter 3 outlines a starting-point for a new form of social theory which starts to overcome some of these problems. It is in fact a survey of a type of theory under development by Marx and Engels in the mid-nineteenth century. Early social theory never took these writers very seriously. And indeed Marxian theory now seems to be falling out of fashion once more. All this is a pity since Marx and Engels are arguably the only writers to have developed a science of the kind that is now needed for an adequate understanding of environmental issues. The following are some of its principal themes:

1. People are a species which, like all other living organisms, have needs like any other species and needs which are specific to human beings.
2. Nature is integral to people's bodies. There is therefore no logical way in which nature can be treated as separate from people.
3. Nature is socially constructed. It is always modified by people. And, in the process of changing nature, people change themselves.
4. Under capitalism, nature is privately owned and exploited. People therefore find themselves becoming alienated or estranged from the nature on which they work. They also become alienated from their own species.
5. The institutions and processes created through social relations and social processes can, however, come to have an apparent life or power of their own. They become fetishised or reified as things in their own right. As such, they become means by which people gain a sense of being in the world. They enable people to organise their lives and experience.

Marx and Engels used some of these themes, especially those of alienation and fetishisation, in their later work. But, as regards people's relationships to nature, they did not take their early ideas much further. Using contemporary knowledge in such fields as biology, psychology, and sociology, Marx and Engels' ideas can now be simultaneously criticised and developed. The core argument of this book is that their ideas would be the best basis for the development of Catton and Dunlap's 'New Ecological Paradigm'.

Perhaps most importantly of all, Marx and Engels' dialectical way of thinking and their realist epistemology provide the soundest basis for the construction of such a paradigm. A 'critical realist' approach as developed by writers such as Bhaskar and Sayer argues for the stratification of knowledge.[2] At a general level relatively enduring generative structures are envisaged. These underly the manifest phenomena of everyday life. Entities, such as humans, other organisms and those of inorganic nature have latent powers or capacities. These are seen as the entities' liabilities, or essential ways of acting. It is at this more abstract level that theory makes its greatest claims. But, centrally for the 'critical realism' which underpins this book, these structures and tendencies are not observable in an unmediated form. They emerge and combine in complex ways with contingent relations and tendencies. Indeed, the contingent factors may be such that the underlying mechanisms or ways of acting may not be experienced or observed. Explanation of manifest appearances critically relies, therefore, on *both* abstract laws and theories and on information of a less abstract kind.

A realist philosophy such as that used by Marx and later developed by Bhaskar and others *starts* by assuming the necessary connections between organism and environment. Each is dialectically dependent on the other. An organism is constituted by ways of acting, but these are realised in different ways according to the contexts in which they are operating. And again, if the conditions are not appropriate for such realisation, the organism's powers may even fail to be realised. At the same time, however, active organisms (including of course human beings) should be envisaged as continually transforming their social and environmental 'contexts'. Chapter 3 concludes by arguing that Marx's original framework offers an understanding of people's relations with nature which is richer and more satisfactory than that offered by much contemporary environmental analysis. In particular, his understanding of people's alienation from nature is an improvement on that offered by much current environmental thinking.

Chapter 4 argues that, after a number of uncertain starts and misleading developments of Darwinism, there are now real and exciting signs that biological science is developing concepts which are very much in line with the paradigm first outlined by Marx in the 1840s. In particular, the abolition of a rigid distinction between organism and environment is a feature of this new paradigm; the one being seen as the product of the other. Furthermore, the working methods of what I term 'the new biology' are also in line with the realist approach first adopted by Marx. Nevertheless, there remains work to be done. Much of biological science still, for example, tends to treat 'environment' as a natural phenomenon and not permeated by human social relations.

Chapter 5 addresses the central question of 'culture' and human beings' distinct capacities in this regard. People have long made an analogy between the earth and a mother or supernatural being. This chapter argues, on the basis of the social psychology developed by Harré and others, that such understandings are partly a product of deep underlying mental structures. But at the same time, they are a product of the everyday social relations in which individuals are involved. Social psychology of this kind helps to provide an improved understanding of what Marx saw as the fetishisation or reification of the natural world. This chapter suggests, therefore, that psychology can provide both a distinctive understanding of humans' relationships with nature and a crucial link between the biological and social sciences. Nevertheless, there remains a tremendous amount of work to be done in this still rapidly developing field.

Chapter 6 draws together some of the earlier themes from biology and psychology and combines them with one aspect of contemporary social theory in an attempt to develop a science more sensitive to environmental issues. In particular, it tries to contribute to and learn from Giddens' recent work. First, his discussion of the relationships between human agency, social structure and locality can be further developed in an 'ecological' direction. Second, however, Giddens suggests that there is a further dimension to alienation which Marx and Engels did not discuss and which in the mid-nineteenth century had not developed very far. This is physical or spatial separation between people's everyday lives on the one hand and their sensuous relationships with the rest of nature on the other.

A characteristic feature of contemporary environmentalism (and related matters such as health and food scares) is that people do not directly experience their continually extending connections with nature. The food they eat, for example, is usually created far away from where they consume it. Similarly, they often remain unaware of the waste they are producing. At this point the significance of the psychological dimension becomes important. People, in order to develop *as* people, develop in relation to their natural as well as their social environments. Yet this form of spreading (which parallels the globalisation of the market economy) undermines a close and active relationship to nature. This, Chapter 6 argues, is a key factor underlying environmentalism and health scares. But, as this chapter also argues, there are many and various ways in which people try to reassert natural and species beings in the face of such separation and alienation. At the same time, the increasingly global connections between people and the natural world are opening up prospects for a new consciousness of the complex relations between people and nature as a whole.

Chapter 7 draws on previously unpublished work in Sussex University's Mass Observation Archive to illustrate some of this book's main themes. It suggests that, in general terms, people are using an idea of nature and their relationships with it as a reflection of their own social, economic and political circumstances. More particularly, the Mass Observation material demonstrates the fetishism in which lay people engage in understanding nature and their relationships to it. Thus a personified 'Nature' is often given a life of its own. People feel small in relation to it. A general sense of insecurity, one which is largely derived from experience of the social world, is transferred to feelings about an all-powerful nature. One result is the quasi-religious one of identifying with nature; people, as it were, throwing in their lot with the natural order by engaging in environmental politics.

One of the dangers in a text such as this is that of eclecticism. This is a result of trying not to exclude approaches which may turn out to have something to offer. I hope, however, that some of these problems will be overcome with the aid of Marx's early work. Particularly important is his realist epistemology and the way it has been recently developed by writers such as Sayer and Bhaskar. Its central significance lies in the stratification and ordering of information and theory. Chapter 8 first returns to this epistemology. It also discusses how the arguments of this book relate to recent debates *within* this philosophy of science.

Finally, and quite briefly, Chapter 8 refers to some critiques of the framework and some of the practical implications of the book. It does so by examining the concepts and programme of the 'deep green' or 'deep ecology' movement. In some respects these closely parallel the framework established by Marx and Engels. On the other hand, the implication is that Marx and Engels were too anthropocentric in remaining principally concerned with people and not with the rest of nature. At the same time, however, the deep greens and other environmental movements such as those linked to anarchism are in real danger of adopting a backward-looking and arcadian vision of small-scale community life. The benefits of modernity, including those of technology and mass-communications need to be recognised and developed rather than rejected. At a more theoretical level, Marx's eventual vision was a single science, one which allowed people to see their place in nature. Such an aim need not, however, only benefit the human species. It can be seen as at least a first stage in developing a non-anthropocentric understanding.

Chapter 8 also argues that the deep green ecologists, and arguably environmentalists more generally, severely underestimate the social and political obstacles to overcoming ecological crises and more satisfactory relations between people and nature. The deep greens in particular place enormous faith in changing personal consciousness. But they give nothing like enough emphasis to changing the social structures within which consciousness is created and changed.

NOTES

1. W. Dunlap, R. Catton (1980), 'A new ecological paradigm for post-exuberant sociology', *American Behavioral Scientist* 24, 1: 15–47. See also R. Dunlap (1979), 'Environmental sociology', *Annual Review of Sociology* 5: 243–73; R. Dunlap (1980), 'Paradigmatic change in social science. From human exemptionalism to an ecological paradigm', *American Behavioral Scientist* 24, 1: 5–13; R. Dunlap, W. Catton (1983), 'What environmental sociologists have in common (whether concerned with "built" or "natural" environments)', *Sociological Inquiry* 53, 2/3: 113–35; R. Dunlap (1983), 'Ecologist versus exemptionalist: the Ehrlich–Simon debate', *Social Science Quarterly* 64, March: 200–3.

2. Readers new to contemporary developments in realism will find the brief summary in the following especially useful. R. Bhaskar (ed.) (1991), *A Meeting of Minds*, Socialist Society: London. Whether, however, there is a necessary connection between socialism and realism is a matter of continuing argument amongst those using realist concepts.

To my father and the memory of my mother

1

SCIENCE, SOCIAL SCIENCE, POLITICS AND THE ENVIRONMENT: SOME UNHELPFUL DICHOTOMIES

In a recent book entitled *The Green Case* Steven Yearley argues that social science can make a significant contribution to understanding environmental issues. This, he suggests, is for two main reasons. First, there are 'major social, political and economic aspects to current environmental issues'.[1] Studies of environmental crisis which he and others have carried out clearly show that issues such as threats to the ozone layer or endangered species clearly have a social basis. Thus 'although most environmental problems are problems of the natural world and accordingly demand expertise in the natural sciences', Yearley argues, 'this demand is by no means exclusive'.[2]

The second part of Yearley's argument is that social theory is directly applicable and useful to understanding green issues. Theories of Third World dependence and underdevelopment can be used, for example, to show that dependent countries are under greater structural pressures to attract investment. Their dependency thus leads them to relax their environmental regulations. Similarly, social theory has a good deal to say about which social classes support 'green' issues. Different social classes are usually associated with different types of environmental demands. The 'deep green' movement, for example, often distances itself from the politics of both Left and Right. But, more generally, environmentalism finds particular support from the well-educated middle classes.[3]

Yearley's argument is in many respects a strong one. There can be little doubt that the causes of contemporary ecological and environmental problems are largely associated with social relations, social pressures and political institutions. As such, environmental analysis clearly cannot be left to the scientists alone. On

1

the other hand, this very acknowledgement itself poses a central problem which Yearley does not address.

Clearly, the social and the natural sciences have all made great strides in their own field of specialism and each now has its own well-developed discourse. But the problem is that they are talking past each other. We have a dichotomous understanding, one based on science, the other on social theory. So, while social theory can certainly continue to make major contributions, the danger is that it will do so within its comparatively watertight disciplinary compartments. Much the same could be said of the sciences, such as physics, chemistry and biology.

One way of stating my argument is to refer to Kuhn's famous book *The Structure of Scientific Revolutions*[4] He argued that most scientific work is of a 'normal' variety which proceeds within broadly accepted paradigms and assumptions. Nevertheless, there come times when the accepted modes of analysis become transparently inadequate. They are no longer doing the business. They are not adequately helping us to understand the structure of the world and the problems with which people are concerned. At such times a scientific revolution occurs, one in which the underlying assumptions which have been accepted for so long are overthrown. A different set of assumptions are created and a new paradigm is established.

Kuhn was writing mainly about change within the natural and physical sciences. His insight can nevertheless be extended to cover social theory. But, still more importantly, the Kuhnian idea can be extended to cover the relationships *between* social theory on the one hand and natural and physical science on the other.

I would argue that a new paradigm is now being forced by environmental issues and related matters such as human health, animal welfare and the application of new reproductive technologies to the human species. Such a paradigm rejects the distinctions between, for example, the life sciences, the physical sciences and the social sciences. It nevertheless entails a combination of these apparently alternative ways of viewing the social and natural worlds, within a coherent epistemological framework. The Kuhnian notion implies what Sayer calls 'an illusion of incommensurability'; one underemphasising concepts crossing *between* paradigms and overemphasising incompatibility between paradigms.[5] A degree of eclecticism, but within a 'critical realist' approach to knowledge, is, I am suggesting, the soundest way forward. 'Critical realism', as I outlined in the Introduction of this book and as I shall discuss later in more detail, holds that there are relatively enduring structures in the social and natural world which lie behind observable phenomena. It also focuses on the relations between organisms, including human organisms, and the structures which both constrain and enable their actions.

It should be clear from all this that we are not just talking of new 'interdisciplinary' approaches necessitated by environmental and related issues; interdisciplinarity has been a hallmark of environmental analysis for a long time and hopefully it will continue to be important. We are talking here about compartmentalised divisions of intellectual labour being broken down and fundamentally new kinds of understanding emerging. This would by no means consist of academics and others all being concerned with precisely the same thing. It is unlikely, for example, that social scientists will become instant experts on the molecular organisation of cytoplasms or that biologists will overnight start examining capitalist labour processes converting inorganic nature into commodities. But they would share common working methods and perceptions. They would share common ways of, for example, understanding organisms (including the human organism) and their relationships with natural-cum-social environments. Perhaps most importantly, they would finally break with a philosophical tradition which insists that there is one rigidly defined science for people (social science) and others (the natural and physical sciences) for nature. Such a break is, to say the least, an ambitious enterprise. But it is not wishful thinking. Such thinking was a feature of Marx's early work and, as I hope to show later, there are now real signs of such a break now actually occurring.

Reconsidering the fundamental bases of Western philosophy (one with its origins at least as far back as Judaeo-Christian thinking) is no easy matter. It would also clearly be exceptionally foolish to reject as useless all scientific and social scientific advances during the past two thousand years. One of the most important effects of such a merger, indeed perhaps the most important effect, would be to abandon the distinction between 'man' (more suitably, 'people') and nature. Contemporary environmentalism often suggests that people are doing things *to* nature and that nature (for example the ozone layer) is doing things to us. Such a picture, while initially persuasive, can be profoundly misleading. Dissolving the distinction between science and social science means that we can start to see people and societies as, in certain respects, *part of* nature. Similarly, we see nature as a part of and integral to human beings as well as to other species.

BIOLOGICAL THEORY AND THE ENVIRONMENT

Later in this book, ecological theory and its relationship to social theory will be given extended discussion. But at this stage some of the difficulties associated with the dichotomy between the scientific and social scientific approach to 'man–environment' relations can be made clear to social scientists by looking at how some of the most influential biologists and ecologists are attemping to use their framework for the understanding of human societies.

Ecology is of course concerned with the relationships between organisms and the ecological systems on which they are dependent. As such it ought to be applicable to the ways in which human organisms relate to their environment. Plants, animals and micro-organisms living in an area constitute what ecologists call a 'biological community' – one in which they are intimately connected to one another. The connections are seen as principally revolving around energy for survival and reproduction; ecosystems being constituted by food chains, by organisms dependent on one another and on the physical climate for their survival and reproduction. The ecological model is of course linked to Darwinian theory. Only those animals sufficiently 'fit' to obtain food and to raise their young are seen by the theory as creating future generations. Natural selection operates, as Colinvaux puts it: 'to make all animals into factories for producing fresh animals out of raw materials wrested from the environment'.[6] According to conventional ecological theory, survival takes place through each species finding a 'niche'. A niche is not only or simply a physical place. Every niche is limited in terms of the numbers of individuals it can carry, a fit individual being one which successfully occupies one of the limited number of places within its niche.

How does Darwinian-cum-ecological theory extend to human beings and their relationships with the environment? 'People, like other animals', Colinvaux states, 'have niches in life.'[7] They have managed to construct a huge 'niche' through using steadily increasing amounts of raw material extracted from the environment. This 'niche' has been continuously increased through the use of technology, increasing divisions of labour and (most importantly of all for Colinvaux) aggressive wars between neighbouring nations. But at the heart of every human society are self-inflating bureaucrats who ensure that the resources which actually are gained during such wars are, almost literally, swallowed up by them. As he sees it, the danger now is that ecosystems are being destroyed and, with them, many organisms dependent on these systems. 'Man' as well as many other species, is under threat.

Up to a point, such a transfer of ecological theory to the human world seems innocent enough. But note first the use of the word 'man'. This 'man' has rather little social, economic, political or of course gender content. There is a reference to increasing divisions of labour and avaricious 'bureaucrats', but the analysis is in fact making very little contact with the central concerns of social theory. In particular, there is no extended discussion of the social relations and processes of capitalism, communism or any other kind of social formation. Property relations, for example, deeply influence people's relationship to resources, but these find no mention. Still less is there any consideration of how all these social relations interact with environmental and ecological systems. Conventional ecological and biological theory is organised primarily around individuals, species or, as we will later see, genes. It simply could not cope with social and political complexities and consequently no attempt is made to stretch it this far. People remain just another set of individuals or species struggling for survival, not only with other individuals for resources but with other species.

Thus ecologists are attempting a form of disciplinary imperialism which does not really work. Stretching their theory into the human world leaves most social theorists deeply sceptical. But, as we can now see, the reverse problem holds for many, though not all, social scientists.

SOCIAL THEORY AND THE ENVIRONMENT

For many years social and political scientists gave little attention to the natural environment. They, like many others, did not see the use of natural resources as in any sense problematic. As Catton and Dunlap discuss, the environment was envisaged as simply 'out there', an infinite resource at the disposal of industrialisation and social progress. Such progress was not seen as seriously constrained by any natural limits. Rather, problems confronting societies were envisaged as wholly social. The limits to social progress lay in property, class and legal relations rather than in the environment within which these relations were developing.

It is only recently, and spurred on by self-evident environmental crises, that social theorists have given serious attention to environmental and ecological issues. And, given that social scientists' stock in trade is 'man'-made culture or society, it again comes as no surprise that their analysis of environmental issues has remained almost entirely social, or what scientists might call 'cultural'. So, in contrast with the biological determinism just outlined, the causes of environmental crisis are almost inevitably envisaged as wholly social or cultural.

Society and environment: the view from the Left

For the Left, an overemphasis on ecological relations are treated with some scepticism. Ryle makes the point analogous to that of Yearley quoted earlier:

Green politics cannot adopt a 'purely ecological' approach: relations between people and classes are at stake the moment one begins to talk about structural economic and social change, even if change is originally advocated because of 'ecological' desires and fears.[8]

Thus for critical theory and practice, explanations are couched almost wholly in terms of the activities of institutions such as multinational companies (with their largely unconstrained capacity for switching investments around the world) or with national and transnational governments which seem to be becoming increasingly distanced from people's everyday lives and demands. Environmental issues tend to be seen, within this paradigm, as an integral part of a fundamentally exploitative, unjust and undemocratic form of society. Here, for example, is Redclift writing of environmental crisis as it affects many of the developing nations:

> Natural resources are systematically depleted in the accumulation drive by both private multinational capital and the state. Ecological degradation in the South assumes emergency proportions through the mindless commitment to the economic growth strategy endemic to developed capitalism. The costs of development are expressed not only in terms of class conflict and economic exploitation, but also in the reduction of the natural resource base on which the poor depend for their livelihood.[9]

In this way multinational producers, including 'agribusiness' and the central drive to accumulate, are put forward by this perspective as the chief causal factors in the scenario. They are seen as the prime wreckers of a society's resources as a result of indiscriminate forms of exploitation and production. They are the driving force, powerfully organised producer interests forcing people to become individualistic and pursuing their own personal interests at the expense of other human beings and other species. This perspective, which certainly contains a number of powerful insights, is linked to distinctive political programmes. If the central cause of environmental crisis is capitalism, then one argument (though now somewhat outmoded) is that capitalism itself needs to be overthrown. This would incorporate the socialisation of the means of production, the acquisition of the capitalist enterprises into the public realm.

An alternative view from the Left shifts away from the more conventional socialist scenario. Bahro, for example, while certainly calling for drastic and large-scale social change, argues that environmental issues are calling for radically new forms of political programme.[10] On the one hand, he still sees the cause of environmental crisis as firmly anchored in the global industrial order. The crisis derives, he argues, from rapid industrial growth in the advanced capitalist societies of the North. It is these societies, populated by high-living consumers and competing with one another to be top industrialised nation, which generate huge demands for raw materials from the developing societies of the South. Ecological crises, which particularly impact on the developing countries, are the result of these relationships. A central part of the solution, therefore, is the de-industrialisation of the North, with the armaments industry becoming a prime target for planned industrial decline.

Bahro is, however, one of a number of activists who recognise that the old socialist programme remains insufficient when faced by ecological and environmental crisis. Class relations in particular will not be readily overturned by the industrialised working class. The latter can no longer be envisaged as the vanguard of fundamental social change. Bahro argues that the new forms of environmental consciousness which have been affecting many social groups and classes since the 1960s should be the starting point for new forms of politics rather than the end result. In short, the environmental issues now widely experienced in Western Europe are seen as leading to a growing critique of capitalism.

But the general point about this type of strategy is similar to that of the older forms of socialism. And it springs largely from the original form of the critical analysis. Ryle, as we have seen, argues that green politics 'cannot adopt a purely ecological approach'. This is clearly true, but neither can green politics be concerned wholly with social processes. Nature makes an appearance as something which is being destroyed by capitalism. But what the 'something' is, and how it relates to human beings, remains very inadequately discussed.

Social scientists, especially those on the Left, thus tend to ignore the sciences. Indeed, they often remain actively hostile to them. This is because they see the sciences as having a depoliticising effect. They argue that science, with its inscrutable technical language and concepts, in effect draws attention away from the central issues involved. The issues are, again, seen as social and political rather than 'scientific'. And, as part of this systematic avoidance of the natural and physical sciences, social theory tends to see society or culture as an area of social and personal life which has no, or at least very marginal, relationships with the various forms of behaviour which have innate biological or psychological bases.

This is again part of the long-held resistance on the part of many critical theorists of any idea that people are in many, arguably most, respects 'natural' or part of nature. Again, this seems to be because the idea of 'natural' humans draws attention away from the social and political relations. They are in danger of being assumed away by the starting-point of the analysis. The effect is, however, to reproduce the old, and in certain crucial respects debilitating, divisions between 'people' on the one hand and 'nature' on the other.

The problem has also surfaced in another area of critical social theory. For some time feminists have been very critical of the notion that there are 'natural' differences between the sexes. The argument that 'biology is destiny' could be used, in particular, to justify the idea that women are predestined to carry out certain kinds of work such as child-raising and housework. There are now, however, moves towards recognising necessary biological and other forms of difference, while at the same time trying to attach alternative values to these differences.[11] I shall return to this important matter in Chapter 5.

Society and environment: the view from the Right

Neo-liberals seem more open to what we might term the 'scientific' view of people's behaviour and their relationships to the physical environment. The special emphasis given by many forms of science to processes innate to individuals seem to have a particular appeal to the Right. And this is no doubt largely due to the methodological individualism associated with much scientific analysis (one concentrating on the individual decision-maker) which is especially appealing to supporters of economic and political individualism.

It is extremely instructive, or at least it should be so, to see F.A. Hayek (perhaps the leading neo-liberal thinker) taking very seriously the insights of contemporary biology and ethology. In the end Hayek's analysis is not a correct one. But his attempted fusion of 'nature' and 'society' is in many respects more advanced than that of most contemporary critical social theorists. He is answering questions which many of his academic and political opponents have not yet even started asking.

In *The Fatal Conceit* Hayek argues strongly that human beings should be understood as having biological as well as human natures.[12] Furthermore, he suggests that there is a major contradiction between these two aspects of human beings. Much like contemporary ethologists and biologists (whose work I will review more fully in Chapter 4), he suggests that we should understand the human species as evolving into its present form several million years ago. Contemporary human beings, Hayek also argues, are still constructed in forms which were well adapted to the life of small hunting and gathering troops and tribes. And their genetic constitution has adapted them in such a way as to interact with a limited number of trusted others in small gathering and hunting communities. Civilisation, as we now know it, has emerged during the last few thousand years and there is no way in which the evolution of the human species could have taken place so quickly during this time as to be adequately adapted to the cultures which human beings have now constructed for themselves.

But, unlike some biologists and ethologists who do not adequately recognise the special characteristics of what Desmond Morris calls 'the naked ape', Hayek argues that humans do indeed have special capacities. These include an especially well-developed brain and a capacity for extended communication. Especially important for Hayek are human beings' capacity for learning from their actions, avoiding purely instinctive actions. This brings us to what Hayek calls 'the extended order', the forms of culture which have evolved during the last two thousand years or so of human civilisation. Biological evolution has been extended by *cultural* evolution. People have evolved rules of human conduct (what he calls 'shalt nots') which are passed on from one generation to the next. These are basically tacit understandings which have allowed the human species to have acquired their special prominence in nature. They include such values as honesty, morality, privacy and recognition of property rights.

Hayek's key point is that cultural relations of this kind now act largely as a constraint on human beings' genetic inheritance. While such relations and values may bring about real benefits in terms of overall human progress, people (with their genetic inheritance essentially based on ancient and tribal ways of life) find it extraordinarily difficult to see how or why they are benefiting from them. An individual or even a society cannot have sufficient knowledge to know why 'the extended order' has evolved in the form it has, but this is not sufficient reason for throwing off the values which slowly emerged amongst human societies.

Unsurprisingly, this view of evolutionary history is closely linked to Hayek's views on contemporary society and his proposals for reform. Here the contrasts with the view from the Left become almost complete. The abstract rules and values which have emerged comparatively recently are, Hayek argues, closely linked to the market economy. He sees modern economies as the principal basis of the extended order. It is an information-gathering process. Adam Smith's 'invisible hand' is coordinating the behaviour of millions of individuals, households and families throughout the globe. It provides signals to the individual decision-maker (such as the manager of a capitalist firm) where such a person simply cannot have total knowledge.

Hayek emphasises the individual and the household throughout his analysis. And this, finally, links to his major assault on institutional planning and control. Contemporary societies and economies are now so complex and far-flung that an adequate knowledge for large-scale planning cannot possibly exist. The best form of 'planning' is that carried out by intelligent and well-informed individuals and households. The main beneficiaries of planned societies, especially of command economies, are the planners themselves. These are classes of bureaucrats who not only ensure that they are extremely well rewarded but create values and priorities for the rest of the population.

These arguments from a leading neo-liberal may seem some way from our central concern with environmental issues. They are, however, important in two ways. First, as I have mentioned, they are beginning to break down the division between 'the social' and 'the natural', a division which is necessitated by environmental and related issues. But also, Hayek's ideas, and those of other neo-liberals, are now being directly applied to the study of the environment and possible future strategies.

Whelan in *Mounting Greenery* and Lal in *The Limits of*

International Cooperation are both working within the neo-liberal
tradition and both make a number of similar points about
contemporary environmentalism.[13] They argue, in some respects
persuasively, that knowledge of peoples' effects on the environment is in fact highly scanty and in some instances even suspect.
They recognise that there are indeed serious pollution problems in
parts of the world. But they say these are not new and are on
nothing like the scale suggested by the contemporary green
movement.

As regards the much-discussed greenhouse effect, for example,
Lal argues that there has indeed been an increase in greenhouse
gases during the past century and this is likely to accelerate. But
beyond this simple recognition, Lal argues that there is simply
insufficient information to justify long-term apocalyptic forecasts.
The relationships between emission of greenhouse gases and
climatic change is very complex and is by no means adequately
understood. Some scientists, Lal shows, argue that the long-term
effect will be that of a new ice age, some that of dramatically
rising temperatures. Thus, depending on which scientist is
consulted 'we could frizzle or we could freeze or there may be no
change'.[14]

Lal argues that environmental effects, in so far as there are any,
will be quite localised. It could well be wetter in East Africa,
Western Australia and Mexico; but it will be much drier in the US
Midwest. So, says Lal, it is quite wrong to talk of global
catastrophe with the whole of humanity suffering. 'Unless we
define "humanity" to be identical with the interests of US farmers,
it is difficult to see how humanity as a whole will be hurt.'[15]

Liberals make a similar point about the ozone layer; another
issue over which there have of course been many alarming
predictions. Again, the scientific evidence, Lal argues, results in
'wild gyrations in theoretical predictions'. It is not at all clear, he
says, that there are indeed strong links between changes to the
ozone layer and the use of chlorofluorocarbons (CFCs). Variations
may well, for example, be linked to variations in the solar cycle.
Furthermore, the links between skin cancers and ultraviolet rays
are also, according to Lal, not at all well established by science.
Similarly, Whelan argues that popularly held beliefs about rain
forests and the disappearance of species should be very critically
reviewed. The Brazilian rain forests may be declining in scale

(although estimates of the extent of that decline vary considerably) but, Whelan argues, *global* levels of forestation are actually increasing. Furthermore, the argument that deforestation in Brazil is resulting in the extinction of species is also treated by Whelan in a sceptical manner. Little is known, he argues, about the number of species in that exceptionally large region. Estimates of extinction rates vary between 100 a year to 100 a day.

So while critical social theory sees capitalism as the main problem underlying ecological problems, liberals see capitalism as the solution. While they recognise, for example, that there are real problems confronting the indigenous peoples of the Brazilian rain forests, they see economic development as the best way forward. 'Economic exploitation of the Amazon offers', in Lal's words, 'the prospect of raising the living standards of many poor people.'[16]

More generally, neo-liberals see the promotion of successful market economies as the principal means by which ecological and environmental problems can be solved. Adam Smith's 'hidden hand' makes another comeback, this time as a means of managing people's relationship with the natural environment. Whelan's faith in the market plus human ingenuity echoes Hayek's philosophy outlined earlier. His strategies fly in the face of most critical social theory and practice: 'The best way to provide for future generations is to exploit resources, not conserve them. Market forces and human ingenuity will always take care of shortage by providing solutions which leave us better off than we were before.[17]

The market, therefore, represents the optimal way forward for this neo-liberal view. Furthermore, it is only through achieving economic success that the resources for tackling these problems can be raised. Similarly, there is no need for government-inspired programmes of sustainable development aimed at stopping the over-use of land or the over-fishing of the sea. Farmers, Whelan argues, have long practised good husbandry. They do so because it is in their own best interests.

This brings us to a central point about the liberals' approach to the environment. Their suspicion of catastrophe-laden predictions and intervention by national and transnational government agencies is very intense. Contemporary environmental scares are, Whelan argues, just one of a series of doom-laden predictions of the end of civilisation as we know it: 'The need to scare ourselves

goes very deep in human nature.'[18] Having abandoned the threat
of God people are now looking for other scares, such as
environmental crisis, which fill this innate need for an external
threatening authority. Furthermore, it is a scare now being
orchestrated and promoted by bureaucrats and state officials for
their own selfish ends. Such people, Whelan argues, have lost the
battle over state socialism. Their ambition now, however, knows
no bounds. They are attempting *global* domination: 'The stage is
therefore set for that ultimate dream of those who prefer
corporate centralised planning to random human initiatives:
world government through the United Nations.'[19]

For liberals, therefore, environmentalism has a sinister hidden
agenda. The greens, with their aversion to consumerism and
economic growth, are finding new ways of pursuing their still
deeply held socialist objectives. Furthermore, it is the better-off
middle-class greens of the Western countries who are attempting
to impose their priorities on those on the edge of starvation
elsewhere. Meanwhile, Whelan argues, scientists, permanent
officials and elected political representatives are promoting
environmental crisis as a way of advancing their own careers:

Why then has the West and the UK in particular launched this eco-
imperialism of an International Green Economic Order? There are
obvious self-interested gains from what economists now call rent-seeking
on the part of the scientists, bureaucrats and diplomats involved. But I do
not think this is all. There is also a natural failing of politicians at work,
which has been accentuated by the growth of a professional politician
class, which has no other career apart from climbing up the greasy pole.[20]

CONCLUSION: TOWARDS AN ECLECTIC BUT UNIFIED APPROACH

So what conclusions can we draw from these two social scientific
perspectives? The first is of central importance in drawing
attention to the social, economic and political structures and
institutions surrounding environmental crises. It manages to
avoid, however, much explicit attention to what 'nature' actually
is and how it relates to society. Are they supposed to be two
discrete categories?

The second is stronger in terms of giving some pride of place to the individual and the household. As part of this it draws attention to genetically based forms of behaviour and to the psychological dimension of environmentalism. Neo-liberals also draw attention to the uncertainty of knowledge surrounding environmental issues. I believe these are all helpful, or potentially helpful, contributions. They are themes which will be developed later in this book. Neo-liberals, on the other hand, are in severe danger in the first place of complacency. Can individuals plus the market really be guaranteed to ensure that no severe problems emerge? Is there really no need for public intervention? Should the state be seen as consisting of no more than self-inflating bureaucrats? These assertions need critical examination.

But, to return to my opening theme, both these perspectives are prone to a deeper-lying problem; that of taking what is sometimes called 'man–environment' dialectic as unproblematic. As I shall elaborate later, this relationship is a highly problematic one and needs considerably more work on it. For the fact is that organisms are creative and make their environments in such a way as to become virtually part of it themselves. But at the same time environments (nature and other people) are active in the making of organisms. In many respects each one of these elements, organism and environment, form part of one another. However, social theory, as it is currently formed, seems largely incapable of encompassing such thinking about these relationships. And, since the relationships between organisms and environment are not going to change to fit in with the concepts of social theory, it is the theory itself which will have to change.

Yearley's demand for an interdisciplinary understanding of contemporary environmental issues must be supported. And yet I am less sanguine than Yearley is in contemplating what such an understanding will achieve. The prospect remains of many 'experts' continuing to talk past each other, generating much heat but rather little light. The basic problem is the dichotomy which remains at the heart of Western culture; that between 'people' (still often referred to as 'man') and 'nature'.

A way forward is the development of a unified approach; one which attempts to overcome this dichotomy. It recognises that people are part of nature and vice versa. But what would such an approach look like? And does this mean that all the knowledge which has so far been amassed by the sciences and social sciences is now redundant? I shall be arguing that there is now emerging a set of epistemologies, concepts and perceptions which can be used in developing such an approach and bringing existing work together. This can be the basis of the new kind of framework which green issues are now demanding. And it can be the basis of new lines of enquiry.

NOTES

1. S. Yearley (1991), *The Green Case*, HarperCollins: London.
2. S. Yearley (1991), *op.cit.*, p. 184.
3. On the middle classes' central involvement in environmental politics see in particular, C. Offe (1987), 'Challenging the boundaries of institutional politics: social movements since the 1960s' in C. Maier (ed.), *Changing Boundaries of the Political* Cambridge University Press: Cambridge. Also P. Lowe, J. Goyder (1983), *Environmental Groups in Politics*, Allen & Unwin: London.
4. T. Kuhn (1970), *The Structure of Scientific Revolutions*, International Encyclopaedia of Unified Science, vol 2, no. 2. University of Chicago: Chicago (2nd edn). I am grateful for Marilyn Strathern's comments on Kuhn.
5. A. Sayer (1984), *Method in Social Science*, Hutchinson: London. For a discussion of interdisciplinarity see chapter 2 of J. Young (1990), *Post Environmentalism*, Bellhaven: London.
6. P. Colinvaux (1980), *The Fates of Nations*, Penguin: Harmondsworth, p. 10.
7. P. Colinvaux (1980), *op.cit.*, p. 19.
8. M. Ryle (1988), *Ecology and Socialism*, Radius: London, p. 19.
9. M. Redclift (1984), *Development and the Environmental Crisis. Red or Green Alternatives?*, Methuen: London, p. 38.
10. R. Bahro (1984), *Socialism and Survival*, Heretic Books: London.
11. See, for example, Chap. 5 of A. Dobson (1990), *Green Political Thought*, Unwin Hyman: London.
12. F.A. Hayek (1988), *The Fatal Conceit*, Routledge: London.
13. R. Whelan (1989), *Mounting Greenery*, Education Unit, Institute of Economic Affairs: London. D. Lal (1990), *The Limits of International Cooperation*, Institute of Economic Affairs Occasional Paper 83, London.
14. D. Lal (1990), *op.cit.*, p. 30.

15. *ibid.*, p. 33.
16. *ibid.*, p. 38.
17. R. Whelan (1989), *op.cit.*, p. 29. It should be noted here that contemporary 'environmental economics' represents an at least partial application of neo-liberal ideals. Thus the Pearce Report, for example, recommends attaching a monetary value to previously 'free' resources (air, water, rain forests and so on) is an optimal way of controlling their use and degradation. And, as taken up by the British and many other governments, this suggestion seems highly compatible with programmes of privatisation. These are seen as a key way of 'promoting market transparency'. See D. Pearce *et al.* (1989), *Blueprint for a Green Economy*, Earthscan: London, H.M. Government (1990), *The Common Inheritance*, HMSO: London, especially Appendix A.
18. *ibid.*, p. 9.
19. *ibid.*, p. 37.
20. *ibid.*, p. 39.

2

PEOPLE, NATURE AND
SOCIAL THEORY

The previous chapter argued that social theory on the one hand and ecological and biological theory on the other are now consistently talking past each other. The result is considerable noise and confusion, with precious little clarification of what is widely seen as a contemporary ecological crisis. There is a special irony about this state of affairs since, as we will shortly see, sociological theory has long maintained a very close relationship with theories of the natural world. Yet, as this chapter will argue, the particular forms of this relationship have been highly problematic. The way sociology has learnt from concepts derived from the study of the natural world has not therefore been especially helpful either to the study of society or to the relationships between society and nature. And, in separating the study of society from that of nature, it has not been especially helpful to nature either.

What is needed, it will be argued here, is a new kind of social theory. It would be one sensitive to the fact that, while humans have distinct characteristics and carry out major changes to nature they are in two senses part of nature. They are a natural being or a species. And, again like all species, they relate in a reciprocal way with their environment. Furthermore, and this is a conclusion to which I will return and which pervades the whole of this book, human beings and their 'culture' should be seen not as a category of behaviour separate from that stemming from genetically inherited tendencies and capacities. Rather, it is a set of capacities which enable people, and other species, to make sense of the natural and social world, their places within it and the possibilities of transforming it.

The 'new' kind of sociology in fact has some precedents in the theories of Tönnies, Parsons and, still more importantly, Marx and Engels. The latter are of special significance for this study, so they will be held over until later. But suffice to say that, since Marx and Engels' work in the mid-nineteenth century which combined biology with an understanding of human societies, the problem has been that of sociology constructing itself as a watertight discipline. And it has done so largely by creating an impermeable division between itself and the natural sciences. Environmental issues, and other recent developments such as genetic engineering, now call for a fusion between the social and natural sciences, one which will inevitably call for changes to both such sciences.

The present chapter reviews in broadly historical sequence the often problematic relationships between social theory and science, especially biological science. It will take an historical overview of the development of sociological theory, exploring why the links between social and biological theory have been largely unsatisfactory. A large part of the problem stems from science being treated as an objective and self-evident set of 'facts'. Clearly, the sciences have made enormous strides in terms of understanding peoples' and other species' relationships to the world. On the other hand, science, including of course the life and social sciences, is constructed in the social world. Both are social constructs and can be used for social and political ends. As such they can be challenged. The difficult job is to know how to incorporate the 'facts' given us by the scientists into a world which is self-evidently social and political. The eventual aim here is to become more positive; developing a new kind of sociology which is not premised on the dichotomy between 'culture' and 'nature' and which allows the insights of the social and natural sciences are fused.

PEOPLE AND NATURE IN EARLY SOCIOLOGICAL THEORY: EVOLUTIONISM AS A FALSE LEAD

Sociological theory, ever since its earliest conception, has engaged in an almost perpetual dialogue with biology; either adapting or contributing to biology's concepts or, more recently, engaging in a radical rejection of this branch of science.

August Comte is often seen as the originator of modern sociology. He consistently maintained that social theory should be based on biology. Indeed, in the long run he envisaged the social sciences as subsumed within biological science. As he put it: 'The subordination of social science to biology is so evident that nobody denies it in statement however it may be neglected in practice.'[1]

If sociology is the science of human beings and their behaviour it was clear, Comte argued, that it must be based on the biological sciences. People after all are partly subject to the laws of biology. Furthermore, like many other early social theorists including Durkheim, Comte found it useful in developing a theory of society to make analogies between the social and natural worlds. The role of an institution or part of society, he argued, was best appreciated in terms of how it contributed to the functioning of society as a whole. And here the metaphor between society and the body became particularly useful. In much the same way as a part of society was best understood by appreciating its function for society as a whole, an organ such as a heart is best understood in its role of maintaining a body through pumping blood throughout the organism.

But it is above all Herbert Spencer who is best known for linking theories of society and social change to theories of biology.[2] Much of British and American sociology has either been a defence or an attack on his ideas. We should note here that Spencer started developing his theories some time *before* the emergence of Darwin's *Origins of Species*. Similarly, it is instructive to note that A. Espinas, the first biologist to suggest that variations in species are a result of environmental adaptation, based his views on Comte's sociology.[3]

This brings me to a recurring point in this study. The fact is that Spencer and the early social evolutionists on the one hand and Darwinian ideas on the other all developed from the same intellectual milieu in the mid-nineteenth century. This was one in which change and development within the social and natural worlds were envisaged as a product of the struggle to survive within an environment. Random natural variations are tested in this environment and the result is the emergence of variations which are well fitted or adapted to the environment. Their characteristics are then passed on to future generations. For Darwinian theory these notions became extended to all forms of species and organisms. The shattering implications of this view for 'man' as well as for other animals do not need emphasising here. At the same time, and as a product of this same intellectual milieu, similar notions or metaphors became extended to human beings and societies.

Yet the fact is that Darwinian theory *did* emerge within a specific historical and social context. Despite its many revelations and disruptions to established ways of thought (including those of nineteenth-century religion) it remains a product of a particular way of thinking. The difficulty is that of simultaneously recognising the significant contributions made by biological theory while at the same time recognising that such theoretical constructs are also what Haraway calls 'visions' embedded in social circumstances and useable to specific ends. Her statement of the potentials and limitations of such visions is highly instructive:

Natural sciences, like human sciences, are inextricably *within* the processes that give them work. And so, like the human sciences, the natural sciences are culturally and historically specific, modified, involved. They matter to real people. It makes sense to ask what stakes, methods, and kinds of authority are involved in natural scientific accounts, how they differ, for example, from religion or ethnography. It does not make sense to ask for a form of authority that escapes the web of the highly productive cultural fields that make the accounts possible in the first place. The detached eye of objective science is a fiction, and a powerful one. But it is a fiction that hides – and is designed to hide – how the powerful discourses of the natural sciences really work. Again the limits are *productive*, not reductive and invalidating. [author's emphases][4]

The extent to which Darwinian theory remains limiting or productive is a matter to which I shall return in Chapter 4. Suffice to say here that in neither the natural nor the social sciences was extended or prolonged consideration given in early Darwinism to the relationships between, on the one hand, species struggling for survival, and the natural environment on the other. A more complete picture, and one which, as I shall later show, is emerging in post-Darwinian biology is that the physicochemical environment is 'fit' for the life to develop. This means that the assumption of purely random variations can be reassessed.

Organisms can be seen as constituted by innate tendencies or
latent forms of development which may or may not become
actualised as a result of the environment of which they are a
part.

   The above is somewhat jumping ahead. But a reminder of the
historical specificity of Darwinian theory is useful when we come
to see how, using Haraway's word, it 'mattered' to social and
political thinkers. Spencer was also influenced by the essays
produced somewhat earlier in the nineteenth century by Robert
Malthus. Malthus had argued that the prospects for progress were
continually threatened by population growth and by the fact that
food production could in no way match such growth. The power
of the population to grow, he argued, is 'indefinitely greater' than
the power of the earth to provide subsistence.[5] The tendency for
populations to increase was due to the 'passion between the
sexes', one which the most diligent of social improvers would find
difficult to extinguish. Malthus argued that providing extra
resources for the poor only increases their numbers and, since it
reduces the incentive to work, further exacerbates their misery. It
also, he argued, artificially raises the price of goods, the capacity
for self-motivation and personal savings. The answer stemming
from the theory became therefore that of benign neglect and a
gradual reduction of state intervention to alleviate poor people's
welfare.

   'Evolution' was, for Spencer, a grand unifying idea. And he was
much more explicit than Comte and other early social theorists
such as LePlay about the role that biological or evolutionary
theory had to play in the study of social change. 'Natural
selection' was the key mechanism around which Spencer organised
his theory. In biology natural selection was, and still largely
remains, concerned with adaptation of organic beings to their
environments. Survival necessarily entails using resources such as
food and protection. But such resources are not available on a
scale sufficient to support all the demands made on them. This,
according to Spencer was because inevitably far more offspring
are produced than the environment can provide for. The result is
that individuals which are well adapted to their environment
survive and have more offspring while those species which are less
well adapted slowly die off. Furthermore, those which have better
physical or other characteristics do not only survive; they pass on

their characteristics to future generations. Later generations are in effect 'naturally selected' to survive and reproduce still further.

Spencer, however, went much further than the Darwinian scheme applied to the natural world. He extended this idea to understand the human as well as the natural worlds, seeing it as a means by which biology and sociology might be united. He therefore extended the concept of 'natural selection' to the social as well as the natural world. Not only were organic and inorganic nature subject processes of growth, transformation and eventual dissolution but so too were human beings and their institutions. These also evolved in relation to one another. And, to be fair to Spencer, there are some passages in his extensive and wide-ranging work where he does appear to recognise the reciprocal relation to environmental conditions. In a little-quoted passage he alluded to constant change both to the social world and to the physical and social spheres within which people and institutions were developing.

It needs but to think of the immense contrast between a wolf-haunted forest or a boggy moor peopled with wild birds, and the fields covered with crops and flocks which eventually occupy the same area, to be reminded that the environment, inorganic and organic, of a society, undergoes a continuous transformation of a remarkable kind during the progress of society; and that this transformation becomes an all-important secondary factor in social evolution.[6]

As this quote implies, however, Spencer's core concern was with people and with social evolution. His key argument was that societies undergo processes of change very similar to those observed in the natural world. A key similarity was increasing differentiation or complexity within the social world. Hunting and gathering societies, for example, appear to have relatively simple social structures. By contrast, later societies such as feudalism or industrial capitalism, are far more complex. They contain far more complicated divisions of labour and often have highly elaborate caste systems and institutions. Advanced industrial societies entail still further complexities and divisions of labour.

In short, social development appears to entail increasing diversity. And it is this phenomenon which was of greater importance to Spencer than the simple idea of using the notion of natural selection. And of great significance, as he pointed out, is the fact that these social and historical processes mirror those

found in the natural world. In the same way that societies develop
and became complex systems of specialised parts, organisms such
as amoeba which remain at the bottom of the evolutionary scale
have very simple physical structures and have little in the way of
nervous systems with centres of coordination in the form of
human brains.·

In some respects Spencer is pre-figuring here late twentieth
century developments in biological science. On the one hand, he
recognises what he calls 'extrinsic factors': the climate, inorganic
nature and other species and individuals; on the other hand, there
are 'intrinsic factors'. As regards the latter an individual has, in
Spencer's words:

physical characters which are potent in determining the growth and
structure of society. He is in every case more or less distinguished by
emotional characters which aid, or hinder or modify the activities of the
society, and the developments accompanying them. Always, too, his
degree of intelligence and the tendencies of thought peculiar to him,
become co-operating causes of social quiescence or social change.[7]

Spencer then says that an increasing mass of the population leads
not only to increasing heterogeneity, complexity and diversity
within society and increasing interaction between neighbouring
societies but, analogous to the brains which have evolved in the
most advanced organisms, it develops increasing levels of control
by the aggregate over the part and the growth of 'super-organic
products' such as complex contemporary forms of culture. We
should note here a criticism often made of Spencer's evolutionism
and that of latter-day evolutionists. He was tacitly advancing a
unilinear form of social progression; one which suggests that the
movement from a simple to a complex social order (an order not
unlike that of contemporary Britain or North America) is pre-
ordained. Every society, Spencer says, must inevitably experience
'progress' in this particular form.

Government intervention over such items as education, sanita-
tion and banking was therefore to be avoided. The effect, again,
was to interfere in the processes of natural selection and promote,
rather than eliminate, the unfit. Better solutions were voluntary
charitable relief on the one hand and eugenics on the other. As
regards the latter, the idea was to dissuade the socially dependent
from further reproducing. As Spencer argued: 'the whole effort of

nature is to get rid of such, to clear the world of them, and make for better. . . . If they are not sufficiently complete to live, they die and it is best they should die.'[8]

As we will see shortly, however, other sociologists did not see such a necessary connection between biological theory and the promotion of free-market liberalism. A more fundamental critique of Spencer concerns not his political and social ideology but the status of biological theory as applied to social change. Society, whether defined at the local, national or global level is clearly not an organism equivalent to an animal or a human being. This being so, it is by no means clear what it means to show parallels between, say, the increasing heterogeneity and diversity of a society and that of organisms.

If we read Spencer's work in some detail, however, it seems he became increasingly aware of this problem. In 'The organic analogy reconsidered', a relatively late (1876) paper in his collected works, he wrote that:

though, in foregoing chapters, comparisons of social structures and functions in the human body, have in many cases been made, they have been made only because structures and functions in the human body furnish the most familiar illustrations of structures and functions in general. The social organism . . . is not comparable to a particular type of individual organism, animal or vegetable. . . . I have used the analogies elaborated, but as a scaffolding to help in building up a coherent body of sociological inductions. Let us take away the scaffolding: the inductions will stand by themselves.[9]

So it is perhaps unfair to suggest that Spencer was engaging in a simple-minded application of biological ideas to the study of society. Some of his early and better-known work does indeed read like this, but his later and less publicised statements suggest that the analogy between society and processes of natural selection was not so much a ham-fisted attempt to envisage society as a super-organism. Rather, it was a means of gaining an overview of societal development and advancing some fairly concrete and testable ideas for the study of social change. An analogy with the natural world was in effect a first stage in the construction of a social theory.

But having, in part at least, cleared Spencer of some of the more frequently made charges against him, there remains a central flaw in his work. Indeed, these are difficulties which are inherited by a

large part of the Western philosophical tradition. Although
Spencer clearly did see that people were in some sense 'natural'
and that 'nature' is also socially constructed, the distinction
between nature on the one hand and society on the other still
persists throughout Spencer's work. This is not especially
surprising since Spencer's chief objective was to construct a new
discipline, that of sociology; one with the status of a firm
theoretical framework. In the end, however, Spencer did not
overcome the 'nature' and 'society' dichotomy. He did not
proceed beyond the rather general proposition that evolution and
natural selection provide a unifying point between the social and
natural sciences.

Spencer's influence was very widespread, although evolutionism
in sociological theory was not always used to imply that society
was made up of competing individuals and the 'survival of the
fittest'. In 1902, for example, the anarchist writer Peter Kropotkin
was arguing in *Mutual Aid. A Factor of Evolution* that the
Darwinian struggle for survival is at least as much constituted by
cooperation as by struggle between individuals.[10] The lessons for
politics seemed just as clear as Spencer's proposal for *laissez-faire*.

And, just as significantly, when taken up in France Social
Darwinism came to possess yet other resonances; those of
harmony and social solidarity rather than rampant economic
competition. As Clark has discussed, French intellectuals had long
had considerable respect for the notion of *reason* amongst human
beings.[11] As a result, they found profoundly discomforting the
notion that a human society was made up of brutish irrational
human beings. Furthermore, middle-class French opinion co-
incided with a tradition of French political thought which
emphasised the tradition of relating the individual to the state.
This particular set of interests and coalitions again suited an
interpretation of cooperation and altruism amongst human beings
rather than one emphasising the competitive and individualistic
struggle for existence.

It was particularly in the United States, however, where
Spencer's ideas and the notion of Social Darwinism were taken up
and developed with alacrity. Spencer's basically free-market
message and the transference of the biological metaphor to the
social world found fertile ground here. But this did not apply to
all American social theorists.

On the one hand, there were indeed those in the United States who took up Spencer's economic and political themes. One of the most influential writers in this respect was Sumner. Adopting both Spencer and Malthus as his conceptual starting-points, Sumner argued that the basis of human society was the relationship between people and land. Where the soil is fertile and the population in sparse the struggle for existence is relatively muted. Where the population is large and land less fertile the struggle for survival becomes intense. It leads to hunger, destitution, mass migrations, military invasions and the development of massive government interventions and state bureaucracies. Sumner argued that access to capital was indeed important, but its significance lay not so much in ownership *per se* but in the fact that it enabled people to gain access to nature.

Undoubtedly the man who possesses capital has a great advantage over the man who has no capital at all in the struggle for existence. . . . This does not mean that one man has an advantage against the other but that, when they are rivals in the effort to get the means of subsistence from Nature, the one who has capital has immeasurable advantages over the other.[12]

But while Sumner saw capital as a means to an end he also saw it as a means which needed promoting. Thus the acquisition of capital and its transmission between generations were of core importance in ensuring social progress. He saw one of the state's main roles as protecting this principle; defending the principle of inheritance and the family or, as he put it, 'the property of men and the honour of women'. As Spencer suggested earlier, the fittest (those with the talent for managing industries and acquiring capital) must be allowed to survive in the interests of ensuring social development for society as a whole. 'The millionaires', Sumner said, 'are a product of natural selection.'[13]

Abstract notions of equality, liberty and natural rights were denied by Sumner. Notions of democracy he saw as a temporary stage in social development. They flourished reasonably in the context of good relationships between people and land but in the long run they should be abolished. There were no rights in the jungle and the eventual objective must be that of freeing individuals to compete in gaining access to nature with the aid of inherited capital. Sumner's parallel between human society and nature is also a telling comment on the relationship, as he saw it, between nature and culture. It is a set of resources to be used for wholly human ends. 'There can be no rights against Nature except to get out of her whatever we can, which is only the fact of the struggle for existence started over again.'[14]

But if one interpretation of Spencer was that of reproducing and developing his insistence on free-market liberalism as the social or cultural equivalent to natural selection, a parallel argument in the United States was again that the theory of natural selection did not actually imply endorsing the continuous social war between competing individuals. Its crudest versions found rather little support from those such as the pragmatists. They maintained a strong faith in the capacity of human effort (and not just the effort of certain 'selected' individuals) to bring about rational and benevolent solutions. They vigorously opposed Social Darwinism.

Social Darwinism was similarly resisted by liberals and ameliorists such as Lester Ward. He was a contemporary of Sumner's but he too attacked the notion that the same principles of evolution could be applied to the natural and human worlds. Evolution of animals in their environmental context he saw – in line with biological theory – as a purposeless process in which the 'fittest' survived through natural selection. But people, by contrast, he saw as having distinctive capacities for rational thought and action. The theory of natural selection could not be applied to human mental evolution. The same theory of evolution could not be applied to the natural and human worlds as Spencer, and later writers such as Sumner had suggested. People, Ward argued, have the very distinctive capacity to stand back, think rationally, coordinate and govern.

All this implied resistance by Ward to the unthinking promotion of *laissez-faire* ideals; government action was to be encouraged. Ward, however, was a long way from promoting socialism. Government intervention must at all costs avoid the growth of large bureaucratic autocracies. Its principal aim should be 'to release the springs of human action'.[15] One of the most interesting features of this particular strand of social thought is a concept of the organism (including the human organism) as constituted by certain potentials, the job of governments and others being to release these potentials. As we will see in Chapter 4, this has some parallels with today's post neo-Darwinian thinking.

TÖNNIES: FROM LAND AND COMMUNITY TO SOCIETY

Much of the heady enthusiasm for Social Darwinism had, by the 1920s and 30s, begun to wane. But Spencer's views, combined with those of other biologists and botanists such as R.E. Clements continued to be influential. They were critically influential, for example, on the Chicago School of Sociology. But, before coming to this group, we should mention another particularly strong theme in social theory as it was originally developed; that is the transition from community to society. If, for example, we carefully read Tönnies – the writer who gave perhaps most attention to this theme – we find that this could have been the basis for a social theory which took the natural world more seriously. He made quite frequent allusions to the disconnection between people and nature during the transition to a modern way of life. And, as part of this concern, he alluded to what he saw as the natural relationships and bonds between, for example, members of the same family. In the event, however, sociology did not retain these interests in nature and in the natural bases of social behaviour as a central part of its intellectual concerns.

Tönnies' famous distinction between *gemeinschaft* and *gesellschaft*, could, therefore, have been a basis on which to construct a 'biological sociology', and one which is more conscious of the relations between people and the natural world.[16] He saw *gemeinschaft* as the old and traditional order, although he insisted that it was a type of society which could and indeed does exist in parallel with modern forms of society. Under *gemeinschaft* people are bound together in an intimately shared order of natural associations. Thus under *gemeinschaft* kin, family and neighbours live and work together, experiencing the common joys and sorrows of regular association within a shared, known and loved territory and operating on the basis of shared values and authority.

Especially important under *gemeinschaft* are kin relations, those 'rooted in the natural bond of blood'. And for Tönnies house and home has a key symbolic significance:

The house constitutes the realm and, as it were, the body of kinship. Here people live together under one protecting roof, here they share their possessions and their pleasures; they feed from the same supply, they sit at the same table. As invisible spirits the dead are venerated here, as if they were still powerful and held a protecting hand over their family. . . . The ordinary human being, therefore – in the long run and for the average of cases – feels best and most cheerful if he is surrounded by his family and relatives. He is amongst his own.[17]

Relationships between husband and wife and between brothers and sisters are of central importance in *gemeinschaft*. So too, for Tönnies, are the relationships between mother and children. This is 'most deeply rooted in liking or in pure instinct'. Women have a key significance in Tönnies' concept of *gemeinschaft*.

All *gemeinschaft* relations are central in forming and supporting 'natural will'; the set of feelings, instincts and dispositions informing people's conceptualisations of the world and their behaviour towards one another. Tönnies argues that people are a particular kind of animal species; one with distinct capacities. These include a well-developed capacity for 'liking', or taking positive pleasure in engagement with the natural and social worlds. They also include a need for 'habit', or regular forms of life activity. They include 'memory' in the form of learning values from others and making them into a set of beliefs which are of core significance to their own lives. *Gemeinschaft* and 'natural will' have a central significance in developing these instinctive human capacities. (Interestingly, and as I shall show later, this also has strong echoes in the ways ethology is now being transferred to humans.) Tönnies points to certain key bonds as underlying *gemeinschaft*: these are relations between mother and child, those between siblings and those between 'husband and wife in its natural or biological meaning'.[18]

Law and culture under *gemeinschaft* are also based on this natural will. Evolved and inherited customs within families and communities combined with the ownership of land are the main means by which social cohesion is maintained. Similarly, education and language takes a particular form, one derived from the home and upbringing as distinct from one imposed from without by the state or other institutions. Paternity, or fatherhood, is seen as the chief way in which authority is upheld under *gemeinschaft*.

Under *gesellschaft* these close personal associations and links to the land are seen as being undermined, largely as a result of rapid developments in commercialism and trade. Under this form of society association becomes a means towards an end. Relationships are seen as becoming individualised, impersonal and shallow; they are based on calculation and manipulation, people become used as means towards ends rather than as other human beings with experiences and emotions which can be shared. Rational will supplants natural will, with feelings being subordinated to reason. Similarly, natural law rooted in past custom becomes formalised law based on contracts between free and autonomous individuals.

Tönnies is in effect describing the development of modernity and, as a result of this, a slow but steady form of alienation. His analysis is not all that distant from the malaise often described by environmental writing in our own era. He shows that *gesellschaft*, though it entails many forms of gain (including escape from the often stifling impositions of family, community and collective norms), also entails many forms of loss. These include blood relations between mother and child, brothers and sisters, long-term relations between man and wife and close relations between people, land and animals. Understanding of self also derives from close and regular *gemeinschaft* relations with neighbours and friends sharing the same experiences.

Gemeinschaft also entails what Tönnies calls the 'unity of being, which is developed and differentiated into *gemeinschaft* of locality, which is based on a common habitat'. This closely links to another key form of form separation; that between people and nature. Thus under the 'will of *Gemeinschaft*':

The people see themselves surrounded by the inhabited earth. It seems as if, in the beginning of time the earth itself had brought forth from its womb the human beings who look upon her as their mother. The land supports their tents and houses, and the more men become attached to their own ground, however, limited. The relationship grows stronger and deeper when the land is cultivated. With the plow furrowing the soil, nature is tamed just as the animals of the woods are domesticated. But this is only the result of the ever-renewed efforts of countless generations, where every step in progress is handed down from father to son. The area settled and occupied is therefore a common heritage, the land of the ancestors towards which all feel and act as descendants and blood brothers.[19]

Tönnies' analysis is quite complex. But it is sensitive to those dimensions of human experience which could form part of contemporary sociology. He is not simply describing a shift from one set of human relationships to another. He is outlining a change first between different relationships between human and the rest of nature and, at one and the same time, a change between human beings' consciousness about *themselves*.

Tönnies is not, however, arguing that all changes are for the worse. He recognises, for example, that new forms of *gemeinschaft* can develop within *gesellschaft* conditions. An example stems from the growing entry of women into the workforce. On the one hand, 'nothing is more foreign and terrible to her original inborn nature, in spite of all later modifications'; and 'for women, the home and not the market, their own or friend's dwelling and not the street is the natural seat of their activity'.[20] On the other hand, he sees the change as possibly heralding a new form of consciousness, one which overcomes the individualism of *gesellschaft* and eventually benefits women's social subordination. I will return to this issue in Chapter 5.

At the same time, Tönnies sees few redeeming features resulting from the separation of people from the land and the rest of nature. People's deep-rooted instincts, their sense of themselves and of others, Tönnies is saying, are fundamentally locked into land:

The metaphysical character of the clan, the tribe, the village and the town community, is, so to speak, wedded to the land in lasting union. The mores have the same function in this relationship as custom in marriage.[21]

So Tönnies could have been a basis for a theory relating people to nature and to social change. As implied earlier, however, he is relatively descriptive. His work contains implicit assumptions about the nature of human nature, about the necessary relations between people and people and between people and nature. It also contains some assumptions about the processes and relationships which have ruptured these relationships and the consequent effects on individuals' consciousness. He does not, however, explore the mechanisms and relationships actually involved. For these, as I shall outline in the following chapter, we must turn elsewhere. But, even though there were drawbacks to his work, one particular theme in his analysis of *gemeinschaft* and *gesellschaft* was society's changing relationship with nature. And it is this theme which became almost wholly neglected by later social theory.

MODERNITY, COMMUNITY AND HUMAN NATURE:
THE CHICAGO SCHOOL OF SOCIOLOGY

Thus the theme of the decline of old-style community has of course recurred in much later social theory. But after Tönnies a sociological concern with the relationships between people and nature becomes very difficult to find.[22] The Chicago School of Sociology, which picked up the theme of a social transition away from community, also neglected relations with nature. But it did at least explore a theme which would be essential to the creation of any new fusion between such disciplines as biology and sociology. They were concerned with *human* nature and the spontaneous ways in which human communities form themselves. They again used an analogy between the natural and social worlds; one which, in the end, proved difficult to sustain. But their work is instructive for our purposes since it explicitly recognises that the behaviour of humans, like that of all species, has a biological as well as purely social, or what they called 'cultural', basis.[23]

The Chicago School was particularly interested in the formation of community lives in large urban areas such as Chicago. Social Darwinism contained the promise to illuminate the relatively unconscious ways in which people organise and adapt themselves spatially as well as socially. The Chicago urban sociologists were thus primarily concerned with society as a product of what they saw to be human nature. They envisaged a Darwinian or Spencerian competition for survival as the main mechanism underlying social change, adaptation and spatial organisation. They used the word 'community' to define this aspect of human behaviour.

The Chicago sociologists, and Park in particular were nevertheless also concerned with the 'cultural' level. This consisted of systems and beliefs, artefacts and technology and non-material cultural forms. And, interestingly, Park includes a fourth item combining with the biotic level to form the 'social complex'. This is 'the natural resources of the habitat'.[24] As I have said, however, Park unfortunately did not give this last item much further consideration in his ecological analysis.

It was the 'community' level of the struggle for survival which the Chicago sociologists used to define what they called 'human ecology'. And, in their attempt to understand human society (including, most importantly, its spatial form) it was to Darwin and Spencer's body of theory that they again turned. McKenzie was perhaps the most explicit of the Chicago writers about this analogy in his essay 'The ecological approach to the study of the human community'. He writes:

> the young sciences of plant and animal ecology have become fairly well established. Their respective fields are apparently quite well defined, and a set of concepts for analysis is becoming rather generally accepted. The subject of human ecology, however, is practically an unsurveyed field, that is, so far as a systematic approach is concerned.[25]

McKenzie and his colleagues had a clear view of human nature, one which is often neglected in commentaries on their work. It was from these human traits that an understanding of the human community should, they argued, be based. McKenzie put the form of this human nature in the following way: 'Man is a gregarious animal: he cannot live alone; he is relatively weak and needs not only the company of other human associates but shelter and protection from the elements as well.'[26]

From this starting-point McKenzie develops an understanding of the ways in which human 'natural areas' grow and develop their internal spatial-cum-social structures. This understanding had its basis in ecological theory. While the Chicago human ecologists were writing, plant ecologists such as F.E. Clements were showing how in plant ecology species compete for survival. They showed how there emerges a 'climax state' in which a particular species (for example, a group of beech trees) comes to dominate the local 'community' of plant life. Nevertheless, such domination is not necessarily permanent. An invasion by another species eventually comes to disrupt the balance between species living in relative harmony. Similar processes, McKenzie argued, take place in the human community. His analogy between the natural and social worlds echoes that made by Spencer some thirty years earlier:

> The human community tends to develop in cyclic fashion. Under a given state of natural resources and in a given condition of the arts the community tends to increase in size and structure until it reaches the point of population adjustment to the economic base. In an agricultural

community, under present conditions of production and transportation, the point of maximum population seldom exceeds 5,000. The point of maximum development may be termed the point culmination or climax, to use the term of the plant ecologist. The community tends to remain in this condition of balance between population and resources until some new element enters to disturb the *status quo*, such as the introduction of a new system of communication, a new type of industry or a different form of utilisation of the existing economic base.[26]

The plant ecologists' notion of 'invasion' no doubt seemed easy to adopt and adapt in studying the social conditions of early twentieth-century Chicago. Between 1898 and 1930 the population of Chicago doubled to approximately three million. This was almost entirely the result of massive waves of immigration, first from the European countries and latterly from the southern United States.

This brings us to the Chicago School's specifically 'urban' concerns. Again using the ecological analogy, they were interested in how different 'species' adapted to one another as they came to live in the same region forming, again in a spontaneous way, 'communities'. Park and McKenzie noted how new groups of people tend initially to establish themselves in zones where they find least resistance. These are frequently in areas close to the central business district. In due course, however, they move out to other areas establishing them as what the Chicago School called 'natural areas'. Race, language, religion, age and sex were amongst the principal factors defining what these natural areas, zones in which personal-cum-social identity were established. In due course these natural areas become a fairly permanent feature of the city's 'climax state', at least until a new wave of invasion and upheaval.

The Chicago School, with its many monographs describing the cultures and forms of distinct natural areas, was in some respects an important culminating point of the Spencerian analogy between the natural and social worlds. There is no doubt, however, that there remain serious difficulties with this work. Not least of these, as Saunders discussed in considerable detail, is the highly problematic notion of 'community'.[27] At some points in their work it is an analytical construct, a means of theorising and describing the spontaneous forms of action in which human beings engage. At other points it is an observable object; an actual community of which people form part.

But underlying this criticism is that concerning the dualism between 'community' and 'society'. Their attempt to amalgamate the 'biotic' and 'social' levels is not adequately developed. They still tend to reproduce the idea that there are indeed two separate forms of behaviour: one 'natural' and one 'social'. The first of these is studied by means of one set of theories (ecology and biology) while the second is studied through, for example, economics and political science.

This split is a point to which I will return, but in the meantime it should again be noted that the Chicago School has distinctively positive elements, despite the considerable criticisms that have been made of it. This group was emphasising certain features of human nature which gave rise to spontaneously formed communities. People were again seen as partly 'natural', with (like many other species) inborn instincts giving rise to forms of community life which are not readily amenable to analysis by the conventional social sciences. This insight has been largely lost in contemporary urban sociology.[28] On the other hand, the confusion between 'community' as on the one hand an underlying mechanism affecting human behaviour and 'community' as a phenomenon observable in the real world left this particular application of Darwinian theory vulnerable and, in the end, largely unworkable.

The declining years of human ecology were largely dedicated to rectifying this difficulty. One effect was to merge the study of people in their environment into the emergent functionalist sociological theory. Again, there seems with hindsight little reason to link Darwinian biological theory with a particular kind of ideology. Rather, it was capable of being interpreted and used by a diverse array of ideologies. The problem remained, however, that of a dominant focus on the human species and its adaptation to the environment – this at the expense of a focus on reciprocal relations between developing organisms and their environment.

One of the last main attempts to use an ecological framework for the study of people in their environment was Hawley's *Human Ecology: A theory of community structure*.[29] This study again maintained human societies as its principal focus, although it was again sensitive to how these societies adapted themselves in relation to external conditions. It once more attempted to define how Darwinian theory might be applied to the study of human behaviour and the formation of community life. 'Human ecology', Hawley writes, 'fastens its attention upon the human interdependences that develop in the action and reaction of a population to its habitat.'[30] It still retains the Darwinian conceptual starting-point. Indeed, it is if anything clearer about this than the earlier Chicago School. As advanced by Hawley, however, its prime concern was with the ways and means by which human beings adapt to their physical and social environment. And Hawley again focuses on the collective aspect of human adaptation. He de-emphasises the Spencerian picture of the struggle for survival consisting of a contest between competing individuals. His interpretation of Darwin for the study of human beings mirrors that of the French and some of the American authors discussed earlier:

Concerning animals, Darwin wrote: 'Although there is no evidence that any animal performs an action for the exclusive good of another species, yet each tries to take advantage of the instincts of the other, as each takes advantage of the weaker bodily structure of the other species.' Darwin is no exception to the general rule. Men everywhere live in association with other forms of life as well as with their fellow men. Few instances of solitary human beings have come to light and, while information concerning these feral creatures is far from satisfactory, it appears that survival in every case was contingent upon the individual adapting his activities to those of other species.[31]

This collective adaptation, Hawley argued, can take two forms. The first, the 'symbiotic', is made up of high levels of mutualism and cooperation. Animals of different types frequently cooperate with one another in the joint struggle for survival and this applies to the human community also. The second is 'commensalistic', whereby similar individuals or aggregates of similar creatures are making demands on their environment. Competition for survival is a feature of this form of adaptation but here too there are, according to Hawley, high levels of collective action in the struggle to live and reproduce. As he puts it, 'organisms with similar requirements frequently combine their efforts to maintain favorable life conditions; an aggregate acting in concert can accomplish what a lone individual cannot.'[32]

Hawley envisaged populations, especially growing populations with increasing demands on their environment, adapting to their environments in other ways. A key process, one again parallel to that in the natural world, is seen by Hawley as social differentiation. The most effective form of social organisation is one with a series of differentiated but closely related individuals and groups.

By organisation we mean an arrangement of differentiated parts suited to the performance of a given function or set of functions. The term implies the interdependence of dynamic individuals whose varied activities are coordinated in a single functional system.[33]

Functional differentiation is not simply, as Spencer argued, a result of growing physical size. According to Hawley it is also the result of such factors as increasing facilities for movement and communication. These enable increasing levels of human association and capacities for an increasing specialisation. Hawley here seems to have been influenced by Durkheim who argues that social organisation is more closely linked to 'social density', or the frequency of contacts and exchanges, than with purely physical density.

As part of such differentiation there emerge, according to Hawley, key units; these having a central role in adapting to the environment. Applying this general idea to the social world, Hawley makes special reference to manufacturing industry. Similarly, there emerge dominant units, those having a high degree of influence over other units and their relationships. In the case of an advanced industrial society like America:

such influence may be exercised directly or indirectly through control over the allocation of space to different activities, the determination of who shall be employed, the regulation of credit, the censoring of news and information reaching the community, and many other ways.[34]

Hawley was therefore attempting to use Darwinian theory to show how human societies adapt to their environment. More specifically, he was using a biological analogy to elucidate how human societies and their environment largely stay in balance, relationships within a delicately organised social web adapting to one another as a result of changes to their social context and the availability of natural resources. At the same time, of course, the environment is itself changing, in what would later be termed a 'cybernetic' way, in relation to humans' actions.

FROM BIOLOGISM TO FUNCTIONALISM

And, as Saunders has also pointed out, in this process of focusing on how human societies adapt to their environment Hawley and the later human ecologists such as Duncan come very close to a parallel set of ideas, those of functionalism.[35] This too originally had its basis in the idea that society is itself a kind of organism. In particular, it stems from Durkheim and his insistence, contrary to Spencer, that society cannot be understood as the product of individual minds and actions. Rather, it is analogous to a body in which the propensities and properties of the whole are far more than the mere aggregation of individual elements. Changes to the social organism cannot be understood as the sum total of the actions and relations between individuals. Indeed, Durkheim went even further than this in arguing that individuals and their behaviour must be seen in wholly social terms.

Functionalist social theory largely dispensed with the explicit analogy between social and natural evolution. It is nevertheless aligned with evolutionism in so far as it is concerned with relating human social life to biologically inherited behaviour. It was like Tönnies and the Chicago School in the sense that it was a possible starting-point for a new, biologically and environmentally sensitive, form of sociology. This potential was never developed, however. And this was partly because of problems with its conceptual starting-point.

Talcott Parsons is the obvious functionalist writer to refer to if we are concerned with theories of social evolution, with people's behaviour having a biological basis and with the relationships between societies and their natural environment. Most importantly, he recognises that human evolution has conferred to the human species 'a generalised adaptive capacity' and, as a result, human societies have the capacity to adapt to changing circumstances.[36]

Parsons also attributes far more significance to the biological organism and its relationship to the external environment than most other recent social theorists. His theory is very clear in arguing that human action is not only bounded by cultural norms which define people's actions. It is also bounded by its physical environment, including natural resources, and by the biological

constitution of other individuals. Parsons argued that there are
four basic requirements for any type of social system, whether at
the smallest or world scale. At its most general, there are four
subsystems to a system of action. These are summarised in Figure
2.1. The first of these, and the most important from our
viewpoint, is what he calls 'the adaptive function'. Here he is
concerned with a society's relationships with the outside social
and physical environment. On the one hand, society must remain
broadly intact but on the other hand it must have some kind of
reciprocal relationship with its environment. It is clearly this part
of Parsons' schema which relates social systems to the natural
environment. And, critically, Parsons sees the human biological
organism as corresponding to the function of adaptation. It is this
which mediates between society and the physical environment,
taking resources from it, exchanging these resources with those
produced by the social system in question, adapting the natural
and social world while at the same adapting *to* it.

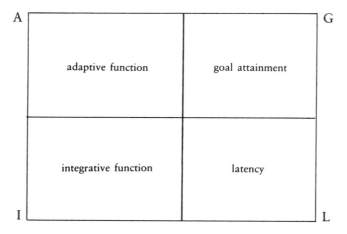

Figure 2.1 Parsons: the social system and its subsystems

Parsons' other functions have some close parallels with those of
earlier functionalists and with Hawley, whom I reviewed earlier.
He sees a social system as having necessarily to act as a
coordinated unit. Ways must be found of setting broad objectives
and mobilising resources to these ends. This function is called

'goal attainment' and it is primarily achieved by the state. Third, societies must operate as a cohesive whole; disruptive forces must be constrained. An 'integrative function' must be present; religion and an array of government agencies usually fill this role. And fourth, there is 'latency' or what Parsons refers to as 'pattern maintenance and tension management'. This means the management of a society's morale and motivation. On the one hand, for example, people have to achieve adaptive, goal-attaining and integrative requirements. On the other hand, they must be able to relax and restore their energies. Leisure and the family are seen as having a key role in this respect.

Thus Parsons' theory outlines the social functions which must be in play for any society to reproduce itself. And the relationship between the biologically and culturally defined and the external world of nature has a central role in the maintenance of social order and social reproduction. But he goes further than this in advancing a theory of social evolution which has some close similarities with evolution in the natural world. He interprets social evolution first as dependent on 'evolutionary universals'; features of all human societies which are necessary for any form of social change to take place. These universals are language, religion, kinship and technology. They are the equivalent in the social world to vision in the natural world. Without vision organisms could not react to their environment, survive and develop.

In Parsons, therefore, we have a remarkable but now largely neglected theory of social evolution in an environmental context, with one affecting the other. All human societies have distinct 'evolutionary universals' which have given them a special evolutionary advantage. And, as regards relationships to nature, these universals not only allowed societies to adapt to the natural world but also to change it: 'This capacity includes an active concern with mastery, or the ability to change the environment to meet the needs of the system, as well as an ability to survive in the face of its unalterable features.[37]

Parsons argued, in a manner which is somewhat reminiscent of parts of Spencer and earlier writers on social evolution, that social change in its natural and social environment context entails a process of increasing complexity and differentiation. The most primitive forms of society such as Australian aborigines were envisaged as fairly simple social organisms. Economic activity was based on hunting and gathering with kinship relations and religion organised around these basic forms of economic activity. There was very little property ownership involved and social hierarchies were not well developed. In an 'advanced primitive society', on the other hand, such hierarchies are much more developed. Economic activity is more differentiated between, for example, pastoral and agricultural work while religion (including the priesthood) becomes less directly related to social life. Further up the evolutionary scale are what Parsons called 'intermediate societies'. These are represented by, for example, Egypt, Rome or China. Economic, political and religious activities become still more distinct at this stage and an emergent feature is a distinct class of bureaucrats. Finally, industrialised societies are seen as still more differentiated and complex; a distinct legal system emerges, for example. Complexity is further increased as a system of democracy emerges in which the population as a whole becomes involved in the political system.

What functionalism actually means in practice becomes clearer if we look at its application by anthropologists. One of the best-known in this respect is Malinowski.[38] He, like many of the other authors I have been examining, is essentially concerned with human adaptation to the environment. Like Parsons he saw society as basically stable and adaptive to internal and external shocks. And, also like Parsons, he sees society as a system of interconnected units. His starting-point for the construction of a theory of society is the range of what he calls 'basic needs'. These include feeding and the disposal of human waste. They also include the reproduction of the human species, the maintenance of a certain level of body comfort, protection of bodily safety, movement (enabling exploration of the environment and contact with other individuals and communities), the ensurance of physical growth and maintenance of health.

Malinowski's basic point is that culture is rooted in people's biologically inherited drives and requirements. In fulfilling their basic needs people create a new, 'man-made', form of environment with houses, tools and so on. At the same time they have developed joint ways of surviving. These tools and relationships themselves need reproducing. Means need to be found, for example, of transmitting knowledge to the next generation. These are what he called 'instrumental' needs. And culture is a response to these instrumental needs. An example is the need to reproduce the ways in which tools and the means of production results in the economic system. The need to reproduce culture and understanding results in an educational system. Malinowski, mirroring Parsons' analysis discussed earlier, also argues that there are 'integrative imperatives' for any society; essentially, means by which a society is held together as a social organism. A set of values, norms and sanctions is thus necessary as are means of social control, legal systems and forms of political organisation. Malinowski sums up in the following way, arguing that even forms of human activity which do not seem directly linked to basic needs are still rooted in such basic demands:

> We can thus see, first and foremost, that derived needs have the same stringency as biological needs, and that this stringency is due to the fact that they are always instrumentally related to the wants of the organism. We see also how and where they come into the structure of human organised behaviour. We see finally, that even such highly derived activities such as learning and research, art and religion, law and ethics, related as they are with organised performance, with technology, and with accuracy of communication are also definitely related, although by several removes, to the necessity of human beings to survive, to retain health and a normal state of organic efficiency.[39]

Malinowski's analysis is, then, that of an anthropologist examining, in small-scale contexts, the detailed interlocking of biologically inherited drives and the creation and transmission of cultures and institutions which are needed to hold a small-scale society together. He forms part of the functionalist tradition which emphasises what it sees as the needs and purposes of societies and the ways in which biological processes, the natural world and social institutions combine to meet these requirements and objectives. The objection to this kind of sociology is, of course, that it overemphasises societies as smooth-running systems with supposed needs which must at all costs be met. What about divisions and conflicts? Surely a description of how societies are integrated is not the same thing as providing insights into how individuals and groups develop purposes and pursue them. In short, the analogy between a society and an organism is still there, albeit in more implicit forms. These are all real enough criticisms of functionalism. But, as I have said, functionalism at least often tried to integrate an understanding of human nature with the rest of nature with the workings of society. What has happened since is a throwing out of the biological and environmental baby with the functionalist bathwater. In short, there is again something there which needs recovering in an improved form of environmental social theory.

PEOPLE AND ENVIRONMENT: THE ARGUMENTS OF LATER MARXISM

It might be expected that, in turning from functionalism to Marxism, we would find the analogies between nature and society as finally dropped. The notion that society is a kind of organism, one subject to its own internal laws and direction of change, is perhaps easy enough to associate with a 'system view' of society. Such a view, as we have seen, envisages society as in some kind of cybernetic balance both within itself and in relation to its external environment. This balance is such that an external stimulus or an internal change to one part of the social organism affects other parts and a new, but still balanced, whole results. And such a view is not unlike that used by biologists and ecologists to understand an organism. Here again is a series of interacting but nevertheless reciprocally balancing parts.

Marxism, with its emphasis on dialectics, permanent upheaval, and irresolvable conflicts between classes would seem incapable of adopting an organismic view of society, one which is in essential balance. Yet even here, biological and organismic ideas and metaphors persist. Indeed, it can be seen as a feature of some of Marx and Engels' own writings.[40] Their periodic insistence on the inevitable progress of history (from tribal, to feudal, to capitalist to communist) has a certain ring of unilinear social progress about it.

And, at a methodological level, their analysis of the mechanisms involved in social change has perhaps more in common with evolutionary theories than is often realised. People, as I shall later show Marx and Engels arguing, actively work on the social, material and natural world of which they are part. And, in doing so, they change themselves. They are not, as in Parsons' theory, adapting it. In much of Marx and Engels' work people are envisaged as engaging with and changing nature. Nevertheless, broad social change, including the transition to communism, is seen as taking place as a result of individuals and social groups struggling with their social and natural contexts. This included the natural world and domination of the nature was seen in much of Marx and Engels' work as a prerequisite for human emancipation.

Thus the Darwinian model is far from dead in this supposedly alternative tradition of social and political thought. Indeed, Marx and Engels held the originator of modern biology in very high regard. Not only did his theory help the human species to see themselves more completely *as* a species, it also served as a model in nature for Marx's view of human change. As Marx wrote, 'Darwin's book is very important and serves me as a basis in natural science for the class struggle in history.'[41]

Marx and Engels were, however, somewhat ambivalent in their admiration of Darwin. They too saw history as an analogy based on competitive struggle in the social world and were aware of the fact that it might make such a struggle seem an inevitable part of nature. Furthermore, as I shall show in the next chapter, there are parts of Marx's and Engels' work which did not adopt such a triumphalist view of nature and stress that the conquering of nature was absolutely necessary for human freedom.

In certain elements of contemporary Marxism we find the organismic analogy somewhat surprisingly alive and well. The contemporary writer Jurgen Habermas entitles one of his best-known books *Communication and the Evolution of Society*.[42] Here he puts forward an evolutionary view of society, albeit one which partly conflicts with Marx and Engels' historical materialism. Habermas sees each type of culture as organised around a basic 'principle of organisation'. Primitive societies tended to be organised around age and sex roles and coordinated primarily by kinship relations. 'Traditional social formations', including early forms of feudalism, were organised around the domination of a particular class, with bureaucracy acting in a coordinating capacity. Under liberal capitalism the relationship between capital and labour is the organising principle with the bourgeois state acting in a regulating capacity. Under contemporary capitalism there are strong tendencies towards monopoly and expansive state intervention. And here the organising principle is that of increasing technical control and rationalisation. Nevertheless, Habermas sees strong contradictions under this contemporary form of capitalism. The state, for example, does not actually own and control the means of production. And this leaves contemporary society extremely unstable.

This view, combined with another feature of Habermas's model, lies behind his confidence in an evolutionary view of society. This might be termed 'collective memory', an idea which appears to have its roots in Habermas's engagement with Hegelian philosophy and the notion that humans have some kind of defining 'essence'. Habermas argued that the characteristic feature of human beings is not, as Marx and Engels argued, their special physical capacities (and especially their erect posture) for carrying out purposive work. Rather, it is their ability to communicate, learn and use language. It was above all this that has enabled *Homo sapiens* to become the dominant species. And Habermas's point in emphasising this capacity is to argue that humans have continually interrogated the organising principle of each society they have constructed. Furthermore, they have been able to store this information and ensure that it is available to future generations.

Thus Habermas sees people as genetically inheriting 'deep-seated general structures'; these being developed in the very early stages of human evolution. These structures roughly correspond to those observable in a young child before he or she starts developing and integrating their cognitive and linguistic abilities. And, on the basis of these structures, many forms of society or culture can be constructed. As he puts it:

Such structures describe the logical space in which more comprehensive structural formations can take shape; whether new structural formations arise at all and if so, when, depends on *contingent* boundary conditions and learning processes that can be investigated empirically. The genetic explanation of why a certain society has attained a certain level of development is independent of the structural explanation of how a system behaves – a system that conforms at every given stage to its acquired structures.[43]

Habermas's picture of social evolution relies not only on social, cultural and political change but on the innate capacities of people to interrogate their social environment and learn from the past. This is an important insight and one I will later discuss. His espousal of an 'evolutionary' model seems, however, to leave him somewhat uncomfortable. He is well aware of the dangers of social evolutionism and at points in his writing seems anxious to distance himself from the concept. He is certainly keen to avoid any notion that social development is unilinear. Thus he sees 'retrogressions' as being quite possible, Fascist Germany being a prime example.

Furthermore, people's capacities for learning and crisis-solving is by no means seen as guaranteeing rationality. Indeed, much of Habermas's writing on contemporary society is concerned with the ungovernability of contemporary societies. The way forward for Habermas here is psychoanalysis. He sees this as a liberating science, one which enables people to see their true selves and capacities as distinct from what he sees as the distorted values and forms of communication imposed by advanced capitalism.

Thus 'social evolution' has a distinct meaning in Habermas's work, and one which, despite its continuing emphasis on *human* evolution at the expense of other species and inorganic nature, is more persuasive than that of the early evolutionists reviewed earlier in this chapter. It implies neither the notion that society is an organism in an environment, nor that it is developing in a definite direction. Rather it means that social change is directly a product of human beings' continuing attempts to realise what Habermas sees as their innate rationality. Thus social change is a product of the inborn special capacity of humans to create knowledge, interpret it, communicate with one another and learn from the past. Social evolution has a logic of its own, one founded in human beings' capacities.

These capacities, however, are seen by Habermas as blocked and distorted by advanced capitalism. The material conditions, inequalities and ownership of the means of production mean, according to Habermas, that these abilities uniquely associated with the human race are being manipulated and perverted. The way forward is through what he sees as 'critical sciences', those in which new forms of action directly derive from understanding. Amongst the most important of these critical sciences is psychoanalysis. This and other forms of consciousness-raising such as aesthetics are seen as a means by which self-realisation and eventually social liberation can start to be achieved.

Habermas can therefore be used to show that the evolutionary tradition as applied to understanding social change is alive and well in the supposedly 'alternative' perspective represeñted by Marxism. Much of it can be developed in evolving a critical, non-functionalist social theory which is sensitive to biological and ecological issues. But as previously mentioned, Habermas can also be used to illustrate another theme, and another problem, within Marxian political economy. While there is certainly a concern here with active human beings and their innate abilities to assess the circumstances in which they are living, communicate with others about these circumstances and develop new concepts which can eventually change circumstances. But the sociology remains 'human exemptionalist' in the sense of not adequately relating personal and social change as it affects the human species, but not relating such change to the rest of the natural world.

Contemporary Marxists still find themselves in acute difficulties when confronting contemporary ecological and environmental issues. This is largely, however, because they have forgotten what Marx originally wrote about the relationship between nature and the human species. Marx's argument was the dialectical one, arguing that the concepts of 'man' and 'nature' would be historically changed as one challenged the other. The human subject is therefore envisaged as both constructing and being constructed *by* nature. As Marx put it in *Capital*: 'by thus acting on the external world and changing it, [man] at the same time changes his own nature'.[44]

Instead of following up this insight much of contemporary Marxist work on environmental issues has become diverted into a debate with Malthusian and other forms of analysis which they see as overly technocratic and 'scientific', and thereby deflecting attention away from what they see as the overwhelmingly significant class bases of resource-use and environmental change. Marxists' concern and engagement in this debate is understandable. Much of the environmentalist literature does indeed concentrate on technical issues and resolutely refuses to engage in political and social matters. On the other hand, contemporary Marxism's involvement in this debate has meant that rather little positive progress has been made in terms of constructing the new concepts and understandings concerning the relation between nature and the human species which, as I shall shortly show, Marx and Engels were originally looking for.

The essence of the contemporary Marxist position was put by the Chinese delegation at the 1972 Stockholm Conference on the Environment.[45] Addressing the specific question of resources, they argued that there was no such thing as scarcity. Western officials assumed this to mean that China possessed vast reserves of minerals and fossil fuels. Yet their argument was compatible with at least part of the line originally drawn by Marx and Engels.

Contemporary Marxists tend to argue, as indeed did Marx and Engels, that needs are not simply the product of biological necessities or, as Malthus argued, that they are held down as a result of rapidly increasing populations. Needs and wants are in large part socially created. In other words, definitions and understandings of wants and needs must be placed in their historical and social contexts. Similarly, 'resources' is also a malleable concept, one subject to constant interrogation and change. While the amount of a given resource may possibly be fixed, the use to which it may be put must be defined in relation to specific levels of technology and levels of consumption. Finally, most contemporary Marxists would place a major question mark over the concept of 'scarcity'. This they see as needing a location in historical and social contexts. Not only is it a product of certain levels of taste and consumption but it is also seen as deliberately created and manipulated by producers. As the Marxist geographer David Harvey puts it, 'Scarcity is in fact necessary to the survival of the capitalist mode of production, and it has to be carefully managed, otherwise the self-regulating aspect to the price mechanism will break down.'[46]

All this leads those on the Left to criticise severely much of the contemporary environmental literature. Much of this literature they see as overly 'scientific', the result again being that of concealing the class and power relations involved. They furthermore agree, somewhat paradoxically, with those neo-liberals who argue that the ecological debate is largely organised and orchestrated by a powerful middle class protecting their own material interests. Here, for example, is Enzensberger an influential and comparatively early critic on the Left, criticising 'eco freaks', hippies and writers such as P. and A. Ehrlich. The latter are neo-Malthusians, seeing the threat to resources and large-scale pollution as primarily a direct result of very rapid population growth:

> On the whole one can say that in the ecological movement – or perhaps we should say movements – the scientific aspects, which derive predominantly from biology, have merged in an extremely confused alliance with a whole series of political motivations and interests, partly concealed.[47]

History shows, Enzensberger argues, a predominantly *class* dimension to resource-shortages, pollution and health problems. The apparent neutrality of biology and other natural sciences is thus seen as no more than a fiction. The 'global' nature of the threat obfuscates the nature of the social interests involved and merely serves to maintain the established social and political order.

The tendency, then, is for those currently operating within a political economy framework to treat biology, the natural sciences and explanations which rely on these disciplines with considerable suspicion, not to say outright hostility. Rather, and in line with their particular conceptualisation of Marxism, they see production and class relations – with the state as supporting the dominant classes – as the chief or even the only processes involved. Blaikie and Brookfield, for example, realise that there is a major gap between how ecologists and natural scientists envisage the environmental problem. But in the end they plump for a particular kind of Marxist explanation, one which does not fully recognise the full richness of Marx and Engels' original insights.[48]

Following a major review of land degradation in societies as far apart (politically, historically and geographically) as Nepal, India, Fiji, eighteenth-century France and South America, Blaikie and Brookfield detect 'one common element'. This they term 'pressure of production on resources'. But this conclusion, even in its own terms, is not persuasive. When we look at the case studies on which it is based we find that, in the Nepal case, lack of capital and resources is advanced as the key factor, in combination with a (Malthusian) population on resources. In India the mechanism involved appears to be private encroachment of common property resources and, again, population growth. In Fiji the problem derives mainly from a rigid system of land tenure. In early modern

France, the empirical work shows that rising population and commercialisation of the land market were the chief culprits. Only in South America (where extensive cattle ranching on grasslands created from an erstwhile tropical forest are causing major environmental damage) can 'pressure of production of resources' be advanced in a fairly convincing way.

So what seems to have happened here is that, in their enthusiasm to overturn what they correctly see as technocratic, scientific and 'value-free' accounts of environmental problems, Blaikie and Brookfield have rushed to a particular version of Marxism. This is a version which insists on political economy and the primacy of production as the only causal generative mechanism. But a Marxism appropriate for contemporary environmentalism should entail a recognition that environmental change also involves ecological and biological systems and that the human organism is itself part of these systems.

There are nevertheless now some signs of change amongst contemporary Marxist commentators. As I shall discuss further in due course, chief amongst these is a climb-down over the 'absolute' nature of resources. Resources, it is now being argued, maybe actually are limited and finite. Such an insistence is not necessarily a fiction put about about capitalists, functionalist sociologists and others anxious to preserve the *status quo*.

Caldwell was one of the first modern Marxists to advance this position.[49] And his work is very significant in terms of linking the 'natural' with the 'social' worlds. He was writing as someone with a particular interest in the overdevelopment of the advanced capitalist societies and the underdevelopment of the 'third world'. And, in line with Catton and Dunlap's insistence on a new 'post exuberant' sociology, he insisted on locating social change in the context of the 'natural limits' represented by fossil fuels. Essentially, he argued that the present levels of population and the levels of affluence enjoyed by a significant proportion of it have all been achieved by transforming the energy contained within the fossil fuels into energy for human beings (food) and energy for the power of labour-saving machinery (fuel).

Fossil fuels, however, are seen by Caldwell as in short supply. And, while solar energy, nuclear power, subterranean heat and other devices may offer some substitutes, there is 'no known or even theoretically conceivable substitute for the fossil fuels in enabling the production of food to remain at its present volume'.[50] This volume is now far in excess of the optimum natural level which would be possible in a society unable to call on fossil fuels. Caldwell is anxious to spell out the social implications of this. In his view the rich nations, 'burdened with an energy addiction' are likely to go to great ends to protect their already high standards of living. Meanwhile, countries in Asia, Africa and Latin America are likely to lose out in the struggle for these finite resources. Nevertheless, there will be struggles and wars. The underdeveloped societies are at some advantage in so far as guerrilla wars against the oil and resource-strong major powers do not entail large-scale use of energy.

Caldwell was in effect introducing the First and Second Laws of Thermodynamics into social and political theory. He started to do this in 1971 but it remains, to say the least, a fairly unusual set of considerations for the social sciences.[51] As we saw in the Introduction to this book, the First Law states that energy can be neither created nor destroyed. When, for example, fuel is burned all that happens is a transformation from potential to kinetic energy. There is no increase in the quantum level of energy. The Second 'Entropy' Law states that transformation in the case of heat energy is a one-way process and is irreversible. Originally free energy has been diffusely dissipated in the form of heat. The key point, and a central part of Caldwell's analysis, is that free or available energy can only be run down. It can never be increased.

It is by no means easy to make the connections between these theories and the social world, but a useful way of envisaging the relationships between these natural laws and social change is to treat them historically. Caldwell argues that hunter–gatherers could, and to a large extent still can, provide for their own and their families' needs with comparatively little labour. Only when population increases to a point at which, given the land at their disposal, they can no longer provide for their group, must they engage in more productive way of obtaining food. This has usually been through settled agriculture. And within agriculture each successive innovation up to and including modern agri-business methods has been made necessary by rapid growing populations and their increasing pressure on existing food-producing techniques.

Agriculture, however, creates new kinds of class relations and new forms of exploitation. The surplus extraction is now coordinated by a ruling class, one which is likely to gain from the particular mode of production. Caldwell's point here, however, is that such surplus extraction is still contained within ecologically possible limits. Furthermore, it continues within the territory at its disposal and with the population control methods and ways of obtaining food that are available to it.

With the rise of capitalism, however, a new international division of labour emerges. And 'an international class system' develops in which one society benefits by the labour of another. And at this stage there is an important spatial division in the ways ecological pressures are experienced. There is an increasing gap between the ecological reality of absolute limits and how ecological problems are actually experienced. With the rise of the international division of labour, Caldwell argues, ecological problems 'are felt at several removes from the locations where new food-obtaining techniques are made the subject of research and of subsequent investment and innovation'.[52] It might be added here, and this is a point I shall take up in Chapter 6, that the *consumption* of the goods provided by the developing countries has also been at some distance from where resulting ecological pressures are actually experienced. The resulting bliss in the developed countries has taken place in the context of continuing innocence of conditions elsewhere.

Caldwell is therefore suggesting that there are objective limits, whatever the type of social organisation involved. It is only quite recently that the extent of these limits has emerged and been recognised. And it is also instructive to note how Caldwell does attribute to population increases a causal significance in ecological problems. Especially important, he argues, have been the huge population rises during the last half-century, largely as a result of considerable advances in medicine and health care. These in turn have put great pressure on agriculture. But the new form of agri-industry is itself highly dependent on fossil fuels and cannot be easily or (given the nature of absolute limits) even realistically adopted in all countries. It was a wrong turning as regards feeding the growing millions.

Caldwell's early admission of absolute limits and the effects of population can be seen as a kind of reconciliation with some of the early social theorists, such as Malthus, whom I reviewed at the beginning of this chapter. His views are still hardly commonplace in contemporary Marxist theory but they deserve far more attention. One Marxist author who did give them credence is Foster-Carter. He sums up the argument concisely in the following way:

Most ecologists have ethnocentrically concentrated on the developed world, and insisted that it will have to experience 'de-growth'. The corollary for underdeveloped countries is that they will never attain the living standards of the presently 'over-developed' world, for two reasons: there are not enough mineral resources to maintain the whole world at such a level, and, even if there were, the necessary energy-consumption would cause a climatic catastrophe (melting of the polar ice-caps, and the like).

For Marxists, abundance is out: arguably it was always an ultimately meaningless notion, but henceforth 'scarcity' will have to be accepted as more than just a bugbear of bourgeois economics defending unequal social relations.[53]

This version of Marxism is one which is particularly worth considering. It needs, however, a better understanding of human beings as possessing certain natural endowments. Furthermore, some insight into how natural limits *combine* with these endowments is needed from this modern version of critical social theory. Such a link was made in an early paper by Benton.[54]

Basing his analysis on Marx's analysis of the labour process, Benton argues for the incorporation of what he calls a 'weak biological determinism'. 'Weak' is relative to 'strong' as implied by early forms of sociobiology. This is an area of work I discuss in Chapter 4, but suffice to say here that this area of biology attributes central significance to genes as the basis of individual and social behaviour. 'Weak' does not, however, imply that biologically based processes are unimportant. Benton includes 'sensory discrimination, cognitive appraisal, symbolic co-ordination of activity and deliberate intervention into natural processes' as inborn features of human beings which must be incorporated into an improved sociological understanding and one which links humans to the natural world.

Furthermore, Benton is arguing that these 'capacities' are realised in specific historical and social contexts and their realisation in such contexts constitutes the acquisition of culture. Thus 'culture' is by no means a feature of individual and social life which is separate from 'nature'. Rather, it is a means by which natural capacities and tendencies are realised. And, since we are now discussing the real historical and social world, the extents and forms of such realisation becomes extremely complex and differentiated.

Benton therefore provides clues as to how political economy approaches might be combined with a serious appreciation of the rules and resources imposed by the natural and social world. These again include, for example, the 'rules' of the Second Law of Thermodynamics or the strictly limited resources of fossil fuels. Like Caldwell, Benton argues that such limits have been given far too little attention by contemporary social theory and by Marxism in particular. Benton sees such resources and rules as enabling and constraining. They enhance, albeit in a socially uneven way, the capacity of human beings to adapt themselves while at the same time acting as limits to what can be achieved. But again, Benton refuses to see such natural limits as *purely* natural. There presumably are finite limits to, say, the amount of coal or petrol buried in the globe. On the other hand, they are only limits to human social activity in so far as the particular practices and interchanges with nature in which they engage are persisted with.

In all, Benton's suggestions have strong echoes of the early Marx and his co-worker Engels. And it is to these people we need to return if we are going to construct a sounder, ecologically based, social theory – one which still concentrates on the human species but sees it in strict relation to the natural world.

CONCLUSION: SOCIETY, NATURE AND SOCIAL THEORY

I have so far reviewed the changing and varied ways in which sociology has related to biological and evolutionary thinking. Much of sociology's history has consisted of a dialogue with biology and Darwinism in particular, but this dialogue has occurred in largely unhelpful forms.

Tönnies' account of the transition from *gemeinschaft* to *gesellschaft* contains a suggestive account of the way in which relations to land and nature become severed with the advent of modernity. But in the end it is descriptive. It gives relatively little attention to the causal factors involved.

Early forms of social theory were largely constructed using analogies between societies and nature. Thus societies were seen as if they were developing like live organisms, or people were seen as struggling for survival in their environment, much in the same way as Darwin had specified in his theories. And, although the Darwinian theory showed itself to be capable of interpretation in a number of different ways, science was seen as immutable. It was not envisaged as *itself* a social product. In all, what was seen as an 'objective' form of knowledge was used to inform the development of social theory. Haraway's view is worth recalling here:

> Just how science 'gets at' the world remains far from resolved. What does seem resolved, however, is that science grows from and enables concrete ways of life, including particular constructions of love, knowledge and power. That is the core of its instrumentalism and the limit to its universalism.[55]

Other problems have arisen from sociology's long-term involvement with biology. One is teleology, the suggestion that society is moving over the long-term towards some improved, more perfected, state. A second is that the *relations* between society and nature have often been sadly neglected. A third is that people are not seen as themselves organisms with natural histories. Some of these problems started to be usefully addressed with functionalist social theory. But at this point social theory started going to the other extreme, seeing social and power relations as almost wholly the result biologically driven individuals relating to their environment. Marxism has not escaped all these problems either. In its many and various forms it too has been guilty of teleology, neglect of relations between people and nature and, Habermas apart, an absence of human beings whose behaviour is in part a product of their evolutionary history.

But perhaps the most important process during this period of intellectual history is the emergence of all the dualisms with which we are now familiar. These are now proving profoundly unhelpful but they were, and to a large extent remain, important in creating disciplines and, not unimportantly, academic careers. As Benton has recently put it:

The distinctive function of the key biology/society, nature/culture, behaviour/action, cause/meaning dichotomies in establishing and legitimating an intellectual division of labour between the natural and social sciences was performed from the latter half of the nineteenth century onwards in Europe and America.[56]

It is the abolition of these dualisms and their replacement by a critical realism which I am proposing here. This emphasises different levels of abstraction. It aims at specifying the powers, capacities and generative mechanisms of organic and inorganic nature and the ways these are realised as they combine with contingent circumstances. Such a framework was offered by Marx and Engels well before most of the social theory outlined above was created. It is to them, therefore, that we must now turn.

NOTES

1. A. Comte (1853), *Positive Sociology*, Vol. 2. (Quoted in G. Jones (1980), *Social Darwinism and English Thought*, Harvester Wheatsheaf: Hemel Hempstead, p. 1).
2. H. Spencer (1972), *On Social Evolution*, University of Chicago: Chicago (J. Peel (ed.))
3. On this point see J. Crook (1989), 'Introduction: socioecological paradigms, evolution and history: perspectives for the 1990s', in V. Standen, R. Foley, *Comparative Socioecology*, Blackwell: Oxford, pp. 1–36.
4. D. Haraway (1989), *Primate Visions*, Routledge: London, p. 13.
5. Quoted in D. Winch (1987), *Malthus*, Oxford University Press: Oxford, p. 19.
6. H. Spencer (1972), *op.cit.*, p. 123.
7. *ibid.*, p. 122
8. Quoted in P. Abrams (1968), *The Origins of British Sociology, 1834–1914*, University of Chicago: Chicago, p. 74
9. H. Spencer (1972), *op.cit.*, p. 138–9.
10. P.P. Kropotkin (1904), *Mutual Aid. A Factor of Evolution*, Heinemann: London.
11. L. Clark (1984), *Social Darwinism in France*, University of Alabama Press: Alabama.
12. Quoted in R. Hofstadter (1955), *Social Darwinism in American Thought*, Brazilier: New York, p. 56.
13. Quoted in *ibid.*, p. 59.
14. Quoted in *ibid.*, p. 58.

15. Quoted in *ibid.*, p. 59.
16. F. Tönnies (1955), *Community and Association*, Routledge: London. (Originally published in 1887).
17. *ibid.*, pp. 48–9.
18. *ibid.*, p. 42.
19. *ibid.*, pp. 239- 40.
20. *ibid.*, p. 186.
21. *ibid.*, p. 240.
22. For a relatively recent review of the state of contemporary community studies see C. Bell, H. Newby (1971), *Community Studies*, Allen & Unwin: London. Rural studies have become relatively neglected by students of modern societies, but see T. Bradley, P. Lowe (1984), *Locality and Rurality: Economy and society in rural regions*, Geo Books: Norwich.
23. See, in particular, R. Park (1967), *The City*, University of Chicago Press: Chicago (originally published in 1925) and R. Park, E. Burgess (1969), *Introduction to the Science of Sociology*, University of Chicago Press: Chicago (originally published in 1921).
24. R. Park (1952), *Human Communities*, Free Press: New York, p. 158.
25. R. McKenzie (1967), 'The ecological approach to the study of the human community', in R. Park (1967), *op.cit.*, p. 63.
26. R. McKenzie (1967), *op.cit.*, p. 68.
27. This point is fully developed in P. Saunders (1986), *Urban Sociology*, Hutchinson: London, Chap. 2.
28. See P. Dickens (1990), *Urban Sociology*, Harvester Wheatsheaf: Hemel Hempstead.
29. A. Hawley (1950), *Human Ecology: A theory of community structure*, Ronald Press: New York.
30. *ibid.*, p. 72.
31. *ibid.*, p. 30–1.
32. *ibid.*, p. 40.
33. *ibid.*, p. 178.
34. *ibid.*, p. 221.
35. O. Duncan (1959), 'Human ecology and population studies', in P. Hauser and O. Duncan (eds), *The Study of Population*, University of Chicago Press: Chicago.
36. For a good survey and summary of Talcott Parsons' work see G. Rocher (1975), *Talcott Parsons and American Sociology*, Barnes and Noble: New York.
37. T. Parsons (1964), 'Evolutionary universals in society', in *American Sociological Review* 29: 339–57.
38. B. Malinowski (1944), *A Scientific Theory of Culture*, Oxford University Press: Oxford.

39. *ibid.*, pp. 124–5.
40. This point is made in, for example, A. Giddens (1989), *Sociology*, Polity Press: Oxford, Chap. 20.
41. Marx is quoted in R. Hoffstadter (1955), *op.cit.*, p. 115.
42. J. Habermas (1979), *The Evolution of Society*, Heinemann: London.
43. *ibid.*, pp. 140–1.
44. K. Marx (1976), *Capital*, Pelican: Harmondsworth, p. 283 (originally published in 1867).
45. See D. Harvey (1974), 'Population, resources, and the ideology of science', *Economic Geography* 50: 256–77.
46. *ibid.*, p. 272.
47. H. Enzensberger (1988), 'A critique of political ecology', in *Dreamers of the Absolute*, Radius: London.
48. P. Blaikie, H. Brookfield (1987), *Land Degradation and Society*, Methuen: London.
49. M. Caldwell (1977), *The Wealth of Some Nations*, Zed Press: London.
50. *ibid.*, p. 13.
51. See, however, F. Soddy (1922), *Cartesian Economics*, Henderson: London; K. Boulding (1966), 'The economics of the coming spaceship earth', in H. Jarrett (ed.), *Environmental Quality in a Growing Economy*, Johns Hopkins Press: Baltimore; N. Georgescu-Roegen (1976), *Energy and Economic Myths*, Pergamon: Oxford.
52. M. Caldwell (1977), *op.cit.*, p. 134.
53. A. Foster Carter (1974), 'Neo-Marxist approaches to development and underdevelopment', in E. DeKadt, G. Williams (eds), *Sociology and Development*, Tavistock: London.
54. T. Benton (1989), 'Marxism and natural limits: an ecological critique and reconstruction', *New Left Review* 178: 51–86. See also T. Benton (1990), 'On the limits of malleability', *Capitalism, Nature, Socialism* 4, June: 68–71. An earlier useful paper connecting the 'biological' with 'the social' is T. Benton (1984), 'Biological ideas and their cultural uses', in S.C. Brown (ed.), *Objectivity and Cultural Divergence*, Cambridge University Press: Cambridge. A sociologist, albeit not one working in the Marxist tradition, who for some time argued for the abolition of the society/nature dualism is Norbert Elias. See N. Elias (1991), *The Symbol Theory*, Sage: London.
55. D. Haraway (1989), *op.cit.*, p. 8.
56. T. Benton (1991), 'Biology and social science: why the return of the repressed should be given a (cautious) welcome', *Sociology* 25, 1: 9.

3

'NATURE AS MAN'S INORGANIC BODY':
MARX'S CONCEPTUAL FRAMEWORK

The last chapter argued that social theory's approach to the natural world has been quite problematic. One reason amongst many is that sociology (and early sociology in particular) borrowed from Darwinism as a conceptual framework. And this borrowing concentrated on a particular interpretation of Darwinism, one which emphasised that evolutionary progress took place as a result of competitive struggle between organisms. The best or fittest organisms were seen as emerging from such a struggle for life.

An alternative version of Darwinism could have been emphasised. As we have seen, early French interpretations of Darwin's thinking gave particular prominence to altruism and cooperative behaviour between species. Dominant social and political concerns in that society led them to see the natural world in that particular way. And this latter perspective, incidentally, is now being taken up by some biologists in our own period. They increasingly see cooperation and harmony as the typical *modus vivendi* between and within species.[1]

Earlier British and North American interpretations of Darwin on the other hand, closely paralleled a particular view of a successful capitalist society, one emphasising the competition between individuals. In terms of producing the 'fittest' individual and progress towards an ever-better form of society. Haraway's cautions about the social construction of the natural world are particularly appropriate here:

Natural sciences, like human sciences, are intextricably *within* the processes that give them birth. And so, like the human sciences, the natural sciences are culturally and historically specific, modified, involved. They matter to real people. It makes sense to ask what stakes, methods, and kinds of authority are involved in natural scientific accounts, how they differ, for example, from religion or ethnography. It does not make sense to ask for a form of authority that escapes the web of the highly productive cultural fields that make the accounts possible in the first place. The detached eye of objective science is ideological fiction, and a powerful one.[2]

But Haraway, unlike many critical social theorists who are wholly persuaded that *their* view of the social and natural world is *the* correct one, is not suggesting that the natural scientists' view is wholly without value. Her argument is far more subtle than this. It is that no one, natural and social scientist alike, can claim to be standing outside of the 'facts' being observed. Such facts are always being discovered and interpreted in line with the values of the observer and of the society in which she or he is living. So rather than dismissing the natural sciences as a fiction designed simply to cloak dominant social interests and the values of competitive capitalism, she is not attempting wholly to invalidate any form of knowledge. Nevertheless, no science (social or otherwise) can be seen as a purely objective form of knowledge.

The second problem we identified was the growing division between the social sciences on the one hand and the natural sciences on the other. The result is what Benton has recently called 'the settled division of labour between the biological and social sciences'.[3] This division may be reassuring for some of the labourers but it is now emerging as increasingly problematic. This is because it insists that one type of science continues to be appropriate for people while another is to be used for understanding the natural world. And, if this is so, the assumption must be that people are not in any sense natural and that their relationships with the natural world are not especially significant. And yet a large part of contemporary social and political concerns are surely pointing to a need for fundamentally reviewing such assumptions. Environmentalism, for example, is clearly drawing attention to the critical connections between people and nature. Concerns with human health place major question marks over whether people can simply be seen as organisms which are socially constructed. Are they not 'natural' in much the same way as other species? And concerns with the rights and welfare of animals also suggest that the attachment of a particular set of sciences and values to humans can all too easily lead to the disadvantage and eventual destruction of other species.

In short, some crucial connections remain to be made. It was back in 1967 that Edmund Leach in his Reith Lectures popularised the phrase 'only connect'. He argued that a new science was needed, one that recognised 'it is not the bits and pieces that matter but the evolving system as a whole'.[4] Such a science would allow people to see their relationships to the natural and social world and their responsibilities towards it. Despite, however, the recent rise of concerns which emphasise peoples' connections with the natural world such a new science remains a long way from being constructed. Even less progress has been made in determining precisely which connections should form the foundations for such a new science.

So what would such a science look like? This chapter will commend the work of the young Karl Marx as providing the foundations for an overarching theoretical construction. Much of the work to be quoted here was written by Marx as early as the 1840s, some fifteen years before Darwin's *Origins of Species* was published. It is somewhat fragmentary and, as I will show, it can be criticised in certain respects. Some of it, especially his idea of an alienated human 'species being' found its way into later work such as *Capital*. But, as Marx increasingly concentrated on the processes inherent to the modern or capitalist mode of production he started to neglect the connections he made in his youth between nature and what (without reminders such as those from contemporary feminism) he called 'man'.

This chapter will be largely devoted to outlining Marx's specifications of these connections.[5] As outlined here, it has four main components. The first is his working method, one which emphasises the reciprocal connections between organisms and their environment. The second is his view of human nature, one which emphasises that people have a 'natural' and a 'species' being. The third argues that under capitalism people's beings are distorted and restricted. Finally, however, he argues that some sense or semblance of human species being can be recovered under capitalism.

Much of Marx's argument, I shall be suggesting, is highly suggestive for our contemporary concerns. To illustrate this I shall later refer to the experience of contemporary indigenous peoples. On the other hand, Marx left us with a range of problems. First, as I shall discuss later, there persists a residual dualism between 'man' and 'animals'. Second, and not surprisingly, his view of the environment and resources on which 'man' depends is inadequate for our contemporary purposes. To push his argument to its logical conclusion we need to consider the environment not as a set of infinite resources but also capable of feeding back on and deeply affecting human beings and their projects.

More generally, Marx's framework can be amended and extended. This book will be largely devoted to understanding how Marx's view of people as natural and species beings can be extended, given contemporary knowledge from the natural and physical sciences as well as psychology and social theory as they have evolved since Marx's day. Such an understanding, while it remains focused on the human species, also helps explain the changing relationships of people to nature.

NATURE, ALIENATION AND PEOPLE: THE EARLY MARXIAN PERSPECTIVE

Of central importance to Marx's approach was his dialectical method. And it is this which makes it especially relevant to the study of the relationships between organisms and environment. His approach was relational. That is to say, he always saw an object such as a human being, a plant or a sum of money not as a thing but as a set of relations. His working method consisted of specifying the potentials or latent tendencies within an object. However, he envisaged these as not necessarily realised in practice. Whether or not they are realised depends on their combination with other factors which are contingent to the latent powers contained within the object. Thus his emphasis was always on connections and, more importantly still, on tendencies which may or may not be released or made manifest.

He rarely applied this way of thinking to the natural world. But one instructive example is his brief comment on the relations between plants and the sun. 'The sun', he wrote, 'is the object of the plant – an indispensable object to it confirming its life – just as the plant is an object of the sun, of the sun's objective essential power.'[6] In other words, a plant is not just a plant. It is much more than this, and indeed much more than is readily apparent from simple observation. A plant is an expression of the sun and its power. It is a way in which the power of the sun is made manifest. At the same time, the sun allows the latent or potential tendencies of the plant (growth and development) to be realised.

This is just one illustration of Marx's broad approach. More generally, he insists that an organism's being resides not just within the organism itself but within its relationships with the rest of the natural (and indeed social) world. 'A being', he argued, 'which does not have its nature outside itself is not a natural being, and plays no part in the system of nature.'[7] And, critically from our viewpoint, this applies as much to people as it does to plants and other animal species.

In an obvious sense people depend on nature for their existence. But Marx's dialectical approach goes beyond such a self-evident statement to suggest that nature is 'man's inorganic body'. Nature is therefore seen as *part of* a person in the same way as, say, a limb or an internal organ. People are constituted by nature and it is therefore wholly incorrect and misleading to insist on the dualism between 'man' and 'nature':

Nature is man's *inorganic body*, that is to say nature in so far as it is not the human body. Man *lives* from nature, i.e. nature is his *body*, and he must maintain a continuing dialogue with it if he is not to die. To say that man's physical and mental life is linked to nature simply means that nature is linked to itself, for man is part of nature.[8] [Marx's emphases]

Linking this to his general dialectical approach, Marx argues that the human species has particular kinds of latent tendencies and potentials which may or may not be realised in their association (or lack of association) with the natural world.

Centrally important here is Marx's conception of human nature. Human beings have certain powers, potentials and needs. 'Powers' are, broadly, capacities and tendencies which people share with all other living species. An organism may, for example, have the power to walk at a certain stage of its development, even if it may not in fact be using this power at any given moment. 'Potentials' are the capacity to develop some capacity in the future. Animals, according to Marx, are characterised by relatively fixed or static types of activity. Humans, by contrast, can develop or be developed in such a way as to acquire new capacities and powers. 'Needs' are the ways an individual feels these basic powers in the forms of drives or wants. But the association between powers and needs is, in practice – as Marx well knew – more complex than this. The way an individual becomes aware of these powers and tries to fulfil them is also socially constructed. Distinct types of society also create distinct forms of need.

Marx's schema also makes the critical distinction between 'natural' and 'species' powers and needs. What does he mean by this distinction? 'Natural' powers and needs are those which people share with all other species while 'species' powers and needs are those distinctive to human beings. Marx classifies labour, eating and sex as examples of the former. They are basic to what a species must do in order to stay alive and reproduce future generations. The bond between the sexes is perhaps the most obvious expression of natural needs shared by humans and other species. Marx gives particular emphasis to this union: 'The immediate, natural, necessary relation of human being to human being is the *relationship* of *man* to *woman*.'[9] [Marx's emphases]

Importantly, Marx goes further to suggest that humans and other animals have needs other than simple survival and reproduction. He implies, for example, that all living species have a need for companionship; one incorporating sympathetic relations with other members of the same species. He also suggests that humans and animals have 'a need to hunt, to roam'.[10] This suggests that human powers and needs, like those of other animals, include those of exploration, seeking variety and the appropriation of surrounding objects. Marx was to take up this point in his later work when he suggested that capitalist labour processes systematically deny such needs.

Again, and most important for us, Marx argued that these internal powers can only be realised or fulfilled through association with a social-cum-natural environment. The objects outside the individual's physical body (other animals, for example, or plants, inanimate objects and the sun's rays) are thus centrally significant in manifesting or confirming these needs. An obvious example is the natural need to eat. 'Hunger', as Marx puts it, 'needs a nature outside itself, an object outside itself to be stilled. Hunger is an acknowledged need of my body for an object existing outside it indispensable to its integration and the expression of its essential being.'[11] Once more, the central conceptual message of this is that in practice there is no discontinuity between organism and environment and an analytical framework which maintains such a discontinuity will finish up by misunderstanding *both* the organism and its organic and inorganic environment.

What of species powers and needs? In parallel with (and rooted in) their status as natural beings people have, Marx argued, qualities which are uniquely their own. 'Man is', he argued, 'a being for himself. Therefore he is a species being, and has to confirm and manifest himself as such both in his being and knowing.'[12] Again, therefore, people have distinctive capacities. But to be a full person, or someone realising their capacities or potentials means a continuing confirmation of species being.

What is this species being and how is it confirmed? Especially important to Marx is the human species' self-consciousness. What, according to Marx, distinguishes humans from other living species is their self-awareness and their capacities for conceptualising and learning. These capacities are used for pre-conceptualising projects and planning them before actually carrying them out. Animals, by contrast, act spontaneously. People, too, have the capacity for seeing themselves as individuals in other individuals; learning about themselves from other individuals and in turn using this learning as a way of understanding the whole human race.

The human species' is seen by Marx as having very distinctive mental and intellectual capacities. So people's interaction with the rest of the organic and inorganic world (including members of their own species) goes beyond simply surviving and reproducing. It is the way in which people develop and use their special intellectual, spiritual and aesthetic potential. Human powers are, once more, being realised through establishing particular relationships with nature, including those with other members of the human species.

Humans, Marx argued, have very distinct 'universal' relations with nature. 'Universality' here has several meanings. Unlike other animals, the whole of nature is the sphere of human activity. People can even produce according to the standards of other species. Universality also refers to the human species as a whole; they operate on behalf of all the human species whereas animals produce on behalf of themselves or their young. Finally, humans produce (or at least are capable of producing) independent of immediate need.

What forms do relationships with nature take? Perhaps the clearest form is what Marx calls 'appropriation'. This involves using the natural world towards the organism's own ends. But, often as part of such appropriation there are other forms of relationship. These are 'perception' or immediate contact with nature and 'orientation', or the interpretation of the natural world and the organism's place within it. It is this latter capacity where again, according to Marx, the human organism has very special capacities.

Whatever type of relationship is involved, however, the young Marx's central assertion is that to survive as a natural and species being people must have a direct and engaged relationship to nature. They are dead in a biological sense without such a relationship. At the same time, they are dead in a spiritual, intellectual and aesthetic sense without such a close association. Human powers operate, but in a distorted fashion. Human potentials, or the possible development of new powers, remain unrealised.

Marx argues, however, that under capitalism this direct relationship is removed. People are systematically alienated or 'estranged' from nature, their inorganic body. Alienation is of course a powerful theme in Marx's thinking and this process of estrangement from nature can be directly linked to wider, more familiar, understandings of alienation in Marx's work. His discussion of this topic is usually most closely associated with his analysis of the labour process. The labourer, he argued throughout much of his writing, works on nature to produce commodities for sale. Before the advent of capitalism and private property,

nature appears as *his* work and his reality. The object of labour is therefore the *objectification of the species-life of man*: for man reproduces himself not only intellectually, in his consciousness, but actively and actually, and he can therefore contemplate himself in a world he himself has created.[13]

But under a system of capitalism and private property such a form of contemplation is denied. People lose control and understanding over the products of their labour. And, since species-being is seen as confirmed in the labour process, they become alienated from their own species-being:

> In tearing away the object of his production from man, estranged labour therefore tears away from him his *species-life*, his true species-objectivity, and transforms his advantage over animals into the disadvantage that his inorganic body, nature, is taken away from him.[14]

The result, according to Marx, is that under capitalism human life becomes distorted to such an extent that it is in a condition appropriate to that of animals. In fact, despite their special capacities and latent potentials, people lose their advantages under capitalism. Animals do at least have a direct relation to nature whereas this is denied under a capitalist mode of production.

One aspect of people's natural- and species-being is, as we have seen Marx arguing, sociality: the need for association with other human beings. Such association helps to realise individual capacities. And, as an inherently social being, people are better able to realise group potential if they are allowed to act in a collective fashion. But again under capitalism this form of natural- and species-being is denied and stunted. Individual people and their capacity to labour are bought like any other commodity. The result is 'the estrangement of man from man'.[15] Species-being is confirmed through association with nature more generally, and community with members of the same species is just part of this wider confirmation. But capitalism again denies such association. People confront each other as alien and competing individuals rather than as members of the same species with individual or communal interests and projects.

Marx's discussion of alienation particularly focuses on the labour process, or the conversion of nature in the making of products, and the forms of human association created and denied through the labour process. Under capitalism a labourer's work on nature to create products entails the loss of association with nature since these products are themselves alienated from the worker's use or control. But Marx's arguments about relations with nature are, especially in his early work, wider than this. Interaction with nature for human beings has a deeper significance. This is again due to what he sees as human beings' very distinctive mental and aesthetic powers and capacities. Nature, and the need to associate with it, has a special significance for human beings in terms of confirming this more extended aspect of species-being. Stones, for example, are made into jewels. Similarly, people's species-being gives special emphasis to the landscape and to the beauty of other animals and inorganic nature. But again, private property and capitalism are seen as denying such species-being. Instead of appreciation in its own right the emphasis turns towards possession. '*All* the physical and intellectual senses have been replaced by the simple estrangement of *all* these senses – the sense of *having*.'[16]

The removal of capitalism and the direct association of people with inorganic nature in a communist society would therefore, according to Marx, allow humans to develop their special aesthetic and conceptualising capacities. The long-term project is the communal appropriation of nature. This would allow the realisation of humans' capacities and potentials:

> The supersession of private property is therefore the complete *emancipation* of all human senses and attributes. . . . Need or enjoyment have therefore lost their *egoistic* nature, and nature has lost its mere *utility* in the sense that its use has become *human* use.[17]

This brings us to the third main component of Marx's theory of alienation. In the first chapter of this book we found neo-liberals arguing that the market is the solution to ecological crises. It can be relied on, they argue, to permit new, more satisfactory, relations with resources and the natural world. By contrast, Marx argued that the market is not so much a solution. Rather, it is the central part of the problem itself. Nevertheless, Marx's conceptual framework can indeed accommodate the apparent freedoms which the neo-liberals say the market can bring.

If the human species loses contact with its inorganic body under capitalism this does not necessarily mean that it always feels this to be the case. A central part of Marx's whole theory of alienation is that people are capable of restoring some sense of the collectivity, association and community from which they have been separated. This is achieved through distinctly human forms of association which, apparently at least, emphasise the equality of individuals. Two examples are religion and the state. The first insists that all individuals are equal before God, whatever inequalities may exist on earth. The second insists that, through such institutions as citizenship, equality before the law and enfranchisement, every individual is in fact equal to every other; this, again, despite the material and real inequalities which persist in the real material world.

But it is in the institution of the market-place where individuals find themselves most systematically and regularly treated as equal individuals. It is here they become sovereign; making choices which allow them to reassert their identities, or perhaps those of their households. Thus it may well be that individuals are indeed systematically alienated or separated from the products of their labour at the workplace. But in the sphere of consumption, the exchange of goods for money, they can once more feel themselves free to make choices about their own lives and lifestyles. Under capitalism, Marx argues, money reconstitutes the individual: 'That which exists for me through the medium of *money*, that which I can pay for, i.e. which money can buy, that *am I*, the stronger am I.[18] [Marx's emphases]

On the one hand, money is 'the alienated capacity of mankind'. Under capitalism people typically sell themselves and their capacities for money. They compete with one another as individuals as part of such sale. In this way, money acts to separate people from one another, and thereby to deny their species-being. But at the same time money is 'the bond of all bonds'. It links individuals to human life and society. It also 'links me to nature and to man'. Thus money has a separating and combining function. Marx sums up its contradictory role by saying that 'it is the true agent of separation and the true cementing agent, it is the chemical power of society.'[19]

What is the significance of this argument as regards the relation between people and nature? As Marx points out, money separates individuals from one another. And since, according to Marx, it is part of humans' species-being to associate with other humans, such species-being becomes lost. But Marx's approach has a more general application. In practice we have been largely separated from nature in the sense of being immediately and sensuously engaged in its relationships and workings. Furthermore, human beings' distinctive and well-developed physical and mental capacities cannot adequately develop in relation to the natural world and the specifics of, say, the particular habitats in which we live. But, despite all this, money provides a sense of connection with nature. It allows us, for example, to buy products and visit habitats in a way which suggests that we are in fact omnipotent. And such forms of consumption help us to gain some sense of personal identity within a group of people engaging in similar forms of consumption. The market economy acts like an extended ecological and environmental system in that it offers to the apparently free individual a series of products to be appropriated and a group-identity to be realised through such consumption.

The market thus realises or confirms aspects of species-being; the human need for appropriation, for individual sovereignty and a sense of association with people and nature. It turns nature into commodities or things rather than items to be enjoyed or indeed to be threatened by. But, still more important for Marx, commodities in the market-place now appear to have a life of their own. Instead of recognising the social relationships, labour processes and alienation of people from the products they have made, commodities in the market-place become treated as ends in themselves. They become, in Marx's words, 'fetishised' or treated like cult objects to be worshipped and compared with one another. Thus social life starts to revolve around the market and the acquisition of reified inanimate objects rather than around work, power and social relations.

Marx's *Grundrisse*, drafted some thirteen to fourteen years after the 1844 Manuscripts, is a way of introducing the idea of spatial and temporal alienation. Parts of this book briefly explore the changing relations between people, nature and community. Taking in turn antiquity, early tribal communes and Roman society he argued that small-scale communes were 'a kind of independent organism'; a close-knit combination or unification of independent subjects.[20] In these societies landed property and agriculture were basic to the economic order and the reproduction of individuals and households. Furthermore, land took the form of property. But Marx's central point is that the individual related to the earth as *communal* or *collective* property:

Property thus originally means no more than a human being's relation to his natural conditions of production as belonging to him, as his, as *presupposed* along with *his own being*; relating to them as *natural presuppositions* of his self, which only form so to speak, his extended body.[21] [Marx's emphases]

So at this point Marx is returning to the idea of nature as an extended part of the individual's body, one forming a unity with another. 'On the one side the living individual, on the other the earth, as the objective condition of his reproduction.' This relation between the individual and nature is not mediated by the private ownership of property in these earlier types of society. Rather, relations with the earth are mediated by the individual's membership of a commune, 'peacefully or violently'. In these earlier social forms the labouring individual therefore has 'an objective mode of existence in his ownership of land'. Preconditions for an individual's existence in the form of property and land are 'a presupposition of his activity just like his skin, his sense organs'.

The type of alienation of species and natural being outlined in Marx's earlier work did not develop in these earlier social forms. Marx outlines the relationships and processes involved in what Tönnies was later to call *gemeinschaft*. The individual is a member of a close-knit community or clan system with a strong communal relation to the land and other species. The fruits of the land were divided although much of the land remained common property. In some instances, for example pre-capitalist tribes, the commune exists mainly as a gathering of families and clans. In other instances, for example the cities of antiquity such as Rome, the commune has a political status. In yet others, such as those in what Marx called the 'Asiatic Form', the commune is the direct proprietor of the land.

But in all these instances, the land lies in predominantly communal ownership. The individual, as a natural and species being and forming part of a communal group, is directly related to the land. And, again, the individual relates to the earth 'as the inorganic nature of his subjectivity'. The latter is realised in this particular historical, social and spatial context. This all means that the individual in pre-capitalist modes of production 'can never appear here in the ant-like isolation in which he appears as mere free worker'.[22] What Marx saw as 'man's essential powers' remain largely realised or confirmed by these early social forms.

Of course, Marx knew that all was not idyllic sweetness and light in these early communal forms of living. Hence his comment that communal relations persisted in 'violent' as well as in 'peaceful' forms. Also an insistence on close working relations with nature does not of course mean that there are no ecological and environmental crises. The point is that the *relation* to nature as people's inorganic being was, whether good or bad, at least understood. And it was, as Marx also argued, to be undermined by capitalism and property relations.

How did these capacities or powers become established as a part of human nature? Engels' remarkable pamphlet 'The part played by labour in the transition from ape to man' is in effect a statement of how people created both themselves and nature through interacting with nature during their evolutionary history.[23] It was first published in 1856 and following a long period of neglect, it is now being recognised by contemporary anthropologists as essentially correct. Ingold, for example, has recently referred to it as 'first class anthropological speculation, whose originality subsequent commentators have been somewhat reluctant to recognise'.[24]

In fact, this essay formed part of a potentially even more remarkable enterprise. While Marx was writing *Capital* Engels was working on no less than the rewriting of science, including human science. 'The part played by labour' was just part of a bigger work, *Dialectics of Nature*. And the latter was a preliminary, and, as it turned out, incomplete, attempt to establish the basic laws and mechanisms of motion and matter *upon which* an understanding of 'man' would be founded.[25] 'The part played by labour' is, as I shall outline below, an account of 'man' arising through labouring on the natural world. This was the culmination of Engels' hierarchical view of the workings of nature, with biology and 'man' as contained within or evolving from the system of mechanical, physical and chemical constituted by the disciplines of physics and chemistry.[26]

'The part played by labour' contains a few problems. But its dialectical approach again represents the soundest way forward in terms of understanding historical relationships between people and nature and how certain behavioural propensities became established as people's species-being. At the same time it alludes to the processes of alienation which Marx had earlier sketched out.

The first phase, according to Engels, was established by the earliest apes. Their upright gait allowed them to make special and additional uses of their hands. These included the creation of nests to protect themselves and, perhaps most importantly, the gathering and holding of food. The earliest people carried this development still further. Their freed hands became still further developed in such a way as to allow them to carry out an increasing range of operations; these included, for example, the fashioning of flints into the form of knives. 'Labour' has a fairly catholic meaning in Engels' account; it refers simply to the appropriation and fashioning of objects.

This development of the hand and with it the extensive appropriation and manipulation of objects, led to the growing 'mastery of nature'. Such mastery increased as people were 'continually discovering new, hitherto unknown, properties in natural objects'. At the same time appropriation necessitated and was enabled by increasingly communal forms of appropriation. Early human beings therefore learned to cooperate and acquire mutual support and joint activity and this capacity needed, and was again facilitated by, a form of speech. Appropriation of nature and communication linked to such appropriation were for Engels the two basic prerequisites of early human evolution. These acted as stimuli for the most crucial aspect of people's development, that of 'the brain and its attendant senses'. And with the development of the brain there arose increasing clarity of consciousness, power of abstraction and of judgement.

These powers of abstract thinking, combined with the functioning of hands and speech permitted the development of modern societies. Agriculture was added to hunting and cattle-raising with, later, spinning, weaving and other forms of industrial production. And, along with trade and industry, 'art and science finally arrived'. Furthermore, the principal means by which people were eventually able to alienate themselves also arrived:

Law and politics arose, and with them that fantastic reflection of human things in the human mind – religion. . . . And so in the course of time there emerged that idealistic world outlook which, especially since the fall of antiquity, has dominated men's minds.[27]

One of the chief effects of advanced mental powers is the possibility of taking conscious, planned, action. Animals, Engels insisted, are quite capable of taking premeditated actions. But this power is especially well developed in the case of humans. It allowed them to develop sophisticated feeding strategies, for example. 'Unlike the hunter', as Engels puts it, 'the wolf does not spare the doe which would provide it with the young next year.' People developed a highly varied diet, using the tool-making abilities to hunt and fish as well as to till the soil for edible plants. And this varied diet again contributed to the development of modern human beings, giving them greater nourishment and physical strength.

But the capacity to reflect and make conscious decisions does not necessarily result in ecologically sound practices. On the one hand, 'the animal destroys the vegetation of a locality without realising what it is doing'. But people, even though they 'master', can do so in still highly destructive ways: 'Man destroys it in order to sow field crops on the soil thus released, or to plant trees or vines which he knows will yield many times the amount planted.'[28] For all this knowledge, however, human beings under capitalism operate in the short term. Their relation to nature is distorted by the principle of private property and profits:

In relation to nature, as to society, the present mode of production is predominantly concerned only about the immediate, the most tangible result; and then surprise is expressed that the more remote effects of actions directed to this end turn out to be of quite a different, mainly even of quite an opposite, character.[29]

Thus Engels shows how the characteristic features of human beings' 'species-being' (communality, language, exploration, powers of abstract thought) were associated with human evolution and dialectical relationships with nature. But, and this is the primary contradiction involved, people's remarkable mental powers have at the same time allowed them to develop concepts which separate them from that same nature.

But Engels, like Marx, was optimistic about the future. In due course the contradictions between man and nature would become apparent and human beings would exercise their well-developed brains and conceptual powers to develop new concepts for understanding the relationships between people and nature:

At every step we are reminded that we by no means rule over nature like a conqueror over a foreign people, like someone standing outside nature –

but that we, with flesh, blood and brain, belong to nature, and exists in its midst, and that all our mastery of it consists in the fact that we have the advantage over all other creatures of being able to learn its laws and apply them correctly.[30]

Engels believed, therefore, that intellectual progress would in due course lead to a realisation that people and nature were one and the same thing. The result would be an overcoming of the alienated condition into which modern people had sunk:

The more this progresses the more will men not only feel but also know their oneness with nature, and the more impossible will become the senseless and unnatural idea of a contrast between mind and matter, man and nature, soul and body, such as arose after the decline of classical antiquity in Europe and obtained its highest elaboration in Christianity.[31]

This one science has, however, despite Engels' best efforts, been a long time coming. For many years since Marx and Engels were writing, biologists and workers in other related disciplines have persisted in developing concepts which have not allowed these connections to be made. Some of their work does indeed place question marks over Marx and Engels' early work. It seems clear, for example, that Engels was assuming a Lamarckian mechanism in his chain of reasoning, one which assumed the doctrine that acquired characteristics are simply passed on to future generations. Human evolution under this assumption is what Ingold calls 'an extended body building exercise'.[32]

Such a model, even though it was also assumed by Darwin, now finds little general acceptance. Few biologists, even the most subversive members of that discipline, would now accept Engels' assertion that organisms and species, including people, simply make themselves through their own life activities and passing on their acquired characteristics to later generations.[33] The tendency now is to see the forms and behavioural tendencies of organisms as having evolved in a way as to be fit for survival and reproduction in particular kinds of environment. But this too is an inadequate specification since 'the environment' has also been constructed by these same, active, organisms. An improved view, and one with which Marx and Engels' model is still broadly compatible, is that organisms are active in making their own environments. But these same environments are organism's 'inorganic body'. They are in turn capable of causing further modifications to the organisms which they house. As I shall discuss in the next chapter, it is towards this kind of concept which some forms of contemporary biology now seem to be moving.

A consistent development of Marx's theory would thus insist on the reciprocal relationships between people and nature. Humans work on nature and, in this process under capitalism, lose their sense of natural and species beings. But Marx's framework also suggests that this worked-on or socially constructed 'nature' should be seen as in turn affecting the species which is modifying it. Such a perspective is the inevitable consequence of seeing the natural world as 'man's inorganic body' and, hence, 'nature' and 'man' are, in the end, the same thing.

In fact Marx did not d   .ss or develop this issue in any detail. In general terms he insi..ed that a materialist view of history should be founded on an understanding that value was based on the exploitation of nature and that human labour power is itself a natural capacity. An example comes from his 1875 'Critique of the Gotha Programme'. His discussion of these events has since proved prophetic:

Labour is *not the source* of all wealth. *Nature* is just as much the source of values (and it is surely of such that material wealth consists!) as labour, which itself is only the manifestation of a force of nature, human labour power.[34]

This abstract discussion of natural outer limits was never fully explored in Marx's writings. Both Marx and Engels were certainly very impressed by human beings' capacities for modifying nature towards their own ends. Indeed, there persists throughout much of their writing a certain triumphalist strain; human beings' capacities are seen as having developed precisely because of their mastery of the natural world. As regards natural outer limits imposed by nature, the assumption seems to have been that such limits, while they existed, would not be reached for a very long time.

As we have seen, Engels seems to have had some reservations about the human races' capacity for infinitely modifying nature without nature finding a 'revenge'. 'The part played by labour in the transition from ape to man' discusses the distinct possibility of unforeseen environmental disasters. It outlines the impacts of early agriculture in Mesopotamia, Greece and Asia Minor. These included the destruction of earlier forms of agricultural production such as dairy farming in the Italian Alps and, in the same region, the creation of large-scale floods by the disruption of streams. From such experiences Engels generalises as follows:

> Let us not, however, flatter ourselves overmuch on account of our human victories over nature. For each such victory nature takes its revenge on us. Each victory, it is true, in the first place brings about the results we expected, but in the second and third places it has quite different, unforeseen effects which only too often cancel the first. . . . Thus at every step we are reminded that we by no means rule over nature like a conqueror over a foreign people, like someone standing outside nature – but that we, with flesh, blood and brain, belong to nature, and exist in its midst.[35]

Such few comments by Engels apart, however, Marx's more typical outlook, and indeed one broadly shared by many later Marxists, was to envisage nature as being unproblematically 'mastered' by communist as well as by capitalist society. The resources were generally assumed to be there to be used. The triumph of 'man' and his enormous conceptual capacities lay in gaining access to such resources. Any limits on their use were seen as not in any way absolute or posing threats to ecological systems. Rather, such limits tend to be seen as *wholly* constructed by capitalist and earlier forms of society. In the case of capitalism they are again the product of private property relations. Marx and Engels' assumption seems to have been that under a communist society relations not only between people but between people and nature would become emancipated. Nature would once more be communally appropriated. But emancipation under communism again implies, as the following quote from Engels' 'Socialism: Utopian and scientific' suggests, that the relation is again one of mastery and domination rather than respect and reciprocal adjustment:

> The whole sphere of the conditions of life which environ man, and which have hitherto ruled man, now comes under the dominion and control of man, who for the first time becomes the real, conscious lord of Nature, because he has now become master of his own social organisation. The laws of his own social action, hitherto standing face to face with man as

laws of nature foreign to, and dominating him, will now be used with full understanding, and so mastered by him.[36]

MARXISM AND THE ENVIRONMENT: CONTINUING DEVELOPMENTS AND DEBATES

As I have shown, Caldwell and Benton's work is an indication of contemporary interest in Marx and Engels' approach. There are now signs of such an approach becoming an increasingly central focus for critical social theory. Recently, for example, Lee has again insisted that the First and Second Laws of Thermodynamics must be taken seriously by social theory, and in particular by critical social theory. The First Law, it will be remembered, says that energy can only be transformed. It cannot be created or destroyed. As Lee puts it:

When a tree grows or when a shed is put up, the energy used is imported from elsewhere. When the tree dies or the shed decays, the energy as such does not vanish; it is merely transformed so that the tree eventually becomes soil, dust and so on.[37]

The Second Law maintains that all processes produce 'entropy'; a simple but somewhat misleading word for 'waste'. The word is misleading because so-called 'waste' tend to be recycled and reintroduced back into ecosystems. To quote Lee again:

When an animal breathes, carbon dioxide is produced; when it shits dung is produced. The carbon dioxide is re-absorbed by the plants in the ecosystems, of which the animal is part; the cow-pat is worked upon by organisms, such as beetles and bacteria, to break it down into elements, which become part of the soil, which sustains the plants, which the animal in turn eats.[38]

Ecosystems are, then, the means by which this energy transfer takes place. The sun's energy passes through the atmosphere, through plant and animal organisms. In the process, the sun's energy is dissipated. But, at the same time, the very conditions in which organisms can live are being created. The biosphere is warmed. The plants produced feed living species and their waste products, and eventually their own bodies, become part of the atmosphere and the soil.

But Lee's point, and that of many contemporary ecologists, is that such an ideal world of living organisms balanced with their environment can no longer be taken for granted. So long as human productive activities involving the transformation of energy have remained on a small scale, ecosystems have indeed been able to reabsorb the resulting waste. Early forms of society and contemporary indigenous peoples have not substantially taxed the laws of thermodynamics. But contemporary industrialised societies now appear to be threatening this. The danger is that of overloading these self-regulating ecosystems and stretching them to a point at which they can no longer cope. At the same time, inputs to these systems in the form of non-renewable forms of energy and matter are being used up at an ever-increasing rate. This latter is another sense in which there are absolute outer limits to industrial development, limits which do not normally form part of social theory's concepts.

Lee's insistence on incorporating consideration of outer limits into social theory clearly makes a lot of sense. It is clearly in line with Marx and Engels' early attempts to relate the human sciences to the laws and emergent tendencies of nature. On the other hand, without the massive, possibly overambitious, schema of the kind Engels seems to have had in mind, there remains the danger that social relations could in the process become ignored.[39]

The way forward here is to return to Marx and Engels and remind ourselves that almost the whole of what we call 'nature' is socially mediated. Furthermore, people (and perhaps other species) have complex symbols for naming and describing what 'nature' actually is. In either case, nature is produced and transformed through human beings' understandings and interventions. Similarly, people possess concepts for understanding absolute and relative limits. They also have considerable capacities for understanding and monitoring these limits. And, as part of nature themselves, they have inner biological and psychological limits and propensities which can deeply affect relations to and modification of the environment. And, in principle at least, they are capable of not only conceptualising these limits but creating new kinds of social relations which are compatible with them. In short, while there is a very welcome extra emphasis in this latest literature on the physical-cum-social conditions in which human agents act, there remains an inadequate sense of that agent's

natural and species powers, and the ways in which they are
developed while manipulating these conditions.[40]

MARX AND ENGELS ON PEOPLE AND NATURE: AN
ASSESSMENT AND COMPARISON WITH EXISTING
ENVIRONMENTAL ANALYSIS

It is often now argued that social theory must stress the links
between people and nature. But the young Marx was the first
philosopher (and, apart from Engels, arguably the only one so far)
to have developed a theoretical construct in which these links are
built in as an essential part of a conceptual framework. They are
not tacked on to a pre-existing scientific or social scientific theory.
This is achieved using a realist approach to knowledge, one which
(as I shall discuss in the last chapter of this book) recognises
different levels of abstraction and one which, potentially at least,
can act as a way of integrating the natural and social sciences. As
we have seen, Marx and Engels' contributions specified in some
detail how biological and social understandings might be
combined. And, having established some specific connections, they
outlined what they saw as the alienating effects of capitalist
markets and social relations on people's relations with nature.

Marx's conceptual framework, and its development by Engels,
is still highly relevant today. As I shall later discuss in more detail,
much of contemporary social life in modern societies can be
interpreted as people's attempts to recover a sense of species-being
and natural-being. And they do this primarily through the market:
purchasing health foods, forms of exercise and so on. But the most
important argument to make at this stage is that Marx's
understanding of people's alienation from nature represents a
distinct improvement on that adopted by the great mass of
contemporary environmental and ecological literature.

In what sense is it an improvement? The version of 'man's
alienation from nature' which currently dominates environmental
analysis and politics adopts what is sometimes called a 'systems
view'. The argument runs as follows. Modern human beings have
long taken a view of the earth and its resources which is borrowed

from Descartian and Baconian philosophy. This treats the earth as passive and inert, a 'thing' to be remorselessly exploited. The task now, it is argued, is to move away from such conceptions and to develop new, more appropriate ideas of the environment and people's relationship to it. These new conceptions emphasise connections between all aspects of life. This is what Capra and others call a 'systems view'. A 'systems view of life' is based on awareness of the essential interrelatedness and interdependence of all phenomena – physical, biological, psychological, social and cultural. It transcends current disciplinary and conceptual boundaries.[41]

Systems, according to this line of thinking, are made up of a number of interrelated subsystems from the smallest organisms, through ecosystems and including even social systems:

Systems theory looks at the world in terms of the interrelatedness and interdependence of all phenomena. . . .
   People form families, tribes, societies, nations. All these entities – from molecules to human beings, and on to social systems – can be regarded as wholes in the sense of being integrated structures, and also as parts of larger wholes at higher levels of complexity.[42]

The 'system' idea emphasises interrelationships, balance, self-repair and self-regulation. This brings us to a key stage in the logic adopted by Capra and others adopting his line of argument. People, it is said, have increasingly come to see themselves as superior to and even outside these systems. Their Cartesian way of thinking has enabled them to believe that they are superior to the systems of which they are actually an integral part. And this in turn has allowed them to destroy nature in the form of rivers, lakes, air, living species and so forth. This is the version of 'alienation from nature' which is envisaged by contemporary environmentalism. Disalienation means that in future humans must learn to live in harmony with nature like all other species.

In what ways is this strand of thinking incorrect and why is Marx's understanding of alienation an improvement? In some respects the above type of analysis is difficult to argue against. An adequate understanding of relations between people and environment surely does entail, for example, the application of a number of disciplines. But what do the relations which systems thinking insists on actually consist of? They do not, under the kind of analysis offered by Capra, consist of social relations. Nor is asocial 'man' involved in or reacting to social relations as they work on nature to produce commodities for the market. Systems analysis was a concept originally developed for military planning during World War Two. It has since found extended application to operational research and the planning of business systems. It is difficult to see how, as a conceptual framework (one with close links to functionalism) it can be satisfactorily addressed to the often contentious issues with which contemporary social theory and environmentalism is concerned.

So if we are looking for ways which allow us to explore connections between social relations, markets and politics on the one hand and organic and inorganic nature on the other, a 'systems' framework is clearly inadequate. Especially problematic is the tacit notion in this way of thinking of a pure, balanced nature or environmental system to which 'man' is doing damage. Almost the whole of nature, as Marx and Engels' early work clearly suggests, is socially constructed. The laws and generative mechanisms underlying the natural world are presumably still intact. But it is becoming increasingly urgent to know how they are combining with one another and how they are now working out in practice. Beyond the most distant reaches of the atmosphere there is presumably a 'nature' which remains untouched by 'man', but down on earth there are few if any pure ecological systems. Indeed, it is not wholly clear when and where such systems actually did exist. Similarly, the seas and the forests have all long been manipulated and changed by 'man'. Now there is even no pure biosphere. In short, an assumption which is far more realistic than that of a pure and socially unreconstructed nature is one that assumes that the causal powers of organic and inorganic nature have always been incorporated into and modified by human social relations and processes.

Thus the view of alienation of people from nature which has so far dominated the contemporary environmental debate is unsatisfactory. Indeed, the assumption by contemporary environmentalism of a pure nature is part of the very problem of 'fetishisation' to which I alluded earlier. To argue that much of current environmental thinking fetishises nature is not of course to suggest that there are actually no environmental disasters. Quite the reverse. Rather, fetishisation has entailed a form of reification;

giving to something which is socially mediated a life and autonomy of its own. A good example is the Gaia hypothesis advanced by Lovelock. He follows mainstream environmental thinking in seeing the earth's biosphere, atmosphere, oceans and soil as a 'totality constituting a feedback or cybernetic system which seeks an optimal physical and chemical environment for life on this planet'.[43] At the same time he names this 'totality' as 'Gaia', after the Greek Earth Goddess. This seems to me a case of fetishisation; a mis-specification of the relationships and mechanisms at work.

Another example of the fetishisation of nature comes from Sheldrake. He argues that organisms are shaped by 'morphogenetic fields'. These are so far unknown to science but they are envisaged as gravitational fields composed of subatomic particles such as electrons and protons. Thus the earth, far from being inert, is full of energy. Its particles and fields form 'a large invisible organising structure, containing the universe within it, underlying all matter and connecting everything together'.[44] These structures or fields are therefore seen as a kind of collective memory. They impose forms on to species which are very similar to those of previous generations. At the same time, existing alive organisms act, in a 'feedback' manner on these morphogenetic fields, influencing their form. Human beings' mental capacities are also a product of these fields shaping the whole of existence. As with the Gaia hypothesis, Sheldrake argues that human beings have become separated, or at least believe they can separate themselves, from these invisible but powerful physical forces. This is the version of 'alienation' on which Sheldrake and much modern environmentalism insists. It is a long way from the more complex but richer understanding of alienation offered by Marx.

The problem with Sheldrake's analysis is not so much the notion of invisible but powerful magnetic fields influencing all aspects of organisms' forms, development and lives. Such fields or structures may well exist and may well be influential. The problem lies much more in the steadfast avoidance of the hard material world in which people actually live and work. And again there is an implicit assertion of a pristine natural world which has somehow escaped becoming an integral part of human beings' social affairs. The analysis may have something to offer but it is, to put it bluntly, socially and politically naive.

DEVELOPING MARX'S APPROACH

But all this is not to say that the conceptual framework laid out by Marx does not contain some problems. These have been extensively spelt out by Benton.[45] He sees Marx's early works as very promising, but he also sees them as flawed. His critique can be summarised with two main points. First he argues that there is a central contradiction in Marx's early work. On the one hand, he suggests, Marx is arguing for a new and close engagement with nature. As 'man's inorganic body' a new, unalienated relation would be a feature of a communist society. On the other hand, Benton says, Marx is arguing for a 'humanisation of nature', one in which the new relation to nature is very much on humans' terms:

If we can be at home in the world, be properly, humanly, connected with the world only on the basis of a thorough-going transformation of it in line with our intentions, then what space is left for a valuing of nature in virtue of its *intrinsic* qualities? If we can 'see ourselves' in, or identify only with a world which *we* have created, then what is left of our status as *part* of nature? Nature, it seems, is an acceptable partner for humanity only insofar as it has been divested of all that constitutes its otherness, insofar, in other words, as it has become, itself, human.[46]

Benton dubs this attitude towards nature 'a quite fantastic species-narcissism'. The quotations from Marx which Benton uses to develop his critique are mainly in the section of the 1844 Manuscripts which is almost wholly devoted to arguing that the supersession of private property is a necessary means towards the end of allowing humans to develop their essential powers. The gist of Benton's critique is therefore that Marx, in his anxiety to overthrow capitalist social relations, has placed 'man' centre-stage, seeing nature as in future simply as a means of developing *humans'* powers and capacities.

There is a potentially sound point here, but I do not think it addressed the central theme that Marx was developing. In this particular part of his argument Marx is not suggesting that 'the humanisation of nature' necessarily entails large-scale transformation of nature. This was indeed to become a feature of his later, more triumphalist, writing where he saw the 'mastery' of nature as necessary for human emancipation. But here, in the early

'Economic and Philosophical Manuscripts', 'humanisation' primarily entails the realisation of human powers through the abolition
of capitalist social relations. If Marx really was proposing a
thoroughly transformed natural world as a result of this abolition,
there could indeed be a major problem of the kind Benton aludes
to. But Marx's next step in this same section of the early
Manuscripts is to suggest that the subsequent stage in the new
relationship between people and nature would be the establishment of a single cross-disciplinary science; one in which 'man' saw
himself as part of nature.

Thus the 'humanisation of nature', as Marx describes it here, is
much more about people realising their potential through gaining
an understanding of nature and their relations to it. Such
'humanisation' is not necessarily at odds with a notion of nature
being part of 'man's inorganic body'. Whether this is a case of
'fantastic species narcissism' depends on the form of the
understanding and the precise ways in which the laws of nature
are used. Some forms of 'humanisation' could, for example, lead
to the powers and capacities of non-human species being
enhanced. 'Humanisation' is not, therefore, inherently problemati-
cal. But there admittedly remains the key question of whether a
new understanding would be used for human emancipation alone.
Would it, for instance, be deployed to eliminate species and
organisms which threaten human health?[47]

Benton's second, and in some respects far more telling, point
concerns the continuing dualism between animals and humans in
Marx's early work. Thus, for all the attempts to create one science
and to envisage people as part of nature, there resides, Benton
argues, a continuing implicit (sometimes explicit) division between
what is truly 'human' and what is truly 'animal'. Take, for
example, the supposed 'universalism' of people relative to animals.
One understanding of 'universalism' is that while animals act on
behalf of themselves and their offspring, humans have a particular
capacity for social cooperation. As Benton points out, however,
subsequent work on animal ethology shows that many non-
human species also act in a social capacity. A similar point can be
made about humans having the potential for developing new
skills, one which other species do not share. Again, this seems to
be overplaying the divide between people and nature. As Benton
puts it:

Many animal species display a complexity, diversity and adaptability in their behaviour which is denied in Marx's view of them as rigidly stereotypical in their species-characteristic modes of life. For many non-human animal species it is possible to speak defensibly of developmental and learning potentials, of simple collective powers, and even to a limited extent of collective potentials.[48]

Finally, a continuing dualism between 'man' and animals can be found, Benton suggests, in Marx's understanding of the human species itself. People are considered to be part-animal, part-human. There is an animal component residing within human beings but at the same time they have an added extra (mind, soul and so on) which makes all the difference. But, as I have outlined, it is capitalism which crushes that difference and reduces them to the level of animals. There are, as Benton points out, an enormous number of problems associated with such a picture. Mental powers are seen as somehow self-sufficient and separate from humans' biological being while humans' supposed animal powers tend to be 'profaned as, perhaps, rather shameful features'.[49]

In sum, the dualistic opposition between humans and animals and between the human and the animal *within* the human seems to inform much of Marx's early work. The question is, therefore, do these difficulties put Marx's conceptual framework out of court? As Benton himself suggests, this need not be the case. It is quite possible to imagine a reconstruction of Marx's approach which retains its power while shedding its difficulties. Marx's naturalism, or his attempt to build a theory across the disciplines associated with science and people, can be retained. But that need not entail the kinds of 'speciesism' outlined above. Benton sums up his approach in the following way:

Each species has its own characteristic species-life. Organisms can 'confirm' or 'manifest' their essential powers only within the context of their species-life, and so can be said to flourish only when the conditions for the living of the mode of life characteristic of their species are met. For each species, then, we can distinguish conditions for mere organic survival – the meeting of nutritional requirements, protection from predators and so on – from conditions for flourishing, for the living of the species-life. But *how* this distinction is made, the specific survival conditions and flourishing conditions which are identified, will vary from species to species.[50]

So Benton's reconstruction of Marx's approach avoids the

dualism of animals and humans by saying that all species have basically common needs. But different species have different ways of satisfying those needs. What we call human 'culture' is constituted by particular methods and means which humans have developed as a way of flourishing and reproducing. The approach therefore makes a crucial distinction between the general needs of all species and the ways they are activated. This does not privilege people as *necessarily* possessing a special something extra. They may well have acquired, on the other hand, peculiarly well-developed capacities, not least well-developed languages and capacities for conceptualisation, enabling them to achieve particularly well what other animals are also achieving. I intend later adopting this approach, especially when it comes to discussing the psychological dimensions of humans' species-being.

NOTES

1. See, for example, R. Augros and G. Stanciu (1987), *The New Biology*, New Science Library: Shambhala, Boston and London. (Note that this book is not a description of 'the new biology' outlined in Chapter 4 of the present study.)
2. D. Haraway (1989), *Primate Visions*, Routledge: New York and London, pp. 12–13.
3. T. Benton (1991), 'Biology and social science: why the return of the repressed should be given a (cautious) welcome', *Sociology* 25, 1: 1–29.
4. E. Leach (1967), *A Runaway World?* (Reith Lectures, 1967), Oxford University Press: Oxford, p. 78.
5. This discussion of the early Marx is based largely on K. Marx (1975), 'Early economic and philosophical manuscripts', in L. Colletti (ed.), *Karl Marx. Early Writings*, Pelican: Harmondsworth, pp. 279–400. (Originally published 1844.)
6. Quoted in B. Ollman (1976), *Alienation*, Cambridge University Press: Cambridge, p. 28.
7. *ibid.*, p. 28.
8. K. Marx (1975), *op.cit.* p. 328.
9. *ibid.*, p. 347.
10. Quoted in B. Ollman (1976), *op.cit.*, p. 80.
11. *ibid.*, p. 28.

12. *ibid.*, p. 82.
13. K. Marx (1975), *op.cit.* p. 329.
14. *ibid.*, p. 329.
15. *ibid.*, pp. 329–30.
16. *ibid.*, p. 330.
17. *ibid.*, p. 351.
18. *ibid.*, p. 352.
19. *ibid.*, p. 378. Note the incorporation of nature into the fetishised market as proposed by contemporary 'environmental economics'. Here society remains envisaged as constituted largely by 'free' individuals or households – in this case choosing between environmental and other 'goods' in the attempt to maximise their (hypothetical) 'utility'. See in particular D. Pearce *et al.* (1989), *Blueprint for a Green Economy*, Earthscan: London.
20. K. Marx (1973), *Grundrisse*, Penguin: Harmondsworth, p. 483.
21. *ibid.*, p. 491.
22. *ibid.*, p. 485.
23. F. Engels (1972) *The Part Played by Labour in the Transition from Ape to Man*, Progress Publishers: Moscow. Also included in F. Engels (1959), in *Dialectics of Nature*, Progress: Moscow.
24. See T. Ingold (1986), *The Appropriation of Nature*, Manchester University Press: Manchester, p. 63.
25. F. Engels (1959), *op.cit.*
26. A hint of Engels approach, including his attempt (using an application of Hegelian dialectics) to identify the underlying mechanisms affecting natural and social life is as follows:

    In nature – amid all the welter of innumerable changes – the same dialectical laws of motion force their way through as those in which history govern the apparent fortuitousness of events. . . . To me there can be no question of building the laws of dialectics into nature, but of discovering them in it and evolving them from it. (*ibid.*, pp. 17, 19)

27. F. Engels (1972), *op.cit.*, p. 10.
28. *ibid.*, p. 11.
29. *ibid.*, p. 11.
30. *ibid.*, p. 15.
31. *ibid.*, p. 13.
32. T. Ingold (1986), *op.cit.*, p. 64.
33. R. Foley (1987), *Another Unique Species*, Longman: Harlow.
34. K. Marx (1959), 'Critique of the Gotha Programme', in L. Feuer (ed.), *Karl Marx and Friedrich Engels, Basic Writings*, Collins: London, p. 153.

35. F. Engels (1972), *op.cit.*, p. 12.
36. F. Engels (1959), 'Socialism: Utopian and scientific', in L. Feuer (ed.), *op.cit.*, p. 149–50.
37. K. Lee (1989), *Social Philosophy and Ecological Scarcity*, Routledge: London, p. 72.
38. *ibid.*, p. 74–5.
39. See T. Hayward (1990), 'Ecosocialism – Utopian and scientific', *Radical Philosophy 56*, Autumn.
40. For a full discussion of the question of 'natural limits' and Marxism see T. Benton (1989), 'Marxism and natural limits: an ecological critique and reconstruction', *New Left Review* 178: 51–86. For a discussion and a suggestion that Benton underestimates the complexity and variety of ecological problems, see R. Grundmann (1991), 'The ecological challenge to Marxism', in *New Left Review*, 187, pp. 103–20.
41. F. Capra (1983), *The Turning Point*, Fontana: London, p. 285. For an argument similar to that developed here see S. Vogel (1988), 'Marx and alienation from nature', *Social Theory and Practice* 14, 3.
42. F. Capra (1983), *op.cit.*, pp. 26–7.
43. J. Lovelock (1987), *Gaia*, Oxford University Press: Oxford, p. 11.
44. R. Sheldrake (1991), 'Is nature alive?', *Human Potential*, Spring, p. 19. See also R. Sheldrake (1983), *A New Science of Life*, Paladin: London and R. Sheldrake (1991), *The Rebirth of Nature*, Century: London.
45. T. Benton (1988), 'Humanism = speciesism. Marx on humans and animals', *Radical Philosophy* 50: 4–18. For another pioneering argument linking biology with Marxism see K. Soper (1979), 'Marxism, materialism and biology' in J. Mepham, D.-H. Ruben, *Issues in Marxist Philosophy*, vol.II, *Materialism*, Harvester Wheatsheaf: Hemel Hempstead. Note in particular her argument that 'human culture comprises a single order in which one never discovers purely "natural" or purely "social" elements instatiated concretely, but which can be studied at different levels of abstraction' (p. 62). Perhaps the earliest modern Marxist to invite an inclusion of biology into social theory was S. Timpanaro (1975), *On Materialism*, Verso: London.
46. T. Benton (1988), *op.cit.*, p. 7.
47. For a parallel and considerably more extended argument see R. Grundmann (1991), *op.cit.*
48. *ibid.*, p. 11.
49. *ibid.*, p. 12.
50. *ibid.*, p. 13.

4

ARGUMENTS WITHIN BIOLOGY:
FROM NEO-DARWINISM TO THE
STUDY OF ORGANISMS AND
THEIR ENVIRONMENTS

Social theory, as we have seen, has largely neglected the biological sciences during the past half century. It is ironic to note, therefore, that the biological sciences (and related areas such as ecology) have not only been making considerable strides in their own fields during the past four decades or so, but have also been making major claims about people, their social relationships and their links with the environment. This chapter will examine how biologists and ecologists understand people and the environment. It will trace the changing nature of this understanding, starting with neo-Darwinism and continuing into socioecology. Most recently, however, there has emerged what I call 'the new biology'; a tendency which undermines the reductionism of much contemporary biology and lays emphasis on close links between the organisms and their relationship with their environments. More particularly, its emphasis is on generative mechanisms and how they are realised or transformed by their contingent conditions. Neo-Darwinism and neo-ecology still very much thrive. Indeed, they represent two of the dominant paradigms within modern biology. But it is 'the new biology' which is now becoming compatible with the type of perspective first developed by Marx and Engels about a century and a half ago. On the other hand, there are some dimensions still missing. The social relations of an organism's environment are not adequately considered.

This and the following chapter will also open up some fundamental questions. These were asked, and answered in a preliminary way, by Marx and Engels. But they are now being asked again. This is a result not only of environmentalism but of a number of related developments such as the animal rights movement. To what are people very special, possessing, for example, cultural and mental capacities which make them wholly unique compared with other species? Or are people best understood as another species, one subject to biological and other restraints along with other species?

But these questions raise still more fundamental issues. They are raised not only by environmental issues but by human debates surrounding the modification of biological reproduction through, for example, *in vitro* fertilisation. How should we see 'nature'? Should we continue following the dominant view of Western science which insists on a radical distinction between 'people' and 'nature'. According to this view a disembodied and detached human 'mind' studies and manipulates an objective 'nature' of which it is not part. This seems an increasingly unrealistic stance. I will be arguing that an adequate understanding of people's relationship with nature now calls for the abandonment of a dualism between 'people', 'mind' and 'culture' on the one hand and 'nature' on the other. People are now so caught up in the modification of themselves and of the rest of nature that they can no longer treat 'nature' as a wholly external phenomenon in which they are not themselves playing a leading role. Similarly, it is very difficult to allude to a 'nature' which is not socially made. Such social construction not only includes its modification in the making of commodities. It includes the way we think of the very concept 'nature' itself. People are an integral part of nature. What we are pleased to call 'the environment' has been deeply implicated in making people into what they are. Again, such a perspective was spelt out in Marx's 1844 Manuscripts and some of Engels' early work.

These issues are extraordinarily complex and reach deep into the heart of how modern people envisage themselves and their relationships with the world at large. At this stage it seems advisable to be treading a delicate path between, on the one hand, developing a new type of theory such as that implied by Marx while at the same time using insights developed under the influence of different theoretical perspectives. We can certainly recognise the force of the argument which wishes to abandon the notion of separate and distinct concepts for 'man' on the one hand and 'nature' on the other. At the same time, it seems unwise to abandon all the insights of the 'old' ways of thinking. How can we use the latter in ways which might be useful in developing a more persuasive overview?

A sensible way forward is to develop a set of relatively autonomous sciences, each with its own comparatively integrated subject matter; biology, physics, chemistry, psychology, sociology and so on. Yet these previously quite disconnected sciences can surely be linked. Their ontologies and their ways of conceiving organisms and their relationships to environments have a great deal to teach each other. Turning now to modern biology, precisely which branch of this subject seems most compatible with the perspective under development here?

A METHODOLOGICAL ISSUE

This chapter will outline, and at the same time be critical of, some of the core themes in biology and related areas of understanding. These themes emphasise procreation, the continuation of biological 'fitness' into future generations, the ways in which bodies are adapted to such purposes and the forms of social behaviour and use of resources and physical environments by organisms towards these ends. At the same time biological science has itself evolved. Over the past twenty years or so there have been considerable debates both within biology and between the biological and social sciences.

But there is one outstanding methodological problem which needs mentioning here at the outset. The general intention here is to use Marx and Engels' framework (including the realist method of working) to develop a more sophisticated view of the relations between people and environment. But such an intention is beset with the problem that more recent concepts and evidence are collected on quite different assumptions. While Marx and Engels stressed potentialities, dialectics and history, much recent work in biology and ecology adopts, explicitly or otherwise, forms of methodological and analytical individualism. This also applies to certain forms of psychology where, again, the individual is the starting-point. Such an approach focuses on the hereditary traits and genetic influences on individuals. As a result of this focus, an important dimension becomes lost. This is the individual as an active and creative being and, just as significant, an individual whose very life *as* a human being is constituted by interactions with other human beings and the natural world and potentialities realised through such interaction. Thus methodological individualism can have a debilitating effect on the analysis. For a long time the very way the problem has been specified has militated against the kind of understanding which seems increasingly important. But there are now signs of such methodological individualism being abandoned and a convergence with the relational perspective being developed here. Socioecology, as we will shortly see, is a case in point. And so too are recent developments in biology.

Despite such criticisms of biological theory, it would still be highly unfortunate if the biological and physical sciences were dismissed or treated in a wholly negative way by the social sciences and particularly by alternative epistemologies. While other ways of conceptualising may certainly pose challenges, they provide at the same time new opportunities for the development of an improved social theory. Biology is, after all, the science of living organisms. As such there should be ways in which this subject is incorporated as part of the social sciences, since the latter are concerned with a particular kind of living organism, *Homo sapiens*. In particular, the emphasis of biology on innate mechanisms affecting individuals and their relationships provides new insights into underlying factors affecting human subjects' actions. Similarly, they indicate the broad processes which underly, but which surely do not absolutely determine, human behaviour. The key value of a biological approach lies in its suggestion that people, and possibly other species, have developed physiologies and latent forms of behaviour which are being affected in complex ways by the very societies which they have themselves made. In our terms, this approach is best at pointing to potential 'capacities' and forms of behaviour.

How then can biological understandings start to be linked with those stemming from sociology? The chapter opens with a relatively brief examination of contemporary ethology and sociobiology. These have been very important in breaking down the 'man' and 'nature' dichotomy and also identifying some of the long-run tendencies affecting human behaviour and some of the constraints still operating over humans' and other species' activities. These approaches have greatly overestimated, however, the extent to which genetic inheritance directly influences behaviour. They also take far too little account of how contingent factors such as the local social and natural environment themselves relate in reciprocal fashion to organisms' behaviour.

The first of these two problems starts to be dealt with by socioecology, a subject discussed in the third part of this chapter. The fourth part introduces very new types of biology which are still more sensitive to how environment is formative in the development of organisms and their behaviour. It represents a move away from the type of Darwinian theory which I discussed in Chapter 2, one concentrating on organisms struggling for survival but giving less attention to the causal effects of environment.

It also raises the central question of mental structures and their application to the study of relations between people and environment. Here, and in line with recent developments in Jungian psychology, Chapter 5 will argue that this provides a crucial link between biological and social theory and perhaps the most basic link in terms of understanding contemporary peoples' relationship with nature. But in itself this is still not enough. Chapter 6 will demonstrate how this kind of biologically and psychologically based understandings of people and their environment can be linked to the methodological and social concerns of more established contemporary social theory.

All this, it perhaps need hardly be said, is not simply a matter of improving 'theory'. Engels, as we have seen, envisaged the development of a more unified science as creating the possibilities for people seeing themselves and their impacts on the natural and social world more acutely. Marx made a similar point. He too believed the creation of a single science must be a central objective:

The idea of *one* basis for life and another for *science* is from the very outset a lie. . . . Natural science will in time subsume the science of man just as the science of man will subsume natural science: there will be *one* science.[1]

Again, such a science remains so far unconstructed. Indeed, it was perhaps always too ambitious to expect the emergence of a *single* science. What now seems to be occurring is a series of semi-autonomous sciences. These are areas of work which have their distinctive concerns but which nevertheless overlap in terms of their methods of working, overarching concepts for understanding the world and the place of organisms (including the human organism) within it.

THE NEO-DARWINIAN REVOLUTION

The 'one per cent difference' between contemporary humans on the one hand and early humans and chimpanzees on the other is one way of underlining the problems in distinguishing between 'man' and 'nature'.[2] This difference has nevertheless been responsible for a considerably enlarged brain, the capacity for speech, the formation of abstract concepts and elaborate forms of communication as well as a number of obvious differences such as an upright posture, bipedal gait and absence of body hair. And it can be seen as responsible for what is sometimes called 'culture'. This is where the difficult dualism between culture and nature starts to emerge.

But, having recognised the differences between *Homo sapiens* and other species, the 99 per cent genetic inheritance remains. A central question is whether, and how, a purely biological understanding of organisms' behaviour can be extended to the human species. There is an immense amount of argument here, especially when it comes to applying a biological understanding of species to human beings. In particular, little attention is given by much of modern biological theory either to the two-way interactions between behaviour and environment or to the inherited mental structures which mediate between organisms' underlying behavioural tendencies and the environment which they are experiencing. Furthermore, and this is an issue that will be taken up in later chapters, there is very little attention given to the broader structures of social and political power within which individuals run their lives.

Since Darwin's day most of the applications and extensions of his theory (or, more precisely, the neo-Darwinian version of his theory) have been concerned with non-human species.[3] One of the chief arguments *within* contemporary biology has been about the unit of adaptation which should be considered and the actual mechanisms leading to the evolution of particular forms and behaviours. As regards the unit, Darwin suggested that a whole species is adapted. Others have argued that the unit of adaptation that should be considered is the social group; it is the group's organisation and behaviour which benefits individuals within it. The present tendency, however, is to see the *gene* as the basic unit of measurement when it comes to understanding behaviour.

This relatively new emphasis on the gene implies that evolutionary change is due to the fact that certain genes increase in number while others decrease in numbers. Differential breeding success is therefore measured and analysed by mainstream biological science in terms of individuals carrying certain genes increasing in numbers while individuals carrying other genes slowly diminish. Thus the physiological and behavioural adapted-ness of any particular organism to its natural and social environment is defined in terms of its ability to contribute more than the average number of its genes to future generations. Genes are seen by neo-Darwinism as the way in which various adaptations and forms of behaviour can be 'cashed out'. Sometimes the emphasis is more immediately on what are called 'proximate outcomes'. Thus the most adapted forms of behaviour may well be considered in terms of the successful acquisition of nutrition and mates and successful encounters with predators and enemies. But the outcome by which such behaviours is ultimately measured is the survival of genes and their acquisition by future generations.

How, according to this version of biological theory, does the transmission of genes to future generations relate to individual and social behaviour? As we have seen, the expectation from Darwinian theory onwards has been that organisms and their behaviour are selected in such a way as they contribute to survival and reproductive success. The implications of our earlier discus-sion on the physical make-up and behaviour of the human species is that natural selection has during *Homo sapiens'* evolutionary history favoured those genotypes (or genetic constitutions of individuals) which participate in or enjoy hunting and gathering. Thus contemporary people can be seen as largely adapted to such activities.

One of the most controversial assertions of early sociobiology (and one which exposes the weakness of seeing people's behaviour as entirely driven by their genes) concerns behaviour based on the reproductive success of the sexes. Even though the theory appears to apply well to non-humans, the controversy derives from its application to the human species.[4] This is partly because it gives little attention to the specifically human ways in which power (in this case patriarchal power) can be exercised in the human world. But it is also because its prime emphasis is on innate mechanisms rather than on two-way reciprocal relations between organisms and environment.

Neo-Darwinism emphasises the fact that sperm is cheap and males can increase their reproductive success by mating with a large number of females. Females can thus be seen as a scarce resource for which males compete. At the same time females are choosing those males with good resources or good genes. Meanwhile the reproductive success of females is dependent on a small number of eggs. Females' behaviour is organised around ensuring that this small number of eggs is safely fertilised. As regards other forms of behaviour, there is an often-repeated story of the distinguished biologist J.B.S. Haldane calculating and announcing in his favourite public house that he would be prepared to lay down his life for two brothers or eight cousins. The basis for such altruistic behaviour is that it would make evolutionary sense. Half an individual's genes are shared with a brother or sister and one eighth with cousins.

Haldane's admittedly tongue-in-cheek suggestion was made in the 1950s but since then his insight has been systematically pursued by neo-Darwinism and used as a means of understanding much of animal behaviour. Actions by individuals as constituted by their genes (or 'genotypes') are seen as organised not simply around the preservation of self but around the passing on of genes into future generations. This leads to a concept of central importance in neo-Darwinist thought, that of 'inclusive fitness' which refers to the total of an individual's genetic fitness (the contribution of one genotype in a population relative to that made by other genotypes) *plus* all its influence on the fitness of relatives.

Inclusive fitness therefore alludes to the total effects of kin selection and kin altruism. But the preservation of genes can also lead to behaviours involving non-related individuals. It can occur via 'reciprocal altruism' with non-related individuals, the central idea here being that non-selfish (or apparently non-selfish) behaviour towards other individuals will be conducted on the tacit understanding that similar reciprocal behaviour will at some stage be paid back in similar measure. Thus the preservation of genes and their preservation into future generations can, according to this line of thinking, be associated with cooperative behaviour within a community of individuals. What Dawkins calls 'the selfish gene' is therefore not necessarily associated with 'selfish' individual behaviour.

People as natural- and species-beings: the contributions and difficulties of neo-Darwinism and ethology

How, if at all, can such ideas be extended to human beings? These biologically based concepts, using the tendency to preserve and transmit genes as an understanding of behaviour, have been almost entirely developed in relation to non-human species. And indeed, to be fair to the community of professional biologists, most such scientists are extremely hesitant about extending their ideas to *Homo sapiens*. For most social scientists, however, very serious problems start when ideas borrowed from biology are applied to human beings. Biologists are seen as not simply trespassing on matters outside their areas of competence but again skating over mystifications and justifications of specifically human forms of power such as sexism.[5]

Such theories are also frequently seen as demeaning the human species; of not recognising the unique and special capacities of humans and the extent to which they are able to rise above the kinds of instincts which govern other species' behaviour. The concepts and understandings offered by biologists and ecologists are therefore seen by many social scientists as unnecessary when it comes to understanding the individual behaviour and social relations formed by human beings.

These are not, however, the primary basis of my objections. These insights from sociobiology or neo-Darwinism are necessary but not sufficient. They are necessary in so far as they have identified how organisms are made. They may even have identified certain generative mechanisms and limits to behaviour. But there remain an enormous number of difficulties: for example, they ignore the complex dialectical relationships between organisms and environment, including the capacities of organisms to construct and modify their physical settings. They fail to recognise how, over the long term, biological evolution has occurred in social contexts.

Second, even in their own terms, biologists and ecologists are now considered to be greatly overestimating the role of genes. As Benton outlires, the theory of 'genetic drift' suggests that the distribution of genes within a population has a large random component and has little to do with 'fitness'.[6] And the more controversial theory of 'molecular drive' argues that long-term changes in the biological constitution of populations can occur quite independently of natural selection. Such changes may have virtually no adaptive value and, interestingly, they may *enable* new forms of behaviour which gain adaptive value. The upshot of these remarks is that this type of biology, despite its many and remarkable insights, has invested far too much in genes as an overarching explanation of form of behaviour. 'The social' and 'the biological' must be intertwined with one another in many complex ways. Furthermore, there is the added question of organisms' evolved mental structures; a complication which has managed to escape not only neo-Darwinism but much of social theory as well.

It is instructive to compare for a moment the neo-Darwinists with Darwin himself. Darwin had few compunctions when it came to extending his ideas to what he called 'the descent of man'. But, compared with the sociobiology of our own era he made many fewer claims regarding the supposedly overarching significance of biology on humans' behaviour. He nevertheless linked what he saw as biologically inherited forms of behaviour to the activities of contemporary peoples. He of course had no knowledge of genes and the precise mechanisms by which inherited characteristics are passed on to future generations during the process of natural selection. But he foreshadowed some of contemporary sociobiological and ethological thinking in his argument that human behaviour evolved in certain ways as a result of the overarching need to survive and procreate. According to Darwin, characteristically 'human' forms of behaviour can therefore be quite adequately explained in biological terms. Early peoples' quite advanced mental capacities led them into various forms of cooperation. Natural selection of tribe-members led to the gradual promotion of qualities with which contemporary people now pride themselves:

In the first place, as the reasoning powers and foresight of the members became improved, each man would soon learn that if he aided his fellow-men, he would commonly receive aid in return. From this low motive he might acquire the habit of aiding his fellows; and the habit of performing benevolent actions certainly strengthens the feeling of sympathy which gives the first impulse to benevolent actions. Habits, moreover, followed during generations tend to be inherited.[7]

Such was Darwin's early recognition of what biologists now call 'reciprocal altruism' and his assertion that certain kinds of supposedly 'benevolent' forms of human behaviour would have been selected for amongst our early ancestors. Darwin's understanding was, however, considerably broader than that of many contemporary biological theorists when it comes to understanding other specifically human forms of behaviour which would have been favoured by natural selection. Praise or blame, or what some social psychologists in our own era would call 'moral careers', are important stimuli in terms of human behaviour. Darwin argued that the instinct to attach moral values to certain forms of behaviour 'was originally acquired, like all the other social instincts, through natural selection'.[8] And, although these values are now much elaborated and encoded into contemporary cultural and religious values, their origins lie in the straightforward need for survival and protection. As such, characteristically 'human' behaviour values are, Darwin argued, not all that distinct from those of other species. We might note here, incidentally, the extent to which Darwin's supposedly scientific understanding of 'savages' in fact reflected the dominant values of his own society:

Even dogs appreciate encouragement, praise and blame. The rudest savages feel the sentiment of glory, as they clearly show by preserving the trophies of their prowess, by their habit of excessive boasting, and even by the extreme care which they take of their personal appearance and decorations; for unless they regarded the opinion of their comrades, such habits would be senseless.[9]

Yet since Darwin's day, the link between biological imperatives and social or 'cultural' activities has been largely ignored by biology and sociology alike. The question whether *Homo sapiens* can be considered as an integral part of the natural world or whether he or she is separate from it has, at least until quite recently, been largely ignored or taken as 'given'. One sensible way forward, as implied by Darwin, is to envisage human beings as on the one hand still subject to a number of inherited forms of instinct and to see their behaviour as governed by outer limits and constraints. These latter include the need to survive, ensure the survival of kin and maintain personal status in relation to known other individuals. But this by no means necessarily implies that these instincts wholly determine what people do or the many and complex ways in which they achieve their objectives. In short, and as I shall discuss in detail later, an approach is needed which stratifies levels of understanding and information. Biologists have established some important mechanisms. But these are modified in many different ways by other factors, including contingent circumstances such as their particular environment.

One result of ignoring the natural bases of human beings' behaviour has been social theory's distinct impoverishment. But such lofty attitudes are, it must be said, partly a result of the sometimes very excessive and deterministic claims made by some ethologists and some ecologists. These concentrate on species rather than genes. Nevertheless, books such as Lorenz's *On Aggression*, Ardrey's *The Territorial Imperative* and Morris's *The Naked Ape* made very large extensions from the understanding of animal behaviour to that of human beings.[10] Few professional biologists and even fewer sociologists would share their views.

Essentially, this work was suggesting that a great deal of human behaviour is not so much a result of latent tendencies and predispositions or of the constraints within which humans live their lives. Rather, such studies imply that behaviour is a direct and unmediated result of people's evolution as a predatory hominid. Lorenz argued that human aggression is innate and largely ineradicable. Rather than trying to stamp out such behaviour, a solution could be found in recognising people's evolutionary past and channelling such genetically inherited instincts into competition, ritualisation and display between individuals and groups. Such instincts would thereby be absorbed into harmless forms. Again, Ardrey suggested that aggression and territoriality amongst human beings was a direct result of their evolutionary past. 'The territorial drive', as he put it, 'as one ancient, animal foundation for that form of human misconduct known as war, is so obvious as to demand small attention.'[11]

And, with a biologically based understanding of human social affairs which seemed almost calculated to raise the ire of most social scientists, Ardrey proposed that his kind of explanation replaced any notions that wars and aggression are a product of the particular ways in which human societies are organised. According to him we are dealing with 'a human instinct probably more compulsive than sex' and this

throws into pale context the more wistful conclusions of the romantic fallacy: that wars are a product of munitions makers, or of struggles for markets, or of the class struggle; or that human hostility arises in unhappy family relationships, or in the metaphysical reaches of some organic death force.[12]

Thus early versions of ethology and sociobiology shared, in their attempt to develop an all-encompassing theory, many of the same difficulties and faults of deterministic and reductionist forms of social theory. Many of their ideas, like those of the early Social Darwinists, look distinctly like 'scientific' rationalisations of the competitive struggle for people to survive in a capitalist economy. In the end they only succeeded in setting social theory's face against biologically based explanation. Early ethology and sociobiology argued that *Homo sapiens* should be seen as an almost *wholly* 'natural' species, one governed by biologically inherited imperatives. In other words, they did not see their theories as implying certain broad tendencies and limits within which a great range of behaviours are possible. This is one reason for the (premature) rejection of their work by social theory.

Less dogmatic and somewhat more persuasive, however, have been those arguments that human beings remain genetically disposed to maintain key social bonds; these again being part of a product of genes which have been selected to promote survival and the maintenance of future generations during the very earliest stages of evolution. This is therefore one way of understanding what Marx called humans' 'species-being'. Tiger and Fox, for example, argue that the mother–child bond is a key one in terms of the preservation of species, one which is shared by virtually all mammals. The obvious reason for such a bond is that of suckling but in the case of human beings and other higher mammals, the bond has even deeper significance:

The further we move from the governance of primary instincts into the arena of learned abilities, the more it becomes essential for the slowly growing young animal to get its learning *right*. . . . Simply on the basis of what we know about the social mammals in general, we can predict that if the mother–child bond does not go right, the unfortunate youngster may never get any of his *other* bonds right.[13] [author's emphases]

The child psychologist, John Bowlby, has similarly argued that there remains in human beings a special attachment between mother and child, one rooted deep in human beings' evolutionary past. The roots lie not simply in suckling and emotional upbringing. According to Bowlby they are part of human beings' 2 million years' history as a gatherer–hunter, one in which priority had to be given to protection from predators.[14]

A more recent but similar type of analysis comes from Odent, a leading contemporary advocate of natural childbirth.[15] He argues that a number of contemporary health problems such as depression, hypertension and heart disease stem from the ways in which infants are brought up in the very earliest stages of their life. In these phases, he argues, infants develop their 'primal adaptive systems'; nervous, hormonal and immune systems which regulate the ways in which the human organisms adapt to later stresses and confrontations in their lives. Unlike people in traditional and older forms of society, those in modern society cannot rely on extended kin and community relations for bringing up infants. A frequent result is, Odent suggests, that the demands of young children forming their ways of 'coping' in the earliest stages of their lives remain ignored. Babies therefore adapt at a very early stage to be 'helpless' and, in later life, they remain unable to cope with trials and pressures which are in fact no worse than those faced by people in traditional societies.

Linking this back to our Marxian conceptual framework, the notion that can be extracted from this work is that human organisms do indeed have a distinct kind of species-being. And, if the capacities with which they are born are not realised during the earliest stages of their development, this leaves them seriously incapacitated for later life.

Tiger and Fox have a still more controversial view of human beings' 'species-being'. They argue that there are other kinds of bond which are part of human beings' latent behavioural tendencies. These again are a product of our evolutionary history. Tiger and Fox argued that the transition of early people to a semi-carnivorous diet was associated with an increasing sexual division of labour. There already existed well-formed divisions. As they put it: 'mature males control and defend the group; the females take care of the next generation; and the young males at the periphery act as guards and watchdogs.'[16] But, Tiger and Fox assert, as males tended to engage in the pursuit and killing of game while females continued with the older form of food-collection (that of gathering), new relations between the sexes and between the young and the old started to evolve. Eventually the processes of natural selection promoted these new forms of social relationship. Particularly important now was the bonding of males around cooperating, collective hunting and defence. Biological evolution would tend to select for such qualities or capacities. At the same time, young male adolescents learned skills; especially those of being loyal to the group, learning from and cooperating with others, risking their own lives in the larger group interest. Again, the tendency would be for these attributes to be slowly evolved during the process of natural selection. And, despite the irrelevance of such groupings to modern industrialised societies, they remain bases on which young male gangs are still formed in contemporary societies.

The problem here is still, though, that of identifying certain broad tendencies which are seen as part of humans' 'species-being', but then assuming that these can be simply read off in the social world. The reasons why young males form gangs are presumably multiple. They may not be especially linked to innate biological factors. But, in so far as they are, we would certainly expect such latent tendencies to combine in undoubtedly complex ways with the contexts in which young people are living. And such a combination may inhibit as well as enable the formation of groups of young males. In all, the picture presented by biologists and ethologists is provocative and useful, while at the same time far too simple and deterministic.

Applying neo-Darwinism to indigenous societies: some predictable problems

One way in which biologically based ideas have been tested in relation to human beings is through the study of indigenous societies. The resulting problems are instructive.

It is all too misleadingly easy to make assumptions about the 'pristine' or 'untouched' natures of groups and their close relationships with one another and the rest of the natural world.[17] Many of them have retained links with societies outside their immediate confines and of course, as was briefly mentioned in the last chapter, the recent history of these peoples is frequently one in which their ways of life and resources have been violently distorted by 'civilisation' in the form of, say, commercially organised mining or tree-felling companies. But some people, such as the aborigines of Western Australia, the !Kung Bushmen of Botswana and the Turkana pastoralists of North West Kenya, nevertheless seem, so far at least, to have remained largely separated from such features as global markets and national governments which now exercise considerable influence over people in the more developed societies.[18] Similarly, although their cultures may be increasingly marginalised, their everyday lives and spiritual practices remain largely organised around locality, other species, the physical environment and networks of closely related kin.

It is therefore to these groups that biologists, ethologists, socioecologists and anthropologists have almost always turned when applying concepts based on genetics and biology to the study of human beings. To use Marx's terms, it is perhaps here where peoples' basic natural- and species-being can be detected and systematically observed. And for sociobiologists, most of whom would have little time for Marx's ideas, there is an implicit search taking place here for a basic human nature; one which modern 'Western' people have also inherited.

There is first a basic problem which applies not simply to the application of sociobiological ideas. It concerns whether indigenous societies can in fact provide any clues as to the living-patterns of our ancient ancestors and, by extension, to an understanding of the behaviour which can be attributed to the human 'genome' or genetically constituted individual. Foley is one of a number of authors who have discussed this problem as it confronts palaeoanthropologists in using modern hunter–gatherers to understand the behaviour of pre-modern peoples. He is particularly concerned about contemporary researchers simply projecting contemporary lifestyles onto older forms of society without allowing for even the possibility of alternative ways of life amongst hunter–gatherers. Nevertheless, in the end he insists that modern hunter–gatherers are indeed useful ways of interpreting the past:

Despite the problems associated with using modern hunter–gatherers as an aid to interpreting the past, they must remain an integral element of palaeoanthropology. Used correctly, they provide important insights as well as being one end of the continuum of evolutionary variability with which anthropologists must deal. As living populations of humans provide the only source of information on adaptation involving technological and material items, they must remain central.[19]

But, returning to the specific issue of sociobiology, a second problem is an even more important one. Sociobiology, despite its extreme explanatory claims may again be useful in suggesting that people too are in many respects a species like any other. But the question again remains whether sociobiology on its own is an adequate basis for understanding *Homo sapiens*. One of the best-known anthropologists in this general area of work is Chagnon and his work implies that sociobiology can be directly useful. He is one of a number of academics who have studied the Yanomami of the Brazilian rain forest. He has, particularly in his more recent work, been applying sociobiological concepts to the study of these people. This has led to heated debates.

Chagnon argues that the concepts of sociobiology can indeed be directly extended to understanding the lives of the Yanomami.[20] The first of his core concerns is kinship and the patterns of alliance-formation, intervillage warfare and community fissioning in which these people engage. The second is the resources (especially food and water) on which these people depend for survival and reproduction of offspring. Chagnon makes direct use of the idea of inclusive fitness and reciprocal altruism. As we have seen, inclusive fitness gives special prominence to the degree of kin relatedness in explaining individual and social behaviour. Altruism is seen as adaptive in the sense that it can be reciprocal; one favour ultimately resulting in a returned 'gift'.

Thus, adopting a sociobiological perspective, the Yanomami are envisaged as designed by natural selection to act in ways that promote, and are indeed still promoting, their survival and reproduction or inclusive fitness. The struggles and relationships of these peoples are then interpreted in this way: the key process taking place is, according to Chagnon, competition between males for mates; coalitions are made between genealogically related males, the object again being to secure marriageable females for themselves, for their brothers and sons. As Chagnon himself puts it:

Viewing Yanomamo society as a system in which there is intense competition among males for reproductive opportunities brings out more clearly the significance of the dynamics of social life on the one hand, and on the other illustrates how demographic reality, kinship behaviour, village fissioning and individual strategies all operate together and constitute a meaningful system.[21]

Resources are seen as directly locked into these processes; biological success entailing access to food and water as well as to mates. Resources are seen as finite; access to them by a group of related individuals being only at the expense of another such group. Thus alliances, kin coalitions, fights between groups of related males and splits in villages are as much about appropriating neighbouring resources for kin and females as well as acquiring females.

Biological success involves, according to Chagnon, intense and frequently violent struggles. Yanomami life is, Chagnon argues, characterised by continuing tribal violence. Some 44 per cent of males have participated in a killing; 30 per cent of adult male deaths are a result of violence and 70 per cent of all adults over the age of 40 have lost a close genetic relative due to violence. In one of his earliest books Chagnon characterised these Indians as 'the fierce people', and his later application of sociobiological theory explains, he suggests, why they are so 'fierce'. Furthermore, this violence is seen by this account as celebrated by Yanomami culture. The 'unokai' (those who have killed) acquire great status amongst women as well as other men. The 'unokai' apparently acquire approximately three times the number of wives and children as the 'non-unokai'.[22]

Chagnon's views have, however, led to heated debate. Other anthropologists not insisting on Chagnon's overarching sociobiological perspective come up with a quite different view of Yanomami society. Their emphasis concentrates on social relations and the relations between people and nature. It is is these, rather than innate processes which give rise to Yanomami culture and everyday life. Furthermore, they extend their emphasis on social relations to those between these tribes and the outside world which is cutting down the rain forests and driving roads through their tribal lands.

THE FIERCE PEOPLE?

One US anthropologist has made his name with a series of books and films, widely used in universities, which describe the Yanomami as 'the fierce people'. He focuses on Yanomami feuding and advances a number of theories trying to explain why they are so 'fierce'. As a result, the Yanomami are often cited as examples of man's innate aggression.

But is he simply wrong? Many experts think so and believe that he has greatly exaggerated Yanomami belligerence.

Survival includes a number of social scientists who have extensive personal experiences of living with the Yanomami. They find these Indians a generally peaceful and fun-loving people, though feuds are not uncommon and do typically end in violence, as they can everywhere. Survival's own anthropologists find the sensationalist attention on Yanomami 'ferocity', promulgated by some anthropologists and some missionaries, to be false and to the detriment of the Indians and their rights.

The Yanomami are neither saints nor savages. They are *people*.[23]

Survival International are arguing here that while there are certainly feuds within Yanomami society, it is surely incorrect to overemphasise the inherently 'fierce' or 'savage' nature of these people, subject to genetic forces over which they have little control. A better way to understand them is through their relationships, both with one another and with the outside world. This view is now becoming somewhat more persuasive. Genetically inherited tendencies are not unimportant but they must surely *combine* with social relations and with the natural world in various complex ways.

There remains, however, the question of how human 'culture' and 'mind' are related to these biologically based understandings. This is a central issue, one I shall pursue in the next chapter.

SOCIOECOLOGY: ORGANISMS IN ECOLOGICAL CONTEXT

The approaches to behaviour reviewed above – which it should be stressed are still being pursued by many biologists and ethologists – were developed largely in response to behaviouristic environmentalism. In this latter approach to human and animal behaviour considerable emphasis was given to the context in which behaviour occurred. More specifically, the suggestion was frequently made that behaviour should be seen as the product of stimuli within the environment; organisms responded to punishments and rewards but their inner workings were envisaged as something of a 'black box'.[24] Sociobiology and ethology, by contrast, gave their greatest emphasis to processes and mechanisms innate within individuals. And, as we have seen, this leads to sometimes quite extreme claims as to the significance of these innate mechanisms in determining human and animal behaviour.

Most recently, however, research within the biological and related sciences (including anthropology) has placed less emphasis on innate processes and long-term behaviour patterns and have once more, concentrated on the context within which such behaviour is taking place. This is certainly a welcome development. The insights of classical biology and ethology have not so much been rejected. Rather, their large-scale claims for an overarching explanation of behaviour have been scaled down and located within particular kinds of environment. At the same time, and as part of this movement, biologically oriented studies have become more empirical in form; examining, for example, particular species in particular places or, in the case of human species, of particular indigenous social groups in particular social and environmental contexts. Crook sees these recent developments as follows: 'As sociobiology encounters problems which its sophisticated but theory-laden approaches fail to resolve, there is a realisation that the way forward must lie in a more extensive development of socioecological and ecocultural field study.'[25]

I will now review this newer approach to understanding behaviour, especially as applied to the human species. As the term 'socioecology' suggests, however, this 'new' direction incorporates some quite old forms of theory; especially that of ecology. Early ecology, like ethology and sociobiology has sometimes, as will be discussed, overextended its concepts into the the area of human social relationships and history. Indeed, as we saw in the last chapter, much of early social theory used ecological theory as a basis for understanding human societies.

This area of work as it has recently developed will be one focus here. Note that we again encounter one of the main themes and difficulties identified in the 'scientific' study of behaviour in environment. This is, again, methodological and analytical individualism. People are typically alluded to as 'man' or 'humans'. And typically these humans remain socially undifferentiated, not only in terms of gender but in terms of class and other bases of social power.[26] This is another product of methodological individualism.

Ecosystems, niches and socioecology

Biology has always had a central emphasis on environment. In the well-established science of ecology every species and its habitat is seen as forming part of a larger system of things. This is what ecologists call an 'ecosystem', a concept usually attributed to A.G. Tansley. As he put it in 1945: 'The modern branch of biological science known as ecology is the study of animals and plants as they exist in nature, and of the communities they form under given conditions of climate and soil.'[27]

In empirical studies the concept is most often used to examine the small scale at which we can trace the interactions between organisms, species, predators and food. But in principle at least it also incorporates energy in the form of sun and other inputs such as wind, rain, water and fuel and materials and organisms which are entering the area in which we are interested.[28] 'Ecosystem' refers too to outputs in the form of processed energy, materials, and organisms leaving the area in question and becoming part of the wider, even global, environment.

The Second Law of Thermodynamics, the 'entropy law' which we referred to in the last chapter, is central here. The ecosystem is degrading to an unavailable or less available form (to heat, for example) energy originally entering the system. Inorganic and organic species are the mediators of this process. The sun is what Colinvaux calls 'the ultimate furnace of life'.[29] Plants catch the sun's light and make use of it to grow. These plants (or, more accurately, some of them) are in turn eaten by animals. They are at the start of a giant food chain, forming part of animals' fuel or energy. The ecosystem is thus seen as consisting of groups of energy consumers and energy producers, all attempting to acquire the most they can and make the most of it in order to survive.

At the end of the food chain are, typically, large, rare and what are sometimes called (with more than a fair dash of anthropomorphism) 'aggressive' animals occupying particular 'niches'. 'Niche' in ecological theory refers to everything a particular species does to survive and stay 'fit' in the sense of contributing to future generations. It refers partly to physical habitat but it refers much more generally to a species' behaviour or way of life within the larger scheme of organic and inorganic nature. Such ways of life are seen as having been fashioned by natural selection. According to conventional biological theory, the numbers that live are set by the numbers of niche spaces in the environment. Thus a population is a function of the carrying capacity of the land for animals of this kind in that specific time and place.

Precisely *which* young members of the species take up the limited number of spaces available within the environment are nevertheless seen as depending on natural selection. Available niche spaces are taken up by 'fit' individuals and a parent's 'fitness' is similarly measured by the number of niche spaces which his or her offspring occupy. Animals such as sharks and tigers, akin to all other species, are attempting to gain sufficient calories to survive and reproduce. But those at the top of the food chain use up large numbers of calories and their particular ways of life or 'niches' are unable to support large numbers of their species. As we will see shortly, this idea of 'niche' becomes quite problematic when we attempt to develop a more dialectical approach to seeing the relations between organism and environment.

For ecology and mainstream biology, therefore, the question of niche and ecology closely links back to that of genetic fitness. It also suggests that there are close links to the biological processes we have outlined above, the ecological system within which species live, the physiology of species, and the forms of social behaviour they adopt are all closely linked. They are adapted to one another.

An example comes from Wrangham's recent work on primates.[30] As summarised by Fox in Figure 4.1, for a particular type of primate, there appear to be close associations between resource environment, digestive capacities, foraging strategies and kin coalition. Certain kinds of primate have a particular capacity to detoxify unripe fruits, seeds, grass and leaves high in tannin and alkaloids. A particular kind of liver enzyme – urate oxidase – is responsible for this digestive capacity. This, in turn, encourages what biologists and socioecologists call 'female kin coalitions' (extended maternal coalitions) to engage in particular kinds of strategy for the collection of secondary food.

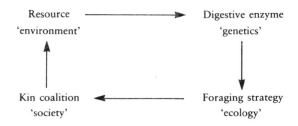

Figure 4.1 Interactions between resources, genetic evolution, ecology and social relations for primates (Source: R. Fox (1989), *The Search for Society*, Rutgers University Press: New Brunswick)

Wrangham, in line with mainstream sociobiological theory, argues that for males other females are the key resource as regards the maximisation of inclusive fitness. For females, however, the environment with which they are most concerned as regards such maximisation is the *physical* environment, in the form of these specific kinds of food which they can eat. For this species, therefore, a particular kind of interlocking system within a particular niche has evolved; one linking resources ('environment'), biological evolution ('genetics'), foraging strategy ('ecology') and kin coalition ('society').

Contemporary socioecology, which has emerged from biology is specifically concerned with evolution of adaptive behaviour in the context of ecological circumstances. It is a fusion of ecological theory with theories of animal behaviour and evolution. Natural selection is seen as benefiting those individuals who adopt behavioural strategies most likely to maximise their gene contribution into later generations. This can be done either through an individual concentrating on its own survival (and using resources to this end) or through putting all its effort into reproduction.

The point according to socioecology, however, is that the actual strategies and combinations adopted will depend partly on local ecological conditions as well as on individual's evolutionary history (or 'phylogeny') and its physiology. Thus ecological conditions now become seen as one of the main factors determining which behaviour patterns are actually favoured. The organism has, in social scientific terms, been 'de-centred'. Crook sums up the significance of socioecology in the context of contemporary biological thinking as follows:

As sociobiology encounters problems which its sophisticated but theory-laden approaches fail to resolve, there is a realization that the way forward must lie in a more extensive development of socioecological and ecocultural field study. While this constitutes the actual testing of socio-biological premises it will also require ... a more holistic model of adaptation which relates environmental, societal and cultural processes to those of genetic selection.[31]

Socioecology, with its much stronger emphasis on how organisms evolve in relation to their environment, represents a considerable improvement on earlier forms of ethology and sociobiology. It also seems broadly in line with our realist approach which suggests that certain powers and causal mechanisms (natural- and species-being) may be influencing individual or group behaviour, and that these develop or otherwise in different ways according to different circumstances. The question remains, however, does socioecology (which, again, is a branch of the life sciences now being actively developed by a number of biologists) still represent an adequate conceptualisation of the problem? Can the understanding of organisms and their relations to the contextual conditions be pushed still further? New concepts, which are arguably not yet part of mainstream biological science, suggest it can.

ORGANISM AND ENVIRONMENT: THE EMERGENT 'NEW BIOLOGY'

The last chapter referred to Haraway's important work on 'primate visions'. She challenges Darwinism's and neo-Darwinism's claim to detached, neutral, objectivity. On the other hand, she is anxious not to dismiss science as 'ideology'. Challenges to scientific 'stories' should, like those to stories in the human sciences be productive rather than dismissive. This line of attack is similar to that adopted by what is sometimes called 'the new biology'. As I shall suggest shortly, this term somewhat exaggerates the extent of the cohesion between all members of this general movement.

A starting-point is the work of Goodwin and Webster.[32] They are part of a small number of biologists concerned with the organism, the principles underlying their form and development and their relationships with the environment. Goodwin, who I take here as a representative of this new tendency, argues that neo-Darwinism, as represented by Dawkins, has been in many respects highly successful. It has been important in terms of providing a theory of biological inheritance and the molecular composition of organisms. But it has tried to describe organisms in terms of the activities of their genes, or the molecules of which they are made. And at this point neo-Darwinism has overextended its enterprise. Organisms are indeed made up of gene product, Goodwin argues, but this in no way explains organisms. It is as if we expected a knowledge of the composition of a liquid to explain its form or its activity, or a knowledge of the composition of planets to explain their eliptical motion around the sun. Organisms, furthermore, have self-organizing principles. They cannot be envisaged as mere machines, made up of predetermined parts and reacting to a fixed environment.

A new starting-point concentrates on the generative mechanisms underlying transformations. It concentrates on establishing the dynamic principles underlying the system in question. Examples are the equations of fluid flow or of crystal formation, or the dynamics of moving bodies. In biology they include statements about the molecular structure of organisms underlying the capacity of an organism to grow and change. In short, the idea is to identify what Goodwin calls 'a generative theory' describing the basic principles or structures underlying the development and the diverse forms of organisms' self-organising behaviour.

But at the same time such an approach gives equal weight to environmental conditions involved in the formation of organisms' forms and behaviour. Thus, in parallel with the approach represented by Goodwin, Ho and Saunders counter established biological concepts of organism–environment relations when they argue that 'the Darwinian notion that organisms are fitted (or adapted) to the environment is incomplete, for it misses the reciprocal in the relationship: the environment is fit for the origination and evolution of organisms.'[33]

The argument here is that the theory of natural selection depends on a neat separation between organism and environment. Evolution supposedly occurs as a result of internal variations within organisms while the external environment selects those organisms which are 'fittest' and most able to survive. On this basis the fit between organism and environment at any one time is seen as the product of past random variations, these being selected according to their adaptive consequences. Organisms are thus seen as mechanical objects, separated from their environment and acted on by selective forces.

Darwin himself had difficulties with this clinical separation between organism and environment. Neo-Darwinism has continued to insist on such a rigid distinction and the metaphor of mechanical organisms 'surviving' within a set of forces over which they have little control or influence. The argument in the new form of biology, and one which closely relates to the conception held by many in the contemporary environmental movement, is that this mental picture is seriously deficient. Ho puts the new paradigm as follows:

When we look at organisms as they are: living, breathing, acting, responding, learning, feeling, developing, and in tune with every aspect of their internal and external environments, it is clear that the fit between organism and environment must arise through reciprocal feedback and adjustments occurring on time scales that range from split seconds to hours and years and even generations. In other words, organisms adapt to the environment and adapt the environment to themselves through continuous processes nested in space and time.[34]

The insistence here is therefore on the intimate relationship between organism and environment. But at the same time, organisms are seen as interconnected wholes themselves; their mental and physical structures being, for example, closely interconnected.

As regards organism–environment relations, this line of attack was in fact established by Lewontin in 1982.[35] He was one of the first to argue that the mental picture of an organism 'fitting' a 'niche' is misleading. The environment in this specification is envisaged as an 'independent circumstance' to which an object is being fitted. An environmental challenge therefore supposedly leads to a response. It is a familiar and powerful metaphor. It is one which suggests that there is a pre-existing outside world with niches and an organism is trying to fit this world. It is like a key trying to fit a pre-made lock or a plug designed for British electrical systems failing to find its 'niche' in North America. Lewontin argued that this concept of organism and environment, one which suggests that remains separated from the organism, is incorrect. Rather, organisms during their individual lifetimes and in the process of their evolution do not simply adapt to environments, they actively construct them. Again, they are not objects of the laws of nature changing themselves to fit the inevitable features of the outside world. They are active beings, changing nature according to its laws. Lewontin summed up his position as follows:

In fact it is impossible to describe an environment except by reference to organisms that interact with it and define it. Organism and environment are dialectically related. There is no organism without an environment, but there is no environment without an organism.[36]

In certain important respects, therefore, biologists such as Goodwin, Lewontin, Ho and Saunders, parallel the early Marx and Engels, in arguing that the organism–environment dualism must be overcome through seeing the two interpenetrating one another. Organisms are envisaged as 'morphogenetic fields' made up of generative mechanisms and interacting with one another in complex ways. Goodwin *et al.*'s insistence that organisms are active, creative and self-organising is also certainly in line with Marx and Engels' conception of human beings.

As Lewontin points out, many animals besides humans adapt their environment in a number of ways; assembling the bits and pieces of the environment to their own ends. 'Nature' is actively made by them. At the same time, animals do not actually live in a raw 'nature'. They have around them an invisible shell of warm air which acts as a protecting boundary between themselves and their environment. All species actively assemble and alter the environment to their purposes. Amongst the best-known non-humans are beavers. Their dam-building has drastically altered water tables in parts of North America, much to the distress of other species, humans included. Organisms instinctively adapt to the environment in different ways. Danger signals, for example, are interpreted by their central nervous systems in ways which release chemical flows of adrenalin and the release of stored sugar. Finally, organisms modulate their environment. Humans and other animals, for example, store resources or body fat in such a way as to modify the effects of their environment on their bodies and behaviour. Similarly, some animals have ways of storing heat. Butterflies' wings, for example, act as solar collectors. Many animals have inbuilt systems of volume control, enabling them to adapt to detect small differences at low levels.

These are all instances of the close, reciprocal, relations between organisms and environment. Clearly such relations apply as much to humans as to non-humans. They too assemble, alter, respond to and protect themselves from nature. Indeed, they have done so in ways which may not only be disastrous but which mean it is now extremely difficult to talk of an unadulterated 'nature'. Furthermore, as I shall outline later, their interactions and modifications are often at a great distance from where they are initiated and experienced.

'The new biology': an assessment and a way forward

There are differences even within what I am calling here 'the new biology'. Lewontin, for example, insists on seeing organisms as the product of history; the product of dialectical relations between the parts of organisms and environments over time. Goodwin and Webster, on the other hand, place much greater emphasis on generative mechanisms at any given point in time. But these differences are relatively minor compared with their joint critique of sociobiology and of neo-Darwinism. Despite their differences, the new view of organisms and of organism–environment relations presented by Goodwin, Webster, Lewontin, Ho, Saunders and others therefore poses a serious challenge to conventional neo-Darwinian thinking. It suggests that evolution and behaviour cannot be simply envisaged as a 'solution' by a species to a given or predetermined environmental problem. This is, again, because active organisms themselves simultaneously determine both the problem they face and the solution which they propose. The Cartesian model of an organism as simply a machine being forced to fit an environment is therefore profoundly unhelpful. These biologists are therefore challenging established biological theory with its considerable insistence on genetic fitness and passing on genes to future generations. They are not, however, wholly denying the significance of either Darwinian or neo-Darwinian ideas. Rather, the suggestion is that organisms, their behaviour and their physical make-up can in no way be *reduced* to genes and genetically based processes.

So if we take this still small but nevertheless powerful critique seriously, genetics would be seen as a necessary but not sufficient basis for understanding. It is necessary in so far as it provides insights into mechanisms affecting both the behaviour and form of human and other organisms. And, as will be discussed shortly, these include and are linked to the crucially important *mental* mechanisms which have emerged in the process of natural selection and which have mediated organisms' experience. At the same time, an understanding is needed which relates organisms as what Ingold calls 'open systems' to their environments.[37] This is not simply to see how these organisms react to their environments but to see these environments, as they are worked on by humans and all other living beings, as in turn active in forming the organisms. This dialectical approach parallels that proposed by Marx and Engels nearly 150 years ago.

In short, this new form of biology threatens to erase the dualism between organisms (including people) and environment. By the same token it also threatens another unhelpful dualism; that between 'genotypes' (the genetic constitution of the organism) and 'phenotypes' (organisms as they have developed under the combined influences of the individual and the environment). It is an understanding which is not generally accepted by professional biologists. Yet it is important in so far as it threatens to dissolve the difference between organisms (including so-called 'man') and 'nature'. And, as we have seen, it is this difference which has long plagued the creation of a genuinely environmental social theory. 'Man' and 'Nature' are now part of one another. The distinction between people and nature is becoming distinctly undermined.

Modern biology, especially the 'new biology' as represented by Goodwin *et al.* is therefore making very considerable strides in its own field. It is this version of biology which seems, potentially at least, to be most amenable to the approach I am developing here. Its immediate main contribution to the social sciences lies in its concepts of the organism, its form, its behaviour and its relation with its environment. Furthermore, this approach has managed to release itself from a model of organisms as automatic pilots propelled primarily by the inexorable workings of their genes. By contrast, the central conception of there being, on the one hand, underlying generative structures which influence the general form and behaviour of an organism and, at the same time, a set of conditions (including, of course, other organisms) which constrain and limit the number of possible variations is surely one of direct relevance to social theorists.

In applying these lessons to their own area of work, social scientists will almost certainly want to overcome incipient methodological individualism. The analysis must become more *social*. Despite its important recent advances, biology still often neglects the ways in which organisms, their biological constitutions and hence their behaviour have evolved as part of *social* relations and processes. But, having made such criticisms, modern biology which emphasises species-specific *potentials* and which examines whether and how these potentials are realised in different types of physical and social environment, seems of enormous potential significance for work outside biology. As Benton has recently argued in the journal *Sociology*, this type of biology suggests that:

Environments, physical or social, may impair or enhance well-being, induce pathologies, or facilitate survival, whilst humans may act on their environments in ways which sustain or undermine the conditions of their own future survival. Sociology, surely, ought to have more to say about how these capacities are actually exercised, and with what consequences.[38]

But what, more precisely, are the implications of the new biology for social theory? This is clearly a matter requiring considerable further analysis and empirical work. But I shall consider this issue further in Chapter 6.

NOTES

1. K. Marx (1975), 'Economic and philosophical manuscripts', in L. Colletti (ed.), *Karl Marx. Early Writings*, Pelican: Harmondsworth, p. 355.
2. See J. & M. Gribbin (1988), *The One Per Cent Advantage*, Blackwell: Oxford.
3. See, in particular, R. Dawkins (1976), *The Selfish Gene*, Oxford University Press: Oxford and E. Wilson (1975), *Sociobiology*, Harvard University Press: Cambridge, Mass.
4. See, for example, P. Kitcher (1985), *Vaulting Ambition*, MIT Press: Cambridge, Mass. and M. Sahlins (1972), *The Use and Abuse of Biology*, Tavistock: London.
5. See, for example, S. Rose, R. Lewontin and L. Kamin (1984), *Not in Our Genes*, Pelican: Harmondsworth. This is a very thorough and effective attack on sociobiology. On occasions, however, it becomes an intemperate attack on all that this branch of biological theory has to offer.
6. T. Benton (1991), 'Biology and social science: why the return of the repressed should be given a (cautious) welcome', *Sociology* 25, 1: 1–29. This is a key paper in support of this chapter's argument and indeed for this study as a whole.
7. C. Darwin (1901), *The Descent of Man*, Murray: London, p. 201.
8. *ibid.*, p. 199.
9. *ibid.*, pp. 201–2.
10. A. Ardrey (1967), *The Territorial Imperative*, Collins: London; K. Lorenz (1966), *On Aggression*, Harcourt, Brace: New York; D. Morris (1967), *The Naked Ape*, Cape: London.
11. A. Ardrey (1967), *op.cit.*, p. 189.

12. *ibid.*, p. 190.
13. L. Tiger, R. Fox (1989), *The Imperial Animal* (2nd edn), Holt: New York. For a measured and critical assessment of how ethology can be extended to the study of human beings see Hinde's important work and in particular, R. Hinde (1967), *Individuals, Relationships and Culture*, Cambridge University Press: Cambridge.
14. J. Bowlby (1984), *Attachment and Loss: Volume 1: Attachment*, Pelican: London.
15. M. Odent (1986), *Primal Health*, Century: London.
16. L. Tiger, R. Fox (1989), *op.cit.*, p. 86.
17. See T. Headland, L. Reid (1989), 'Hunter–gatherers and their neighbours from prehistory to the present', in *Current Anthropology* 10, 1: 43–51. Also P. Mellars (1989), 'Major issues in the emergence of modern humans', *Current Anthropolgy* 30, 3: 349–85.
18. See, for example, R. Dyson-Hudson (1989), 'Ecological influences on systems of food production and social organisation of South Turkana pastoralists', in V. Standen, R. Foley, *Comparative Socioecology*, Blackwell: Oxford.
19. R. Foley (1987), *Another Unique Species*, Longman: Harlow, p. 77.
20. N. Chagnon (1979), 'Mate competition, favoring close kin, and village fissioning among the Yanomamo Indians', in N. Chagnon and W. Irons (eds), *Evolutionary Biology and Human Social Behavior*, Duxbury: North Scituate, Mass.
21. N. Chagnon (1979), *op.cit.*, p. 127.
22. N. Chagnon (1988), 'Life histories, blood revenge and warfare in a tribal population', *Science* 239, 26 Feb.: 985–92.
23. Survival International (1990), *Yanomami*, Survival: London.
24. See, for example, B. Skinner (1971), *Beyond Freedom and Dignity*, Knopf: New York.
25. J. Crook (1989), 'Introduction. socioecological paradigms, evolution and history: perspectives for the 1990s', in V. Standen, R. Foley (1989), *op.cit.*
26. Odum, for example writes of 'human-made catastrophes'. See E. Odum (1989), *Ecology*, Sinauer: Sunderland, Mass., p. 62.
27. A. Tansley (1945), *Our Heritage of Wild Nature*, Cambridge University Press: Cambridge.
28. D. Owen (1980), *What is Ecology?*, Oxford University Press: Oxford.
29. P. Colinvaux (1980), *Why Big Fierce Animals are Rare*, Allen & Unwin: London, p. 22.
30. R. Wrangham (1980), 'An ecological model of female-bonded primate groups', *Behaviour* 75: 262–300.
31. J. Crook (1989), 'Introduction: socioecological paradigms, evolution

and history: perspectives for the 1990s', in V. Standen, R. Foley, *op. cit.*

32. See B. Goodwin (1991), 'What is an organism?' (mimeo, Dept of Biology, the Open University, Milton Keynes and *New Scientist*, forthcoming); B. Goodwin (1990), 'Structuralism in biology', *Science Progress* 74: 227–44. See also G. Webster (1989), 'Structuralism and Darwinism: concepts for the study of form', in B. Goodwin, A. Sibatini and G. Webster (eds), *Dynamic Structures in Biology*, Edinburgh University Press: Edinburgh, pp. 1–15. For a recent overview of this area by a sociologist see in particular T. Benton (1991), *op.cit.*

33. M.-W. Ho and P. Saunders (1984), 'Pluralism and convergence in evolutionary theory', in M.-W. Ho and P. Saunders (eds), *Beyond Neo-Darwinism*, Academic Press: London, pp. 3–14. See also M.-W. Ho, P. Saunders, S. Fox (1986), 'A new paradigm for evolution', *New Scientist*, 27 February; M.-W. Ho 'Evolution in action and action in evolution', in P. Bunyard and E. Goldsmith (eds) (1989), *Gaia and Evolution* (Proceedings of 2nd Camelford Conference on the Implications of the Gaia Thesis) Wadebridge Ecological Press: Cornwall; M.-W. Ho and S. Fox (eds), *Evolutionary Processes and Metaphors*, Wiley: Chichester.

34. M.-W. Ho (1988), 'On not holding nature still: evolution by process, not by consequence', Chap. 7 of M.-W. Ho, S. Fox (eds), *op.cit.*, p. 122.

35. R. Lewontin (1982), 'Organism and environment', in H. Plotkin (ed.), *Learning, Development and Culture*, Wiley: Chichester. See also Chap. 10 of S. Rose *et al.* (1984), *op.cit.*

36. R. Lewontin (1982), *op.cit.*, p. 160.

37. T. Ingold (1990), 'An anthropologist looks at biology', *Man* 25: 208–29.

38. T. Benton (1991), *op.cit.*, pp. 24–5.

5

'NATURE AS ALIVE': SOCIAL RELATIONS AND DEEP MENTAL STRUCTURES

The problems which emerge in transferring biological concepts direct to human beings are therefore raising some very fundamental philosophical and even political questions about how, if the dualism between 'man' and 'nature' is to be avoided, a satisfactory fusion can be developed. At the back of the problem are notions of 'mind' and culture'. How can we resolve this problem and how does it help an understanding of the relations between people and nature? Here I shall draw on elements of contemporary psychology to argue that some of these complex issues can be addressed by adopting a view of culture which refers to the human beings' biologically inherited capacities for drawing analogies between different areas of experience. However, I shall be using Harré *et al.*'s model of the human mind to insist that these capacities are a product of, and combine with, the social relations in which people are necessarily caught up.

This view of the human mind helps, I shall argue, in overcoming the division between 'man' and 'nature'. It also undermines the dichotomy between 'biology' and 'culture'. Furthermore, it begins to explain why humans engage in what Marx called the 'fetishisation' of things which they themselves have constructed. To explore the implications of this approach I shall turn to two specific issues. First, I return to the study of indigenous peoples with this new emphasis on humans' mental capacities. Second, I turn to the highly contentious matter of species-being in the form of natural differences in male and female consciousness.

THE EVOLUTION OF MIND

On the one hand, much of biology suggests that humans are not so unique as many of us might like to think. As Darwin himself argued, other animals share a wide range of capacities with *Homo sapiens*.[1] To varying extents other species can, for example, communicate with one another, use signs and symbols as a means of such communication, choose between alternative behavioural strategies, use tools, recognise themselves *as* 'selves' in mirrors, create (as do ant populations) elaborate divisions of labour and even cooperate with other species as part of their strategies for survival and reproduction.

But on the other hand, human beings do seem to have at least some extraordinarily well-developed capacities. Speech, the formation and use of abstract concepts and an elaborately codified language are unique to the human species; a facility which seems associated with human beings' exceptionally large brains and their capacities for social interaction and cooperation. Language and mental powers were, according to Darwin, the main distinguishing feature of human beings. He wrote: 'the lower animals differ from man solely in his larger power of associating together the most diversified sounds and ideas; and this obviously depends on the high development of his mental powers.'[2]

'Culture' in the form of speech seems to have started evolving during human beings' gathering and hunting phase. It was further developed with the relatively recent development of agriculture. Thus the originally primitive repertoire of sounds in early people was eventually given grammatical structure. Speech allowed the supplementation of other kinds of communication such as gesturing. It facilitated the making of concepts and the construction of moral judgements.

This suggests that it would be fruitful to envisage the notion of mind or 'culture' as historically developing. Its pre-modern forms were the outcome of the human organisms' dialectical relationships with nature and with other human beings. In other words, as Engels in particular argued, it is precisely through such interaction that humans came to form themselves *as* human beings able to construct and communicate abstract concepts. People and their capacities for communication therefore evolved in a dialectical way in the process of handling and managing their social and natural environments.

Both Marx and Engels were quite dismissive about what they called 'the fantastic reflection of human things in the human mind'.[3] Thoughts, they believed, only originate in their material needs. To think otherwise was to indulge in idealism. Yet more recent work in the Marxian tradition and non-Marxian tradition of anthropology and psychology lends more credence to relatively separate and autonomous mental structures and needs. Thus so-called 'fantasies' and 'myths' can be seen as integral to human beings' constitution. To put this another way, human beings developed more than the considerable mental capacities recognised by Engels. As I shall discuss shortly, one theme in psychology is that they evolved mental structures organising their experience of the world in ways which allowed them to feel secure within that world and at the same time to communicate this experience to others.

BIOLOGY AND THE PROBLEMATIC NOTION OF 'CULTURE'

The relationships between 'nature' and 'culture' have continued to haunt the biological sciences. The basic question is how to incorporate an understanding of human culture into the kinds of understanding developed by neo-Darwinism. So far there has been very little satisfactory progress towards answering this question. I suspect that this is because the artificial distinction between what is 'nature' and what is 'culture' is difficult to sustain and, in the end, impossible to recombine in a coherent form.

Dawkins, who is of course well-known for his theory of the 'selfish gene', comes to what he agrees is a 'surprising' conclusion regarding the importance of genetics for the understanding of modern peoples' culture. He argued that: 'for an understanding of the evolution of modern man, we must begin by throwing out the gene as the sole basis of our ideas on evolution.'[4] He suggested that the characteristic feature of modern human societies is that genes and the genetic basis to behaviour are slowly *ceasing* to be of significance. In the human case, culture is supplanting genetics. What he calls 'memes' are acting in a way similar to genes:

Examples of memes are tunes, ideas, catch-phrases, clothes fashions, ways of making pots or of building arches. Just as genes propagate themselves in the gene pool by leaping from body to body via sperms or eggs, so memes propagate themselves in the meme pool by leaping from brain to brain via a process which, in the broad sense, can be called imitation.[5]

Dawkins is nevertheless implying here that 'culture' is of a different order to 'nature'. Although he has rejected genes as a way of understanding culture, he is using an analogy with genes in trying to understand how the human species develops its cultural forms.

A related understanding of how biology relates to culture comes from Lumsden and Wilson with their theory of 'gene-culture coevolution'. Their theory suffers from something of the same problem, although in explaining human behaviour they do insist on a higher degree of genetic determinism.[6] On the one hand, they argue, genes prescribe the ways in which the human mind has been assembled and the 'epigenetic rules' which affect how a human organism develops and interacts with its environment. Given such an inheritance the mind grows by absorbing the existing culture which it experiences. On the other hand, in Lumsden and Wilson's formulation, culture is itself changing. Each generation of people makes fresh cultural innovations. These new forms of culture are in turn experienced and monitored by a new generation of human beings, with the epigenetic rules inherited by some individuals allowing them to survive and reproduce better than others. And, as culture changes the human species itself evolves, its genetically inherited epigenetic rules themselves being slowly modified. Thus they envisage a dialectic taking place. As Lumsden and Wilson put it: 'culture is created and shaped by biological processes while the biological processes are simultaneously altered in response to cultural change.'[7]

The idea of society and people dialectically interacting in this way is initially appealing, even though Lumsden and Wilson do not discuss what modern 'society' actually is and how it relates to the developing organism. But there are a number of problems here. The first is the continuing issue of methodological individualism; there still seems little scope here for the 'epigenetic rules' of humans and other species having an inherently social or collective form. Second, they are still operating with the dichotomy of 'biology' on the one hand and 'culture' on the other.

It again remains very difficult to see how these two categories can be blended. The categories themselves are, I believe, a large part of the problem.

Wolfe is one of the few social scientists to have explored how social theory can be connected to the insights of disciplines such as ethology and biology, and his argument is helpful here in so far as it points to mental as well as purely social evolution.[8] He gives a central place to 'mind' in distinguishing the specific features of human nature. He does not ignore the genetically inherited characteristics and forms of behaviour to which the biological sciences give such prominence. Rather, Wolfe argues, it is mind and the sense of 'self' which characterise the human species and which can allow them to override their biologically inherited instincts. 'Human distinctiveness', he argues, 'lies in the power given us by the existence of selves to alter the rules that govern our evolution.'[9] Thus modern societies, he suggests, are where respect for the individual self are most likely to predominate. They are also societies in which 'deterministic theories of human behaviour associated with either genetic or cultural structures ought to play less of an explanatory role and those stressing the autonomy of mind and self ought to play more.'[10]

Wolfe is surely correct to introduce the question of mind in considering *Homo sapiens'* species-being. And such consideration shows how it is indeed possible to consider human beings as simultaneously part of nature and yet still the dominant species within it. On the other hand, Wolfe does not adequately state what 'mind' consists of, why it is such a distinctly human capacity and why it should be considered to make people autonomous from their instincts and evolutionary history. Assuming that 'mind' refers in some way to extremely well-developed mental capacities, there surely remains the possibility that people's minds (like, presumably, those of other species) have themselves developed as part of a process of evolution.

However, the most important problem surrounding the socio-biologists' attempts to relate their theories to the question of 'mind' and 'culture' is that they are still committed to an inadequate conceptualisation of the human agent. And this brings me back to my concern with methodological individualism and with the contexts within which individuals act. People's practices may in part be a product of genetic and evolutionary imperatives.

But this need not divert us from the fact that people, and other species too, are active, creative, beings. Their natures are not simply a product of genes or forms of behaviour stemming from their genetic inheritance. As I argued at the end of the last chapter, their unfolding capacities, and what they communicate with one another are also a product of relationships between individuals and between people and the environment; furthermore, they are a product of people's understanding of these relationships. Neo-Darwinism on its own is incapable of incorporating such an understanding. The individual is still an automatic pilot, his or her life being guided by commands. Ingold makes this point about sociobiology as follows: 'Individuals are still seen as *products* which are assembled, if not entirely from genetic instructions, then from genetic *plus* cultural instructions.'[11]

Finally, there remains the closely related problem of 'culture'. There are, I believe, better ways of addressing this issue.

THE MIND: ERODING THE CULTURE–NATURE DISTINCTION

Thus it is largely inadequate to see humans as simply, in Dawkins' term, 'survival machines' possessed by their genes. Indeed, it is probably unwise to see any organism in this way. While their behaviourial propensities may well be generated from their genetic inheritance and while such inheritance poses constraints over such behaviour, this is hardly a total specification of an individual. But the way of giving them greater explanatory power is not, I believe, to try clipping on another category; that of 'culture'. The way forward is to start by allowing for different levels of abstraction and understanding.

As I shall discuss in more detail shortly, biologically based mechanisms and tendencies associated with what we call the human 'mind' *combine* with a large range of contingent circumstances and conditions. These latter are the rest of inorganic and organic nature (including of course other humans) and the generative mechanisms underlying their constitution and behaviours. They are again part of, and unfold in relation to, their environmental context, this being partly constituted by other organisms and mechanisms. This way of proceeding would replace the biology–culture dualism. It would envisage what is sometimes referred to as 'culture' as deriving directly from the distinctive, biologically inherited, capacities which humans (and no doubt other species) have evolved as a species. But it would also stress the interactions of these capacities and latent tendencies with the rest of the social and natural world.

But what are these distinctive biologically inherited capacities? A useful starting-point here is anthropological work which sees 'culture' as the capacity to transfer understandings derived from one area of social life to another. In short, people (and, again, perhaps other species to some lesser degree) make sense of themselves and their relationships through making analogies between different areas of experience. Furthermore, analogies and metaphors are important as symbols by which humans can communicate with one another. These are fairly familiar themes in symbolic anthropology. They have been most effectively developed in recent years by, amongst others, Strathern. Here she summarises her approach:

There is more to communication than just disseminating ideas. The anthropological analysis of culture also points to the way in which we make – replicate, reproduce – ideas out of other ideas. We create by analogy. We make new concepts by borrowing from one domain of life the imagery by which to structure other areas. . . . Where we borrow from and what we borrow has consequences for the way we think.[12]

So, taking this view of human culture, it consists of our making relationships and artefacts which in turn are used to give form and shape to the way we construct *other* artefacts and relationships. This is very useful as a starting-point. It also links up well with recent developments in biology and psychology which are emphasising the continuity between 'mind' and 'body' and the major difficulties in using this dichotomy as an explanatory device. Humphrey, for example, argues on the basis of his work with primates that mind or what he calls 'intellect' enables sophisticated social interaction and confers distinct evolutionary advantages.[13] Humans and other species which have acquired well-developed capacities for reflection and monitoring their own and others' behaviour are able, for example, to protect their young for long periods and to ensure that offspring are able to learn from their elders' experience. They can thus engage in complex forms of social interaction and in the process become dominant over other species. Furthermore, as Humphrey points out, capacities for reflective interaction can be extended to relationships with inorganic nature. Humans, and perhaps other species with similarly developed capacities, can adapt their behaviour in the process of interacting with the emergent properties of, say, plants and the biosphere.

But intellect or mind developed and deployed in such ways can be used for other purposes. It has, for example, enabled humans to develop sophisticated religions, myths and philosophies. These have provided people with particular understandings of their relationships with one another and with nature. Such understandings again often entail the capacity for analogy-making; an understanding of an individual's relationships to society can, for example, be transferred to an appreciation of her or his relationship with an animised or personified 'nature'. Such investing of living qualities into an apparently alive 'nature' may well be inappropriate and indeed highly misleading, but it nevertheless continues to affect human beings' appreciations and interactions deeply. Furthermore, as I will now discuss, it seems quite possible that the human species has evolved in such a way as to predispose it not only towards generalised analogy-making but towards the adoption of particular analogies. These again deeply affect their understanding of themselves, their social relations and their relationships with nature.

AN UNDERSTANDING OF THE BIOLOGICALLY EVOLVED MIND

At this point I turn, with some hesitation, to the work of Carl Jung. My hesitation derives from those interpretations of Jung which reduce the whole of psychic and social life to the unmediated workings of deep mental structures. This is a problem to which I shall return very soon. Jung argued that there indeed are deep structures of the mind which organise or pre-figure the concepts we use. A key element of Jung's thinking is of course the notion of archetypes. According to this notion an individual's experience of life is conditioned by the collective evolutionary history of human beings.[14] A person's experiences and actions are therefore seen as not just the product of her or his life history but of the evolved social history of the human species. Archetypes are what Jung called 'pre-existent forms of apprehension'. They have been formed during the millions of years when the human brain and human consciousness were emerging and evolving from their earlier animal states. 'Ultimately', Jung wrote, 'every individual life is the same as the eternal life of the species.'[15]

According to this perspective, therefore, an individual's archetypal endowment both reflects and influences the typical and primordial experiences of human beings in general. It includes and links such themes as good and evil, gender, power and mortality. It can also be seen as presupposing a life cycle. This includes being mothered, experiencing and engaging in the environment, adolescence, establishing a position in the social hierarchy, raising children, hunting, gathering, fighting and eventually preparing for death. It nevertheless still relates to and informs the 'ego', the focal point of consciousness and the mediator between inner and outer worlds.

Archetypes, according to this line of thinking, are thus seen as having evolved to reflect the central themes with which human beings have struggled throughout history. They can be seen as genetically inherited liabilities or ways of acting. They help to structure and give order to everyday life. They make sense of it, respond to it, communicate about it and create a sense of personal security in relation to other people and to their environment. Note that this is a theory about people as a biologically evolved species. It links the life sciences to psychology. It also, I believe, links to social theory in the form outlined by Marx. As I have shown, Marx argued that people do tend to fetishise or reify things as though they had lives of their own. Jungian psychology (and indeed other forms such as those of Freud) suggests that human beings are predisposed to 'fetishise' in this way; through, that is, the systematic projection of myths and metaphors onto their perceived world.

But, to return now to the problem of psychological reductionism, many social theorists will feel distinctly unhappy with a formulation which gives primary significance to the evolved structures of the mind as themselves governing human behaviour.

Surely the mental constructs people make and the analogies they use all combine with, and are a product of social relations of which they are part? This is clearly correct. Furthermore, there is an understanding of the human mind which attempts to combine both these forms of understanding: it is that represented by Rom Harré and his colleagues.[16] Figure 5.1 represents their understanding of the mind – one which *stratifies* this complex apparatus. At the top level (Level 1) are, first, the deep structures of the mind. These can be seen as analogous to those discussed by Jung and his later followers. Here is what might be called the 'biological level' of the mind. At the same time, and on the same level in the figure, are the social relations in which people find themselves. As I have implied above, and as my earlier insistence on the avoidance of a biology–society dualism would imply, there must be complex connections between these two. Social relations develop in relation to the underlying substrata of the mind, and of course vice versa. An extension of Harré *et al.*'s diagram would be the relationships and mechanisms of the natural world within which the human mind has also evolved.

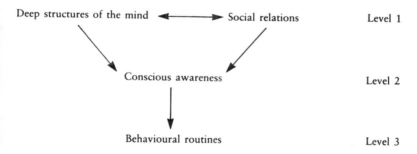

Figure 5.1 The levels of the human mind (Source: R. Harré, D. Clarke and N. DeCarlo (1985), *Motives and Mechanisms*, Methuen: London)

At the middle level of the figure is what Harré *et al.* call 'the information-rich level of decision'. It is here that awareness is located and where people exercise conscious control over their relationships and their environment. Planning, decision-making, conversation, language and communication are the defining characteristics of this level. Note, however, the underlying, archetypal, deep structures of the mind and the social relations

(what Harré *et al.* call 'social orders') of 'Level 1' still influencing
this middle level. The significance of the archetypes is that they are
what Harré *et al.* call 'generalized summaries of the success and
failure of different policies'.[17] In effect, they are acting as a kind of
monitor to the workings of the conscious brain; influencing and
constraining the range of images and metaphors which inform
action. But, again over the millions of years of humans' evolution,
this conscious level of the mind can be seen as affecting the
evolving form of the mind at the higher level.

The lowest level of Harré *et al.*'s stratified level is that at which
organisms experience and respond in a virtually automatic way to
the physical and social environment. Raising the voice to make
oneself heard or instinctively withdrawing from a source of heat
are examples of the types of behaviour represented by this level.
Note, however, that even this level is ultimately connected to the
subconscious structures of the mind as well as to the social
relations of which an individual forms part.

Harré *et al.*'s work takes us back to a kind of psychology which
is only now finding the full recognition it deserves. In stressing the
development or unfolding of individuals' capacities within distinctive types of environment, they are following and developing the
work of the distinguished Soviet psychologist, Lev Vygotsky.
Working mainly in the 1920s and 30s, his approach was very
much modelled on Marx's dialectical thinking. He examined how
mental functions such as memory, attention and perception first
emerge in 'elementary' and then in 'higher' forms. Children
initially appropriate public forms of language. But as they develop
they acquire increasingly individualistic forms of discourse, the
capacity for reflection on and regulation over what they are saying
and the use of complex signs to communicate their feelings. At the
same time, of course, each individual becomes part of a social
context; developing adults influencing the language of developing
children and so on.[18]

SOCIAL RELATIONS AND NATURE AS 'ALIVE'

How do all these above understandings of Marx's 'species being'
and its relationship to the material world link to our central theme

of human society and its links to nature? I return, again with some reservations, to Jung. He envisaged his conception of the collective unconscious as underpinning the production of myths, visions, cosmologies, religions and dreams which were common to various cultures. Authoritative power figures are seen by Jungian psychology as a core element of the collective unconscious. The Wise Old Man and Great Mother were the names ascribed to such figures. The latter has a special significance here.

The female figure, with both a creative and a destructive nature, is seen not as a mother image as such but what Stevens calls an 'inner dynamic'. The mother figure has its basis in the early sustained mothering of a child. It goes, however, much further than this. Such nurturing in an infant's early years gives rise to a much more *general* sense of trust that the world as later experienced actually is as it appears to be.[19] This means that a developing being, as it later acquires its own identity, can still feel confident in engaging in the social and natural world. The sense of security in the world created by the mothering of the child is thus transferred into a sense of security about the social and natural world in general.

The physical expression and symbolism of the earth as an alive organism can, however, take diverse and even contradictory forms. Indeed, it is not always a female figure. The 'green man' is another way in which the earth is sometimes characterised or personified.[20] But, as Neumann has shown, it is particularly the female archetype which is very common across many societies. It represents on the one hand, fertility, nourishment, creativity and growth and, on the other hand, chaos and even death.[21] Neumann clearly shows how for scores of millennia early people have attributed this contradictory and paradoxical nature to a living female organism. She is seen as both creative and destructive, caring and yet hateful. She is someone on whom the individual is totally dependent. On the other hand, she is unpredictable, can exert revenge if mistreated, and so must be treated with caution and respect.

The analogy between relations on earth and nature as a living being of which humans are part can therefore be seen as an important underlying propensity affecting all humans and their construction of the natural world. Perhaps too it is a feature of other species. But note that in the case of humans the expressed form this takes is very considerable. And this returns me to the problem of psychological reductionism. Expressions of 'Mother Earth' have occurred very widely across cultures. They can, for example, take the symbolic form of a Moon Goddess, expressing the periodicity of both womanhood and nature. They can also take the form of divine animals; the bear protecting her children or a celestial cow nourishing the earth with milky rain. But what Neumann and others interested in this and other mental structures do not show or discuss is the circumstances in which these archetypes and constructs have developed and in which they are used. Presumably they emerge in the context of specific social and natural conditions. In other words, there may be latent human propensity to make analogies between the known human world and the relation between people and nature. But we need to know much more of the circumstances under which such analogies are formed, why they finish by being so different from one another and what they actually mean to an individual's development. Harré *et al.*'s diagram (Figure 5.1) again needs recalling.

And Merchant has indeed shown the extent to which the Mother Earth metaphor has been adaptable and flexible. Furthermore, she very usefully relates it to changing conditions and contexts. Merchant summarises the pre-modern perception as follows:

Central to the organic theory was the identification of nature especially the earth, with a nurturing mother: a kindly beneficent female who provided for the needs of mankind in an ordered, planned universe. But another opposing image of nature as female was also prevalent: wild and uncontrollable nature that could render violence, storms, droughts and general chaos.[22]

Furthermore, under modern conditions the analogy of Mother and Earth has unfolded into a form very different from the earlier version. The organic metaphor and its imagery of nurturing and coexistence was, with the rise of the industrial revolution, largely replaced by one emphasising the mastery and exploitation of nature rather than dialectical interaction. In other words, there developed a competing version of Mother Earth, one which emphasised machinery and dominance. As Merchant puts it in relation to early modern mining: 'The organic framework, in which the Mother Earth image was a moral restraint against mining, was literally undermined by the new commercial activity.'[23]

Psychology of the kind I have been outlining suggests, therefore, that the notion of the earth as an alive organism can be considered as a mental structure or predisposition. It is a part, and an important one, of the deep structure of the human mind; one based on an analogy between the person and real people, especially real parents. But, in line with Harré's stratified model of the mind, it not only guides the concepts and metaphors which people use to organise and communicate their experience, it also combines and develops in relation to the organisms (human and otherwise) constituting the human organism's physical and social environment.

ALIENATION AND FETISHISATION: RETURNING TO THE YANOMAMI CASE STUDY

Thus the concept of the mind developed by Harré *et al.* allows for the idea that humans have evolved effective structures and ways of acting. And these usually enable them to meet much the same needs as other species, though in what we often deem to be more 'sophisticated' ways.

An illustration can be given to suggest that these ideas help towards a better understanding of changes to actual civilisations. A regular feature of contemporary social and political life is the constant throwback to a lost arcadian and rural world. But Raymond Williams in particular points out how predominantly *social* crises are often associated with notions of returning to a lost world with close connection with nature and with other people.[24] This is also a feature of much contemporary environmentalism. It especially applies to the 'deep-ecology' movement: their vision of an ideal world of close-knit communities closely integrated with nature can be seen as a critique of existing society. It is easy to categorise these movements as 'ideology'. Perhaps, however, it is not too far-fetched to suggest, that they are attempts to recover a more connected relation with nature. To put this in Marx's terms, they are the attempted recovery of an un-alienated species being.

A more developed kind of understanding provides a fuller account of relations and practices in societies composed of both humans and nature. It certainly provides a better picture of indigenous peoples; one in considerable advance of the pure sociobiologically based studies as advanced by Chagnon. As we saw, his was a controversial picture, one which saw Yanomami society as principally organised around sexual reproduction and kin relations. But recognising people's capacities for creating a culture based on transferred experience allows a more complete picture.

Contemporary studies of indigenous peoples usually stress their close working 'fit' and indeed close spiritual relationships between human species, other species and inanimate nature. The fit is again of a two-way nature: people and their behaviour are adapted to their environment, but the social and natural environment is in turn 'fit' to support the peoples in question. Their behaviour and indeed their whole beings are formed through interaction with their context, one constituted by other people and by other species. At the same time, and most importantly, the peoples have usually remained attached in emotional or spiritual terms to their environment.

In this sense, though not as a result of the processes identified by Marx for capitalist societies, they 'fetishise' nature in a way which allows them to picture it and their relationship to it. This picturing involves giving it a life of its own, one paralleling and combined with their own social relations. Such fetishisation is in part a product of the way they organise their lives. The Yanomami work for only about four hours a day. And the arrival of new tools is used to shorten working time still further: 'Intelligence and imagination are applied instead to the leisurely observation of nature and to the development of elaborate ritual and ceremony. It is an attitude to life which has ensured a balanced and restrained use of the forest.'[25]

This respect for, and learning from the natural world is very closely linked to the Yanomami spiritual order. And, as is so often the case with indigenous peoples, the spiritual order closely links everyday life with a degree of fear of the natural world. Not only is this a form of 'fetishisation', but it is one based on very definite ideas about social relations. These are again borrowed from human society and transferred to the supernatural world:

For the Yanomami, the world of everyday life is part of a larger spirit-world which they treat in the same way as they do one another. Thus, when they garden or gather or hunt, taking from nature, they are incurring a debt; arousing the vengeful spirits of dead plants and animals. These attack the Yanomami in their dreams and are said to account for much illness. They can only be controlled by special song and dance by shamans (spiritual healers) which bring the aid of 'helpers' from amongst the creator spirits. These are imagined as little Yanomami, personifying the forces of nature in human form and circling down from their Yanos in the sky to drive away the disease-causing spirit.[26]

Thus understandings of earthly relations between people, animals and plants have been transferred into a set of articulated beliefs about the relationships between people and their controlling spirits. A fusion has taken place between the known social and natural world on the one hand and the relation between that world and an assumed cosmology on the other. This seems a far more rounded account than the sociobiological understanding offered by Chagnon. It is also, as I shall describe later, not wholly unlike the lay understandings of people in supposedly advanced societies.

'WOMEN AS NATURE': CONSCIOUSNESS, NATURAL DIFFERENCES AND ENVIRONMENTALISM

Notions of 'mother earth' or 'mother nature' raise the thorny question of natural differences. Should women be viewed as somehow 'natural'? Linked to this is the issue of relationships between gender and environmentalism. The approach under development here seems to have definite implications for these vexed matters, though I am well aware that the literature here is multifaceted and very considerable.

There are now a number of different relationships between feminism and political ecology.[27] Some branches of ecofeminism make a particular case for a close connection between women and nature. And, in doing so, they attempt to restore what they see as distinct but suppressed feminine forms of consciousness. Here, for example, is Shiva writing of women in the developing countries.

She argues that there is a special connection between women's priorities and the natural environment:

> To say that women and nature are intimately associated is not to say anything revolutionary. After all, it was precisely just such an assumption that allowed the domination of both women and nature. The new insight provided by rural women in the Third World is that women and nature are associated *not in passivity but in creativity and the maintenance of life.*[28] [author's emphasis]

The suggestion is, therefore, that many women, especially those in the Third World, perceive nature and people's relation to it in ways which wholly contradict the dominant mechanistic and reductionist paradigm influencing modern peoples' relations to nature. Their viewpoint stresses interactions between people and nature rather than nature as a resource to be exploited. Here, again is Vandana Shiva:

> Women in sustenance economies, producing and reproducing wealth in partnership with nature, have been experts in their own right of a holistic and ecological knowledge of nature's processes. But these alternative modes of knowing, which are oriented to social benefits and sustenance needs, are not recognised by the reductionist paradigm, because it fails to perceive the interconnectedness of nature, or the connection of women's lives, work and knowledge with the creation of wealth.[29]

At the same time there are, as I outlined in Chapter 3, difficulties with any simple concept of 'the interconnectedness of nature'. It can easily suggest that there is a pure nature, one which has not been socially constructed or modified. Furthermore, the envisaged connections are all within nature (albeit a nature which incorporates people) and not between environment and social relations, labour and so forth. The danger with such an image again is that of fetishising a pure 'nature' and 'pure' human beings, all of which have somehow become disconnected from the real material or social world.

Many feminists remain deeply sceptical about any notion that women have a special connection with nature. They are even more sceptical about ideas of an innately 'feminine' form of consciousness. To them the notion that, for example, men are more 'cultural' while women are more 'natural' is a clear and misleading nonsense[30] which draws attention away from social processes and institutions which form such differences.

The logic of my position is that gender identities are both socially constructed *and* subject to naturally inherited predispositions. Indeed, this is a point made in an early commentary on these complex issues made by Kate Soper.[31] As regards conceptualising natural differences and their implications for environmentalism, an appropriate strategy again seems to be that of differentiating between levels of abstraction. At the most abstract level the two sexes may well be constituted by distinct generative mechanisms which lead to different forms of inherited behavioural dispositions or propensities. But this is not saying very much, since they combine in many and complex ways with contingent circumstances.

How does this relate to our concern with environmental issues? It is very difficult to envisage a necessary link between sex and gender on the one hand and environmentalism on the other. First, as I have said, an unhelpful proposition is that a special link between environmental politics and women is a result of women being somehow more 'natural'. Men too are 'natural', though perhaps in different ways. Second, even Jung and his later followers do not suggest that the Mother Earth archetype is associated with *either* women *or* men. Such propensities are ways in which both sexes conceptualise the social and natural worlds. Third, Shiva's argument that there is a special association between women and environmentalism is, I suspect, very much a comment on the very specific circumstances of the Third World.

If women do indeed have distinctive biologically inherited propensities towards the maintenance and nurturance of life, there are a number of ways of achieving that objective. One would indeed be the maintenance of the physical environment. Others, particularly perhaps for those in modern or 'Western', societies, might include the development of an efficient social environment or, more specifically, the acquisition of a well-paid job. So again, it may be possible to say that distinctive innate mechanisms influence the consciousness and practices of the two sexes in different ways, but such a recognition on its own does not tell us much about the precise forms of these practices. Still less does it lead to a special association between one sex or gender and the physical environment. This is because in the same way as nature itself is socially constructed, the biologically inherited propensities influencing human behaviour are mediated and modified in diverse ways by the contingent social circumstances of which people are part. Amongst these are of course the ways in which the two sexes are socially constructed, or gendered.

NOTES

1. C. Darwin (1901), *The Descent of Man*, Murray: London.
2. *ibid.*, pp. 130–1.
3. F. Engels (1972), *The Part Played by Labour in the Transition from Ape to Man*, Progress: Moscow, p. 10.
4. R. Dawkins (1976), *The Selfish Gene*, Oxford University Press: Oxford, p. 205.
5. *ibid.*, p. 206
6. C. Lumsden, E. Wilson (1983), *Promethean Fire*, Harvard University Press: Cambridge, Mass.
7. *ibid.*, p. 18.
8. A. Wolfe (1990), 'Social theory and the second biological revolution', in *Social Research* 57, 3: 615–48.
9. *ibid.*, p. 647.
10. *ibid.*, p. 646.
11. T. Ingold (1990), 'An anthropologist looks at biology', *Man* 25: 208–29.
12. M. Strathern (1990), 'The meaning of assisted kinship', Paper to British Association for the Advancement of Science, Swansea, August 1990, p. 2. See also M. Strathern (1990), 'Enterprising kinship: consumer choice and the new reproductive technologies', *Cambridge Anthropology* 14,1. Strathern's work is part of the more general field of 'symbolic anthropology'. For a recent account see R. Wagner (1986), *Symbols That Stand for Themselves*, Chicago University Press: Chicago.
13. N. Humphrey (1983), *Consciousness Regained*, Open University Press: Milton Keynes.
14. A. Stevens (1982), *Archetype*, Routledge, London.
15. Quoted in *ibid.*, p. 40.
16. R, Harré, D. Clarke and N. DeCarlo (1985), *Motives and Mechanisms*, Methuen: London. Note also Benton's recent plea for the idea of 'levels' of psychological as well as sociological and biological organisation (T. Benton, 1991, 'Biology and social science: why the return of the repressed should be given a (cautious) welcome', *Sociology* 25, 1: 20).

17. R. Harré *et al.* (1985) *op.cit.*, p. 27.
18. See J. Wertsch (1985), *Vygotsky and the Social Formation of Mind*, Harvard University Press: Cambridge, Mass. Also A. Kozulin (1990), *Vygotsky's Psychology*, Harvester Wheatsheaf: Hemel Hempstead.
19. A. Stevens (1982) *op.cit.*
20. On 'personification' by the human mind, see in particular J. Hillman (1977), *Re-Visioning Psychology*, Harper & Row: New York. On the 'green man' archetype, see W. Anderson (1990), *Green Man*, HarperCollins: London.
21. E. Neumann (1955), *The Great Mother: An analysis of the archetype*, Routledge: London.
22. C. Merchant (1980), *The Death of Nature*, Harper & Row: San Francisco, p. 2.
23. *ibid*, p. 41.
24. R. Williams (1973), *The Country and the City*, Chatto & Windus: London.
25. Survival International (1990), *Yanomami*, Survival: London, p. 9.
26. *ibid.*, p. 11.
27. See Chap. 5 of A. Dobson (1990), *Green Political Thought*, Unwin Hyman: London. See also L. Birke (1986), *Women, Feminism and Biology*, Harvester Wheatsheaf: Hemel Hempstead; A. Jaggar (1983), *Feminist Politics and Human Nature*, Harvester Wheatsheaf: Hemel Hempstead; J. Sayers (1982), *Biological Politics*, Tavistock: London; R. Sydie (1987), *Natural Women, Cultured Men*, Open University Press: Milton Keynes.
28. V. Shiva (1989), *Staying Alive*, Zed Books: London, p. 47.
29. *ibid.*, p. 24.
30. See, for example, D. Fuss (1989), *Essentially Speaking. Feminism, Nature and Difference*, Routledge: London. See also references in note 27, especially R. Sydie (1987), *op. cit.*
31. K. Soper (1979), 'Marxism, materialism and biology', in J. Mepham, D.-H. Ruben, *Issues in Marxist Philosophy, Vol.II Materialism*, Harvester Wheatsheaf: Hemel Hempstead.

6

SPREADING 'MAN'S INORGANIC BODY': SOME IMPLICATIONS

Towards the end of Chapter 4 I discussed aspects of what I called 'the new biology' and the notion that organisms develop and unfold in relation to neighbouring contexts of other organisms and inorganic nature. The present chapter might have been subtitled 'human organisms unfolding, but in relation to what?', my main interest being in the global and temporal spreading of these fields and the implications for human beings.

I can start here with the work of Tim Ingold, someone writing from an anthropological perspective who has made direct use of the 'new biology'.[1] He has extended its use to the study of *human* organisms. He argues that the lesson of the new biology to the social sciences is that human consciousness simultaneously encapsulates or 'enfolds' the social relations of which it is part. Simultaneously, however, it unfolds *within* these relations. Thus Ingold, like the biologists such as Goodwin, Ho *et al.*, is resolutely refusing to accept the organism–environment dichotomy, insisting that one is integral to the other. His general argument could quite readily be extended to the relations between human organisms and those aspects of organic and inorganic nature constituting their environment. Indeed, this environment is envisaged by Goodwin, Ho *et al.* as constituted by the generative mechanisms represented by physicochemical laws as well as those represented by other organisms.

Such an understanding of the relations between organisms, including the human organism, and the environment, is very suggestive. It is arguably, however, most helpful in studying the kinds of society which anthropologists traditionally examine: small-scale, relatively static communities. There arise, however, difficulties when we turn to modern societies where the relationships between human organisms and their environment are not only complex. My central point here is that they are far more attenuated. They are *stretched* over time and space in a v₂ay which makes the 'new biology' model of organism–environment relations quite difficult to apply in a straightforward fashion. To put this another way, the environment which the human organism experiences and with which it deals is decreasingly that which influences its growth, development and well-being. And this raises a number of subtle difficulties for the organisms in question.

In this chapter I shall be dealing with this matter by returning to those aspects of modern sociology which discuss the global spread of social life and some of the implications for psychological and social identity which derive from such spreading. To relate this back to my initial theoretical starting-point, globalisation represents an extra dimension to the analysis of alienation offered by Marx, one which has particularly developed since the days when Marx was writing. Second, I shall illustrate how the global spread of 'man's inorganic body' raises new difficulties of identity and combines with the forms of alienation and forms of fetishism which Marx outlined. As an illustration I shall be referring to recent concerns with health and food; here, in a very literal sense, we are concerned with nature as 'man's inorganic body'. But, this body is becoming increasingly globalised.

SPACE, TIME AND MODERNITY: ASPECTS OF GIDDENS' ACCOUNT

Giddens' emphasis on time and space needs approaching, in the first instance, through his 'theory of structuration'.[2] His objective is to overcome a dualism that has long haunted social theory and which was a particular problem with the structuralist version of Marxism prevalent in the 1970s. This is the division between social structure and human agency.

Social structures, according to Giddens, can be defined as resources and rules. 'Resources' are of two kinds. The transition from gathering hunter to modern forms of society are directly linked to the control of nature by human beings and the storage of what Giddens calls 'allocative resources'. The second type he terms 'authoritative resources'; these are primarily information. Information is power and authoritative resources are the main means by which societies are regulated and held together. 'Rules' refers to 'procedures of action' or 'techniques of generalizable procedures applied in the enactment/reproduction of social practices'.[3] They are understandings in which human actors regularly engage. Language is one example. It contains rules or generally agreed procedures for human intercourse. Such rules can be changed but at the same time they constrain and enable forms of communication in which people regularly engage. Rules and resources thus facilitate as well as limit human action. They are drawn on by active human subjects. And, in being drawn on, they are reproduced. Thus 'social structure' and 'human agency' are deeply implicated in one another. And they change each other over time.

Particularly in his later work Giddens gives special significance to questions of space and its role in 'the problem of order'.[4] People's interactions and the remaking of social structures do not occur on the head of a pin. They are all embedded in contexts or 'locales'. At the same time, however, social systems are increasingly stretched over time and space. International markets, telecommunications and multinational corporations are all part of a process whereby society is taking on an increasingly globalised character. In linking the problem of social order to the question of space, Giddens distinguishes between 'social integration' and 'system integration'. The former refers to face-to-face interaction between people in the context of 'co-presence' or 'high presence availability'.

'System integration' refers to the ways in which social systems are spread across time and space and are at the same time maintained under circumstances where people are not physically 'co-present'. The central question here, therefore, is how do active human subjects relate to and communicate with each other and to the social system of which they are part? And how are such relationships maintained in the context of the spreading of social and economic life, or 'time–space distanciation'? At this point the scales and ways in which allocative and authoritative resources are stored have a critical significance.

Giddens argues that in the earliest societies, including feudalism, the prime locus of both such types of resource was the city. But with the global extension of industrialising societies the chief site of power becomes the nation-state. This, then, is part of a long historical process whereby daily life and routines (which remain largely limited to small-scale locales) become increasingly removed from the institutions and processes which are deeply affecting such practices.

The rise of the nation-state closely relates to the question of system integration. Central to Giddens' approach are the differences between traditional or 'tribal' forms of society and globalising modern society. In the former, system integration remains largely based on small-scale, face-to-face, interaction. Thus in this case social integration is virtually the same thing as system integration. Modern forms of society, however, depend to a decreasing extent on such small-scale, face-to-face interaction and engagement. And this poses particular problems for the maintenance of social order or system integration. It is at this point that the modern nation-state is seen as having a central role.

Globalisation, however, is seen by Giddens as not only threatening the maintenance of large-scale social structures. In line with his parallel concern with human agency, he argues that small-scale interaction of the kind so important to older forms of society has a special significance for the self and personal identity. Daily routines and interactions whereby people have a relatively clear sense of their identities and circumstances are centrally important in creating and confirming individuals' sense of 'ontological security'. This is their sense of 'being' or 'being in the world'. In Giddens' words this is 'confidence or trust that the natural and social worlds are as they appear to be, including the basic existential parameters of self and social identity'.[5]

In his most recent work Giddens has gone on to develop these ideas and concepts. He remains, however, centrally concerned with the relationships between the self and the transition to modernity and, as part of this, with the dialectical relations between social structure and human agency. Furthermore, he remains concerned with the spreading of social life and its impacts on the self. Modernity, he argues,

increasingly tears space away from place by fostering relations between 'absent' others, locationally distant from any given situation of face-to-face interaction. In conditions of modernity, locales are thoroughly penetrated and shaped in terms of social influences quite distant from them. What structures the locale is not simply that which is present on the scene; the 'visible form' of the locale conceals the distanciated relations which determine its nature.[6]

A central effect of modernity is what Giddens calls the 'disembedding' of social life from local contexts and small-scale interaction. Traditional societies are where acquaintance or enmity is primarily based on knowing and trusting individuals or persons who are continuously available and deemed reliable or otherwise on the basis of continuing familiarity. The transition to modernity sees a fundamental change to a society in which interaction takes place with persons whom we hardly know. He asserts two main mechanisms as responsible for this disembedding. One is money and the market-place, this again linking up with small-scale integration yet placing it within a much larger social system. Another is the rise of 'science', expert knowledge and expertise. This professionalises local knowledge, extracting it from its immediate context and placing it in the hands of experts with more abstract expertise.

Such disembedding again poses particular problems for active, or 'reflexive' human beings. In traditional cultures, for example, knowledge frequently takes the form of passed-on tradition, this being a culture based on a close monitoring of the local social and natural world and the transmission of knowledge from generation to generation. Under modernity, however, tradition cannot be relied on in the same way. Individuals must place their trust in abstract systems and professionalised knowledge. In short, the ontological security which individuals need for the preservation of their selves entails a transfer of trust from that between known individuals and towards abstract systems.

But Giddens makes an important point here concerning what he calls 're-embedding'. The 'access points' at which individuals and groups use and influence abstract systems are of course managed by individuals. One of their key roles is to exhibit 'manifest trustworthiness' to the individual confronting the abstract system. Therefore, in some respects the declining significance of face-to-face association in traditional society becomes re-established in modern forms. But at the same time Giddens argues that such 're-embedding' is not simply imposed by abstract systems on gullible and passive persons. In some important respects it is recovering the face-to-face relations between known individuals which are a feature of traditional societies, 'providing encounters and rituals which sustain collegial trustworthiness'. Re-embedding, is therefore also a product of active, reflexive, individuals. And the result, again, is the transformation of social life itself. 'Modernity's reflexivity', in Giddens' words, 'refers to the susceptibility of most aspects of social activity, and material relations with nature, to chronic revision in the light of new information or knowledge.'[7]

SOCIETY AND NATURE: DEVELOPING AND USING GIDDENS' ANALYSIS

Giddens is not attempting to combine the biological and social sciences as proposed in the present study. There are nevertheless a number of dimensions to his work which closely parallel the perspective informing the present analysis and which can be combined with it. One is an emphasis on the active individual and his or her relationship to 'structures'. Human beings are envisaged as not only changing society; they are seen as constrained and enabled by social structures and institutions. But the notions of 'structures' and 'resources' in Giddens' work clearly needs developing to include the generative mechanisms, resources and limits represented by the rest of nature. Resources cannot be assumed as 'given' and unproblematically available for consumption.

As regards human agency, Giddens' notion of 'ontological insecurity' places a premium on human beings' attempts to find some sense of being and psychological identity in the natural and social world. The notion of the human mind borrowed from Harré and outlined in the last chapter needs recalling here. If broadly correct, it would suggest that such insecurity derives in large part from tensions between, on the one hand, those archetypal propensities which enable people to make sense of their direct sensuous experience but, on the other hand, the spreading relationships in which people in modern societies are necessarily caught up. In short, the incorporation of human subjects' biological and psychological species-being implies a still more profound sense of 'ontological insecurity' than that outlined by Giddens.

There is also an implicit parallel between Giddens and Marx in their common concerns with the process of modernisation. This entails the slow shift away from a small-scale community life based largely on face-to-face interaction towards modern, market-oriented societies. For Giddens the particular significance in these changes is the problem of social order and the maintenance of self-identity. But he does not make the explicit suggestion, as did Marx, that human beings' innate capacities and potentials unfold or are realised in relation to their social and natural environment. Nor, in his historical account does he suggest that human species-being was more readily realised in earlier forms of society where land and resources were held in common. In short, Giddens' work can be further developed with the notion of organisms unfolding within or enfolded by neighbouring social and the natural worlds; but with modern society again drastically extending those worlds.

Giddens' emphasis on 're-embedding' again stresses active individuals' capacities for reasserting their social and psychological identities; this being a respose to social change while at the same time contributing to such change. Like Marx, Giddens suggests that the market-place is a central way in which personal identities are created. But, unlike Marx, he does not stress the market-place as 'fetishising' the social relations, processes and institutions which are involved in the transformation of nature into commodities. Marx's understanding of markets and the exchange of commodities seems very much worth holding on to here.

Thus, although there are clear differences in method and theory, Giddens' conceptual framework can be linked to the general perspective under development here. Most important to this study's theoretical perspective, however, is Giddens' emphasis on contemporary social life being locationally embedded, on 'time–space distanciation' and on the psychologically unsettling effects of this tension on human beings. My central point is that these notions apply to people's interactions with nature and not just to the social relations and processes to which Giddens gives such emphasis. Indeed, there is a sense in which an understanding of nature must be incorporated into Giddens' own project. Social relations are constituted through engagement with and transformations of nature. 'Locales' are environmental as well as social systems. And 'time–space distanciation' is increasingly affecting, and socialising, the whole of the supposedly 'natural' world. One of the themes of McKibben's book *The End of Nature* is precisely this spreading and socialising of nature. As he puts it:

> Man's efforts, even at their mightiest, used to be tiny compared with the size of the planet – the Roman Empire meant nothing to the Arctic or the Amazon. But now the way of life of one part of the world in one half-century is altering every inch and every hour of the globe.[8]

Thus nature is certainly still 'man's inorganic body' in modern societies. But the distancing over time and space between producers' and consumers' daily relationships with this inorganic body is increasingly stretched and, like association between people, of a less direct form. This militates still further against the kind of sensuous or direct understanding of this relationship which Marx insisted characterised the 'humanisation of nature' and the further realisation of human potential.

Giddens' work draws us, therefore, to a central paradox. On the one hand, nature is becoming increasingly socialised. In that sense society and nature are indeed becoming increasingly integrated. But on the other hand it is precisely through such socialisation, and the attendant spreading of the social relations and institutions involved in its production, that people lose tangible association with the processes and mechanisms of the rest of nature and the circumstances surrounding their manipulation. The fact is, as Marx pointed out long ago, that such spreading is largely taking place by courtesy of the private ownership and manipulation of the rest of nature.

Not only does the form in which the integration is taking place seem to militate against a direct, engaged, involvement with nature of the kind which Marx saw as essential to the realisation of human capacities and potentials. But, as I shall outline in more detail shortly, under these circumstances a purified, commodified and fetishised version of 'nature' seems to thrive; one which consumers encounter in the market-place or through the mass media. But this is to offer a wholly negative picture. Contemporary environmentalism seems to suggest that full-scale integration of 'the social' with 'the natural' could also prove to be the basis of a new kind of integrated understanding; possibly even a popular basis for the creation of Marx's 'one science' linking biology and social theory. Thus the integration of society and nature also contains positive prospects for social action and eventual large-scale social transformation.

NATURE AND THE TIME–SPACE DISTANCIATION OF SOCIAL LIFE

The spatial and temporal separation of people from nature under modernity can be illustrated with the aid of Figure 6.1. The figure represents the relationship between a late nineteenth-century European town (based on a local economy of coal and steel) and nature. This is the type of town that was to emerge after the earlier forms outlined by Marx; indeed, such towns did not really begin to develop for some time after the young Marx was writing.

The town itself is the 'site' at the centre of the diagram. But clearly it is just part of a vast stretched-out open system relating people to nature. To the left are the inputs to the town. Local links include those to supplies of water. In the town's earliest stages these needs would be met by wells. River water is later tapped. In due course enlarged reservoirs are constructed, often at some distance from the town. Raw materials can be produced locally, regionally and globally. The same applies to food. But as the town grows the sources of supply again become greatly enlarged and local consumption starts to have increasingly global impacts.

The town also has outputs. The industrial plant discharges effluents and wastes into water courses and the atmosphere. Mine-drainage and mine-tips are likely to acidify surface water. The sulphur dioxide from coal burning will take the form of sulphuric acid in rain. Sewage output is likely to reduce the diversity of life in the river near the outfall. In the nineteenth century this frequently resulted in local water contamination and disease. But all these outputs are again increasingly regional and global.

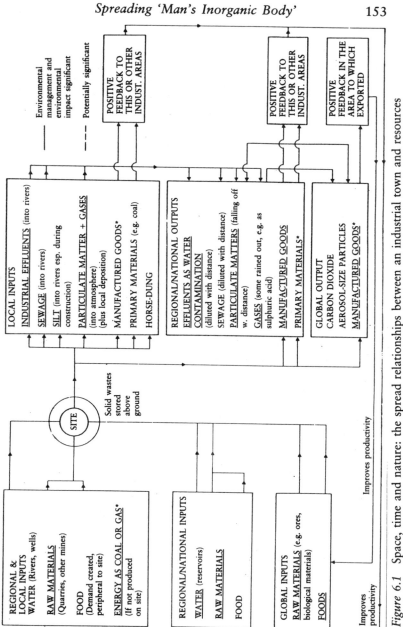

Figure 6.1 Space, time and nature: the spread relationships between an industrial town and resources (Source: A. Simmons (1989), *Changing the Face of the Earth*, Blackwell: Oxford)

Dilution may be accompanied with distance but key outputs (such as carbon dioxide and the products of aerosols) are increasingly modifying the atmosphere on a wider scale. As Simmons puts it:

Just as the inputs become global in their connections, the outputs begin to achieve a universal distribution on Earth. Aerosol-sized particulate matter from chimney stacks and dust from bared areas of land start to go into the global circulation and be deposited in what are now detectable quantities in the Greenland ice-cap, for example. The burning of coal produces more carbon dioxide than can be scavenged out by the world's biota and so its concentration in the atmosphere begins to rise to the levels currently detected.[9]

Marx correctly gave central prominence to the alienation of the industrial workers in such a town. He saw them as estranged from the commodities they produced while working on the raw materials of nature which were to be sold and used in, say, Birmingham, Pittsburg and Dusseldorf. Such processes are still the central way in which people are alienated from nature. And those increasing numbers of people in modern societies who distribute, sell and maintain the commodities which others have made from the raw materials of nature are still further removed from their 'inorganic body'.[10]

Marx's main emphasis was therefore on social relations, social processes and the alienation of commodities. It was not on space and time. He did not comment on the emerging temporal and spatial separation between people and their inorganic bodies in these circumstances. But under modernity and what Giddens calls 'time–space distanciation', man's inorganic body becomes simply an input from an increasing distance. To use Giddens' word, people have become 'disembedded' from it. Similarly, the results of working on nature become an increasingly remote output. They are experienced at increasing distance from where they are created. At the same time, people remain, in Giddens' terms, 'co-present' with their local social and ecological systems. The overall effect of modernity is therefore to undermine understanding and direct or sensuous experience of these increasingly complex links between the transformation of nature on the one hand and the experience and consumption of such transformation on the other. Such sequestration, as Giddens implies, can be seen as having a profoundly unsettling effect on people's sense of security and being in the world.

TIME–SPACE DISTANCIATION COMBINING WITH
ALIENATION: THE INSTANCE OF FOOD AND HEALTH

These assertions can be developed and illustrated with a particular and topical worked example, that of food and health. Table 6.1 gives an indication of the increasing, and in many cases dramatic separation of food from consumers as it emerged during the nineteenth and early twentieth centuries. The data are of course a testament to new forms of production, storage methods and emerging forms of faster transport.

Table 6.1   Food and time–space distanciation: average distances over which types of British food exports were moved, 1830–1913

Import Type	Average distance from London to regions from which import type derived (miles)				
	1831–5	1856–60	1871–5	1891–5	1909–13
Fruit & vegetables	0*	324	535	1,150	1,880
Live animals	0*	630	870	3,530	4,500
Butter, cheese, eggs, etc.	262	530	1,340	1,610	3,120
Feed grains	860	2,030	2,430	3,240	4,830
Flax and seeds	1,520	3,250	2,770	4,080	3,900
Meat and tallow	2,000	2,900	3,740	5,050	6,250
Wheat and flour	2,430	2,170	4,200	5,150	5,950
Wool and hides	2,330	8,830	10,000	11,010	10,900
Weighted average	1,820	3,650	4,300	5,050	5,800

Note: * Indicates no significant imports.
Source: J. Peet (1969), 'The spatial expansion of commercial agriculture: a von Thunen interpretation', *Economic Geography*, 45:4.

Such processes of separation persist in our own time. Indeed, they have considerably escalated. Cheap, very often Third World labour and transport are generally a more profitable, solution than the 'home grown' solution. In the words of Clutterbuck and Lang:

It can be cheaper to collect phosphate and cheap labour from another part of the globe than lump farmyard manure around the farm. It is cheaper to have a workforce around the world, including the transport of labour, than it is to employ it locally.[11]

As this quotation again suggests, underpinning such time–space distanciation is the globalising market economy. One of the key features of the contemporary food chain is that the solar energy flowing through the chain can be greatly enhanced by a range of fuels, machines and fertilisers. These are run and organised by a few multinational corporations. Amongst these are the large food-processing companies taking the raw materials, processing them and selling them to consumers. Clearly this process has delivered many benefits, not least the large amounts of relatively cheap food. But the net effect has again been that of separating producers and consumers from commodities, adding to the alienation at the point of production outlined by Marx. Fertilisers, for example, have largely replaced farmyard manure while pesticides have replaced knowledge of local species and ecosystems. As Clutterbuck and Lang put it: 'there is no money to work on the daily rhythms of a ground beetle, but there is to work on an insect of 'economic' importance.'[12] Capital investment has placed 'farming' into a set of practices which can (almost literally) insulate working practices from local environmental conditions. Greenhouses, genetic engineering, refrigeration and rapid transport mean, for example, that the significance of local environments and seasonality is being increasingly eliminated.

Much the same detachment applies to the consumer. Self-provisioning and food-production in the home are being steadily eliminated. Now, instead of choosing food on the basis of direct sensory information, it is bought in inpenetrable packets with 'scientific' information as to its contents and calorific value. Again, the distancing of humans' 'species-being' from the seasons and from the conditions of production becomes more complete. Gofton expresses the time–space distanciation of consumers from food in the following way:

The year's round of food, which meant that certain vegetables and fruits, and the foods which are made from them, were only available (and only intentionally consumed) at certain seasons, certainly no longer obtains. Tradition still boosts the sale of turkeys, and fish on Fridays perhaps, but certainly these 'substantializations' of the cycle of the year are no longer strong.[13]

Such spatial and temporal separation is I suspect, a major factor underlying contemporary concerns over food and health. It combines with the specific form of alienation at the point of production which was at the heart of Marx's analysis. To use Giddens' terminology again, these modern scares are largely the product of 'ontological insecurity'; this deriving from the distancing over time and space between humans and the nature on which people depend. This dependence takes a psychological, as well as more obvious material, form.

'Food panics' are by no means new. Bread riots were a recurring feature of medieval Britain, and, from the fourteenth to the nineteenth centuries magistrates were charged with the considerable duty of monitoring the quality of, as well as the price of bread. During the nineteenth century death due to the adulteration and contamination of food was a regular event amongst the industrial poor. Contemporary scares in Britain (which has recently experienced widely publicised scares over eggs, cheese, yoghurt, apples, drinking water, chicken and beef) seem, however, based on a different set of concerns. These are as much a result of psychological fears based on lack of direct experience and understanding as on real threats to physical health.

Food now may or may not be fit for consumption. The central problem is that the processes and locations of its production and preparation ensure that there are few people who can know with an acceptable sense of certainty. The old forms of trust (based on observation, direct experience and lay knowledge) have been largely displaced by 'scientific' expertise and knowledge as produced by what Giddens calls 'abstract systems'. And now, with a rising suspicion that such supposedly detached knowledge has been hijacked by dominant interests, even this latter form of certainty comes under intense questioning.

But as Giddens also argues, the adoption of an 'alternative' form of eating or lifestyle itself involves a transfer from one type of belief to another:

A person may go to great lengths to avoid eating foods that contain additives, but if that individual does not grow everything he or she eats, trust must necessarily be invested in the purveyors of 'natural foods' to provide superior products. Someone might turn towards holistic medicine after becoming disenchanted with the orthodox medical profession, but of course this is a transfer of faith.[14]

Thus the alienation of people from products they have made is supplemented by the physical and temporal separation from their necessary relations with nature. This takes many forms, including separation from the experience of waste as well as that of the supply of commodities such as food. As I hope to have indicated, such separation is above all the product of social processes and social relations. It is primarily, I would argue, a result of the ways in which the capitalist production, distribution and consumption of commodities has been developed and modified in the interests of increasing profitability.

TIME–SPACE DISTANCIATION, CONSUMPTION AND THE REIFICATION OF 'NATURE'

So far, I have offered a picture of combined alienation, spatial and temporal separation from the human subject's context and what Giddens calls the 'ontological insecurity' deriving from such separation. But it is important to recognise that human subjects will still try to gain some sense of reassurance about their well-being and identity. They will try to restore, or to use Giddens' word 're-embed' their natural- and species-being.

Let me return to the example of food and health. 'Re-embedding' here takes the contemporary form of trying to gain a better understanding of what they are eating and the effects it may have on their health. And acquiring such an understanding entails various forms of fetishisation of food, 'nature' and the factors affecting peoples' health. What is meant by fetishisation in this context? Here we return to something much closer to Marx's idea of commodity fetishism, the notion of 'green consumerism' being the key. This form of market-based environmentalism is often criticised by elements of the green movement for promoting the further purchase of commodities as a solution to the world's environmental problems and failing to recognise that further consumption of resources is the problem, not the solution, to environmental crises.[15] There is much to be said for this critique. But the significance of green consumerism is actually more profound than this. It incorporates very distinct and subtle notions as to what 'nature' actually consists of and how people should relate to it. Nature again becomes re-fashioned as wholly pure and unsullied by the interference of human beings. Furthermore, the social relations involved in the making of 'green' commodities apparently remain unproblematic.

Such fetishised abstractions again turn a blind eye to relations and conditions of production and celebrating 'natural' commodities as having mystical powers of their own. As Coward has usefully noted in relation to contemporary 'health' products, the predominant idea of 'nature' contained in such notions is that health is to be found through *individual* action; especially, of course, individual action in the market-place.[16] Green consumerism generally, and 'healthy' products and lifestyles in particular, contain quite precise notions about how an individual should consider his or her well-being. Not only is the market-place celebrated but an understanding of the 'natural body' itself becomes fetishised and idolised. Normality seems to have wholly dispensed with bodily illness and pain. Perfection is the norm, and one that can be gained through acquiring the correct products and perfecting the body. To quote Coward: 'The corporeal body is no longer something which holds us back on our quest for perfectability. Instead, it has become the place where this perfectability can be found.'[17]

This understanding of 'health' and 'nature' is quite different from one which emphasises the real or material connections between people and nature and the social relations involved in the modification of nature and of the body. As Coward puts the argument in relation to the alternative health movement:

[It] is significantly different from ideas of nature in ecological movements and politics. There is no requirement here for external action to preserve some hypothesised proper relationship between mankind and the environment. Instead, nature can be found by attending to the inner being.[18]

Parenthetically, we could note here that contemporary definitions of 'natural' are also quite different from those of past eras. Contemporary insistence that healthy food should not touch the mouth or food of others would not, for example, have been recognised in the Middle Ages. Modern definitions of 'natural' and 'healthy' have been socially constructed over a long historical period.[19]

Adoption of contemporary versions of 'nature' and 'health' is, not surprisingly, the province of the more affluent consumer or customer. As I and others have shown elsewhere, there are a number of different versions of green consumerism.[20] Perhaps most importantly in the light of the above arguments, the main distinctions are between those of different ages. Young adults, those deemed to possess the nearest approximation to the perfect body, and especially those with sufficient resources to engage in the market economy, are the subjects principally engaging in the new culture of health and exercise. And it is of course they who acquire most attention from those vested commercial interests promoting this culture.

Other versions of green consumerism and the healthy lifestyle relate to class and levels of education. The less well-paid but better-educated middle classes lead a seemingly less alienated lifestyle in so far as they incorporate not only 'healthy' eating but high levels of exercise into their lives. They also, due to their lower incomes do not engage in high levels of consumption and material production. Other social groups, particularly the more affluent workers in the leading sectors of the economy, adopt a version of the 'healthy' lifestyle but try, in a contradictory fashion, to combine it with high-living consumerism.

To different extents all such groups are adopting fetishised, market-oriented, versions of 'nature' and 'health' in an attempt to restore some sense of their natural- and species-being. Furthermore, the unrealisable ideal for all these groups again becomes that of the fetishised young, supposedly natural, body. It would be wrong, however, to dismiss all these reifications of nature and health out of hand. No doubt one result is the creation of more long-living and active individuals. Furthermore, the creation of collective identities through these forms of consumption partly realises what Marx saw as a central element of human beings' species-being, their sociality. On the other hand, some social groups (young affluent adults in particular) are proving more successful than others in reasserting their natural- and species-being.

This particular kind of market-based reification is, however, combined with other ways of fetishising a dominant 'nature'. Marx showed that under capitalism the market-place is the prime means by which people reclaim their relationships with a version of 'nature' and with other people. But this is not the only sphere in which individuals ascribe to products of their own making certain mystical, autonomous and eventually dominant qualities. Another is religion and the supernatural.

Recent anthropological work on 'lay epidemiology' in Britain confirms that much of people's perceptions of what constitutes 'healthy' living and eating does indeed take seriously the recommendations of 'green' or alternative consumerism.[21] But in practice these understandings are combined with notions of health and disease which frequently resort to another version of 'nature', one emphasising superstition and the irrational. While bad eating-practices and lack of exercise are widely seen as amongst the many factors leading to ill health, there remains what Davison *et al.* call the 'residual bad luck category'. People can try to eat the correct things, take the correct amount of exercise, worry less and so forth. But in the end fate or destiny is seen as taking its toll. People die, to use a commonly used phrase, 'when their number's up'.[22] Thus in addition to all modern 'scientific' explanations (Giddens' 'abstract knowledge') are those more homespun accounts which dignify as 'natural' a quasi-religious force dominating human affairs.

Such understandings are relatively easy to appreciate and easy to adopt. Indeed, we will shortly encounter other similar understandings in modern society relating to climatic change. Like the quasi-religious worship of commodities they may perform an important psychological purpose in terms of reasserting a sense of personal security and sovereignty. But the central problem remains that the complex, globally organised mechanisms and relations materially linking people, classes, labour processes and nature become obscured and mis-appreciated in the process.

NOTES

1. T. Ingold (1990), 'An anthropologist looks at biology', *Man* (New Series) 25: 208–29.
2. See A. Giddens (1984), *The Constitution of Society*, Polity: Oxford, Chap. 1.
3. *ibid.*, p. 21.
4. *ibid.*, p. 17.

5. *ibid.*, p. 375.
6. A. Giddens (1990), *The Consequences of Modernity*, Polity: Oxford, pp. 18–19.
7. A. Giddens (1991), *Modernity and Self Identity*, Polity: Oxford, p. 20.
8. B. McKibben (1990), *The End of Nature*, Viking: London. Quoted from jacket.
9. A. Simmons (1989), *Changing the Face of the Earth*, Blackwell: Oxford, pp. 211–12.
10. For a recent discussion of the labour process as the link between ecological analysis and political economy (an analysis which borrows from and develops Marx's early work) see T. Benton (1989), 'Marxism and natural limits: an ecological critique and reconstruction', *New Left Review* 178: 51–86.
11. L. Clutterbuck, T. Lang (1982), *More Than We Can Chew*, Pluto: London, p. 72.
12. *ibid.*, pp. 65–6.
13. L. Gofton (1986), 'The rules of the table: sociological factors affecting food choice', in C. Ritson, L. Gofton and J. McKenzie (eds), *The Food Consumer*, Wiley: London, p. 146. See also L. Gofton, M. Ness (1991), 'Meaty horrors and poisoned delights', *Times Higher Education Supplement*, 8 Jan.
14. A. Giddens (1991), *op.cit.*, p. 23.
15. See, for example, S. Irvine (1989), 'Consuming fashions? The limits of green consumerism, *The Ecologist* 19, 3.
16. R. Coward (1989), *The Whole Truth*, Faber and Faber: London, p. 33.
17. *ibid.*, p. 43.
18. *ibid.*, p. 33.
19. N. Elias (1983), *The Court Society*, Blackwell: Oxford, Chap. 6.
20. M. Savage, J. Barlow, P. Dickens and A. Fielding (1992), *Property, Bureaucracy and Culture. The Anatomy of the Middle Classes in Britain*, Routledge: London, Chap. 6.
21. C. Davison, G. Smith and S. Frankel (1991), 'Lay epidemiology and the prevention paradox: the implications of coronary candidacy for health education', in *Sociology of Health & Illness*, 13: 1–19. See also C. Davison, S. Frankel and G. Smith (1989), 'Inheriting heart trouble: the relevance of common-sense ideas to preventive measures', *Health Education Research* 4, 3: 329–40.
22. C. Davison, G. Smith and S. Frankel (1991), *op.cit.*, p. 14.

7

NATURE REIFIED: A CONTEMPORARY CASE STUDY

A reified version of 'nature' is therefore one which draws attention away from social relations and attributes an autonomous existence to a nature which has been socially constructed. It is this latter fetishised existence which comes to dominate human affairs. This can take the modern market-based form adopted by green consumerism or it can take the supposedly old-fashioned form. The latter is where an analogy is made between an actual social relation on the one hand and the individual and nature as an alive deity on the other. Such a form of reification is often associated with indigenous peoples. But it is also a 'lay theory' frequently adopted in modern societies. Here I shall develop this argument further.

Chapter 6 argued, with the aid of Harré et al.'s psychology, that people construct a version of 'nature' in modern or advanced societies based on fusion between, on the one hand, latent archetypal structures of the mind and, on the other hand the actual social relations and processes in which they are caught up. This chapter develops these themes in the form of a more extended case study. It uses material from the Mass Observation Archive based at Sussex University. From time to time during recent years the Archive has asked a large number of its correspondents to reply to directives on specific topics. It too is a form of anthropology, one applied to a modern society and providing an invaluable resource as to how lay people understand and relate to major issues of the day.[1]

The particular Directive on which I have concentrated mainly concerns a hurricane which hit southern parts of England on the night of 15–16 October 1987. It also referred to a series of floods

163

in parts of Wales shortly beforehand. Questionnaires were mailed out to 1,047 individuals. Replies were received from 621 individuals, the majority understandably being from the areas most affected. The Directive elicited feelings during these disasters plus experiences of tidying up, insurance, getting repairs done, the adequacy or otherwise of government responses and reactions to local environmental change. A further question concerned the role of the media. Did it reflect a bias in favour of the South East?

I used this Directive to explore whether, and how, the concepts of alienation and fetishism outlined in this study have relevance to the people of an advanced society such as Britain. A secondary theme for exploration was the 'time–space distanciation' and 'ontological security' as outlined by Giddens. Almost every reply contained something of interest in both these respects. Most of the material stemming from this Directive consists of detailed descriptions rather than what might be termed 'lay philosophies' about nature and natural disasters. It is nevertheless clear from the contributors to Mass Observation that what Marx called 'fetishism' and what others might call 'superstition' or 'religion' remain alive and well in a modernised nation. What emerges more generally is that people are making analogies between the globalising social relations in which they are caught up and their relations to nature. Modern peoples' perceived relation to nature is in part a mirror image of their relations to one another.

Some of the main themes to be developed here can be introduced with the aid of a leaflet sent by one of the correspondents (see Figure 7.1). The leaflet was produced by 'Good News for All', a group of evangelical Christians and is composed of five closely connected themes. First, using selected biblical scriptures, the pamphlet suggests that the hurricane is the product of an all-powerful God. Second, human expertise in the form of weather forecasters, are unable to predict God's will accurately. Third, earthly mortals remain powerless and helpless in the face of divinely inspired natural forces. Fourth, the hurricane is just a harbinger of an even stronger future storm: God's wrath will in due course be visited on the population on a scale which will make the hurricane seem puny by comparison. For this group of evangelical Christians, the message is clear enough. Finally, the only effective shelter to be found from the forthcoming, still more apocalyptic, hurricane is to be found in combining with Jesus, the originator of the hurricane. Let me now take these five themes in turn

Nature as an alive and superior being

The general message of this pamphlet seems to have featured in some Sunday sermons. This may have been in less apocalyptic forms. But, as the contribution from one correspondent with the Archive shows, it could also be combined with the message advising against the acquisition of material gains:

'From time to time GOD SHOWS HE IS MASTER' The theme of our Parish Priest's Homily the Sunday after the gales. 'Man may get to the moon, do wonderful things with technology, think he can have all the material things of this life, BUT just now and again he does something like that just to prove that He is Master of all'.

Very few people, however, wholeheartedly adopted the notion of the hurricane being identified with an all-conquering God. But there is nevertheless a more typical lay version of a rather similar account. This is the notion of 'fate'; one which is also seen as operating according to an intelligent and intelligible logic. Here, for example, is the account of an English teacher in London (this also raises the notion that people remain relatively powerless in the face of such a fate):

Many theories have been expressed relating to the question of why the path of destruction and damage was as it was and why wasn't everything in its place flattened?. . .
   The first states, it was chance, there was no apparent reason for the winds, they just happened, without warning. This presupposes that life is a gamble and only the unlucky people were touched by the Hurricane, in the game of life, that has no pattern or purpose to it.
   The second theory, again brings up the questions that are unanswerable by man. Was it part of a major plan? One of the stages of the development of man? Showing man that nature, or the force or energy of whatever name one gives to the creation of man and the universe always seems to cause man's efforts to pale into insignificance. However developed and advanced man appears with modern technology there is

Figure 7.1 Reifying nature: the case of evangelical Christianity. People's understanding of their relation to nature can reflect their experience of the social world

always something more superior that will have the final say in anything working or happening. There are many more theories and opinions, but these are the two that have emerged when questioning the local farmers, woodmen and public affected by the hurricane.

The failure of modern scientific analysis

Very few of the Mass Observation correspondents unreservedly adopted the explanations of disasters offered by modern environmental science. Thus people such as the librarian below remain very cautious about the idea that they are the result of the greenhouse effect. What she calls 'a more general belief in the irrational' is much more common. At best the expertise offered by science is combined with more homespun knowledge of natural forces.

My family and colleagues have a general belief that the weather is 'changing' due to ecological abuse of the environment. Any manifestation of change in the British weather is held up as proof of this. The 'greenhouse' effect is cited, and dire warning of 'radiation'. I suppose this *might* be true, but I'm not very convinced. I suspect this is part of a more general belief in the 'irrational'. However, during the last few days (February 1988) I heard on the radio that domestic insurance premiums are likely to go up because there have been more weather disasters in the UK during the last few years, so maybe this general belief is right after all.

The failure of rational or scientific expertise is a common theme in the Mass Observation Archives. This focused on one unfortunate television forecaster. A lay member of the public had heard that a hurricane was approaching the South of England and she had asked the forecaster whether this was indeed so. This query was briefly alluded to by the weatherman but dismissed in the same breath. Modern technology and science, as many of Mass Observation's correspondents suggest, remain incapable of coping. Older, more tested, forms of prediction are just as likely to succeed. The following contribution from a full-time housewife in Harrogate is quite typical:

The weathermen GOT AWAY WITH MURDER. I am not a fan of TV

AM and Jimmy Greaves but on that day he condemned weathermen he was TOTALLY in his rights. Some say what good would it have done to know in advance? Well, firstly, they SHOULD HAVE KNOWN IN ADVANCE since they push constantly all the old codswallop about mod cons, satellites. . ., space stations and so forth (old Alice's corns were always much more reliable in forecasting bad weather!) and if they had at least warned the public and heeded the advice given them by a member of the public who had phoned them I am sure some lives would have been saved. People seem to forget that SOME PEOPLE ACTUALLY DIED! [Mass Observer's emphases]

The helplessness of the human subject

Closely linked to the supposed inadequacies of technology and science to predict disasters is the theme of personal helplessness. A recurrent theme amongst the contributors to the Mass Observation Archive is that nature is all-powerful and there is little people can do to predict or control it. The following extracts illustrate this – they also show how 'Nature' can at this stage again become personified, or treated as a human being with a will which is nevertheless unknowable:

Perhaps when touching on the subject of weather and its vagaries you would think that people would be reminded we are still but mere specks of dust in relation to the events of the Universe and our brief moment of time in its history.

Instead we want to punish those whose job it is to 'PREDICT'? when they get it wrong.

(Unemployed male, Cardigan)

We have taken no action against future storms, always feeling 'small' by comparison with the Universe and all Mother Nature's Mysteries. . . . It certainly always puts man in his place and is a constant reminder that man is, in fact, a creature of low degree when it comes to the angry elements!

(Female housewife/carer, Gomshall, Surrey)

The weather pattern is supreme in all things relevant to our planet. It is virtually unpredictable despite all meteorological aids available to man. We are, individually and as a whole, at its mercy, on land, sea and in the air. It cuts us all down to size.

(Retired male, Fair Oak, Hampshire)

Amid some of the press hysteria that usually accompanies such an event and demands for this change or that action it is easy to lose sight of the fact that it is impossible to create a perfectly safe world.

(Male local government officer, Addlestone, Surrey)

The fact that mortals are being controlled by 'Nature' is by no means seen as necessarily a bad thing. One clerk touches on a theme which many psychologists (Jungian and otherwise) would instantly recognise. There is a strong sense in which people actively want to feel that something or someone else is in control of their destiny. Significantly or otherwise the following Mass Observation correspondent works for the Department of the Environment!

In a weird kind of way I find it reassuring that 'Nature' is still in control and, for all our sophistication, we are still to a certain extent at the mercy of the elements. Perhaps in the year 2087 man may solve the problem of the motorcar, but I feel in the final analysis Nature will have the last word.

Some of the same themes are present in the following extract from an artist based in Wisbech, Norfolk. At the same time, his contribution touches on our third theme. Nature is no respecter of the socially privileged. Indeed, it may be involved in dispensing social justice.

The hurricane had very little effect here in East Anglia, I'm afraid and there were no floods whatsoever. . . .

But it did affect me in other ways. It made me feel how insecure life is and how I wish it wasn't. I think the South of England is privileged in many ways but even there a bleeding great wind can come along and whip the roof of your house off. It also made me selfishly glad that it didn't happen to me. . . .

Beyond that it made me think that perhaps true maturity consists of coming to terms with life's insecurity and looking it in the face. This can only mean that I'm not truly mature or anything like it.

Nature taking revenge on society

During and after these disasters the social world for many people
became in many respects projected onto the natural world. At a
fairly trivial level this took the form of, for example, a reflection
on the irony of the affluent and soft South East finding itself
battered by winds of the kind other parts of the country had long
suffered. The fact that the media is itself South-East dominated is
further seen as overemphasising the South East's plight. As one
woman from Scotland put it: 'I'm afraid I laughed at the news. To
see the 'Southern English' facing a bit of adversity was quite
amusing.'

But this connecting of society with nature takes other, more
profound, forms. Some of them link with the idea of a divine
social purpose in nature. As I have shown, this is a feature of some
religious thinking. But, in different ways, it is also very much a
feature of some lay understandings. And this does not take the
form articulated by mainstream environmentalism. It does not see
society causing irredeemable changes *to* nature. Rather, the
process is seen as operating the other way round. Nature is in
charge. It is a controlling force meting out justice onto an unjust
society. A strong impression here (although it can only be put
forward as an impression based on correspondents' job descriptions and the ways in which they express their feelings) is that
such sentiments are particularly prevalent amongst those with
little formal education and those with only a marginal position in
the labour market.

Below is an example from a disabled and unemployed man in
Derby. The hurricane is seen by him as delivering social
retribution. As he saw it, punishment was being exacted by an
intelligible force on the Southern 'yuppies'. Some of them are seen
as now escaping to Northern parts of the country and the strong
winds were a way of stopping them in their tracks. Note,
incidentally, that this correspondent is simultaneously well aware
of the 'the arguments of the "Greenhouse" effect' while at the
same time animising this effect and giving it an overall purpose:

October 1987, the arguments of the 'Greenhouse' effect were brought
vividly home as very strong winds, comparable with hurricanes across the
USA struck across Britain.

It did not escape notice who suffered the most from this. . . . The 'yuppies' are in our village now as they move northward and are openly talking of forcing the poor out their council houses to go further North so they can take over all the houses here. . . . So it does make one wonder if the odd warning is being sounded to deaf ears and dead hearts.

Finally, more than one correspondent noted that the hurricane occurred the night after a major stock market crash in London and the other major financial centres around the globe. And for some the question arose as to whether this was mere coincidence; perhaps the two were related to one another. Again echoing the theme of the explicitly religious commentators, perhaps both such disasters were a sign of a supernatural force avenging its wrath on a wicked world. One correspondent (a man from Telford 'doing professional jobs', but currently unemployed) went so far as to assume that there was a connection, but allowed room for argument. As he put it:

There is just the possibility that the balance of nature might, having been upset, make considerable advances [sic] in drastic weather patterns and couldn't have any connection with the Stock Market crash.

From personal fears to a realignment with an all-powerful nature

This last quotation, equating economic and social apocalypse with the hurricane suggests that, for some people, analogies are being made between, on the one hand, unpredictable natural disasters and, on the other hand, the feeling of insecurity deriving from (increasingly globalised) economic and social conditions. This suggests that some people are, albeit unconsciously, projecting their personal fears in the social world onto the natural world. The result is a profane version of the Evangelists' call to Jesus; a throwing in of their lot with an all-powerful but unknowable 'fate'.

It would be difficult to argue, therefore, that the deterioration of the physical environment is, on its own, the cause of the recent resurgence of environmentalism. Rather, such politics are at least as much a commentary on people's social circumstances, analogies being made between these circumstances and their sense of alienation from other aspects of society. Thus an understanding of relationships in the social world is, in Strathern's words, 'giving form and shape' to an understanding of individuals' relationships to nature.[2]

The following extracts from a Mass Observer illustrate, albeit in a schematic way, some of the connections between personal estrangement on the one hand and engagement in 'green' politics on the other. Here the observer is responding to another Mass Observation Directive, one seeking impressions of the most important developments during the 1980s:

Funnily enough 1980 to 90 were some of the most significant in my life, I had a nervous breakdown, sloughed off my conditioning and laid down new base rules which I believe at present to be correct. . . .

For twenty odd years I had been bringing up a family earning my bread by running a mobile shop round the houses and working twenty four hours a day, making as much money as I needed and ploughing all the spare back into the business.

One day the van broke down and I was sitting in a phone box waiting for the breakdown truck to come and tow me back to the garage for repair, when I thought what the hell am I waiting here for. All my profits this week will go to repairs and all I get out it is another long week of work and work and I went home, stopped all my supplies and went down the DHSS and signed on for supplementary benefit. . . .

This episode was to have a long-term effect on this Mass Observer – he was already involved in environmental politics but at this stage he became more fully engaged in the Green movement:

Some time before I had joined the Ecology Party and was engaged in a lot of debate with my friends etc and went to Worthy Farm Somerset to a Green Gathering. I had sold my van and bought a moped as being the cheapest form of transport than a bike which I thought I was too old to ride for long distances.

At Glastonbury I was involved with the Women for Life on Earth who were walking from Wales to Greenham to try and stop Cruise coming. For three days we sat in a marquee in a circle and debated whether it should be women only in order to get press interest. Although it was called Women for Life on Earth there were men involved as members and as husbands of members. There we decided the men should leave the march. . . .

This man goes on to describe his deepening involvement in the environmental movement, culminating in mass demonstrations by

the Campaign for Nuclear Disarmament in London (he was then
appointed to a regional secretaryship of CND):

Then I read the theory of Gaia and everything became very clear to me
that the earth had evolved me in ninety six million years for the sole
purpose of looking after her, in other words as her gardener and so in
pure self defence, since I could not survive without the world, I must
make sure the world did [*sic*] survive. Since then I have stood as candidate
for the European Parliament for the Green Party and am currently
engaged in the [named region] Green Party.

If I make something happen every day then I am having an effect on the
Chaos which is the world. I try and grow my own food and so have as
little to do with the social system as possible except to change it.

This last Mass Observation correspondent provides a key
insight into contemporary environmentalism. In the material
social world people are subject to massive and unknowable forces
and relations. The way in which people and nature are
constructed by contemporary environmentalism is none other than
a mirror of that self-same social world. Bearing in mind Giddens'
work on the 'ontological insecurity' deriving from modernity, the
insignificant individual facing an apparently all-powerful, globally
organised nature is an analogy between peoples' relations within
nature and their relations within the modern social world.

Similarly, the distrust of weather experts is just part of a deeper
distrust in what Giddens calls 'abstract systems'; those institutions
which undermine lay understandings and consciousness. Ecological calamities may well be threatening, but my point here is that
the *way* they are conceived is a reflection of how contemporary
social life is experienced. As Marx wrote in *The German
Ideology*:

We set out from real, active men, and on the basis of their real life process
we demonstrate the development of the ideological reflexes and echoes of
this life process. The phantoms formed in the human brain are also,
necessarily, sublimates of their material life process, which is empirically
verifiable and bound to material premises.[3]

But, as I have argued in Chapter 5, 'the phantoms formed in the
human brain' do not directly reflect the mechanisms and emergent
properties underlying the experience of nature and society. Such
'phantoms' are also a product of complex mental structures which
simplify by animising such complexities. The Mass Observation

participants show clearly enough that such animising is by no means limited to people in supposedly 'primitive' societies.

NOTES

1. Details of Mass Observation Archive from Dorothy Sheridan, University of Sussex Library, Falmer, Brighton. The extracts on the hurricane are taken from replies to Directive No. 24(2), Autumn/ Winter 1987.
2. M. Strathern (1990), 'Enterprising kinship: consumer choice and the new reproductive technologies', *Cambridge Anthropology* 14, 1: 2.
3. K. Marx (1976), *The German Ideology*, in L.S. Feuer (ed.), *Karl Marx and Friedrich Engels. Basic Writings on Philosophy and Politics*, Fontana/Collins: London, p. 288.

8

SOCIETY AND NATURE:
FROM THEORY TO PRACTICE

The Mass Observation correspondents seem to be indicating that there is more to environmental politics and relations to nature than hurricanes and environmental degradation. Feelings and insecurities about relations within the social world are being, subconsciously or otherwise, transferred to an understanding of peoples' relations to the natural world.

In the first part of this final chapter I wish to develop this line of analysis. I will be using a realist strategy for organising knowledge and indicating how aspects of biology (specifically the human capacity for analogy-making) combines with the social world. Realism is the epistemological strategy which informed the work of Marx in his early studies and in later work such as the *Grundrisse*. And allusions to this way of working have been made throughout this book. Here I shall discuss this type of knowledge in a little more detail.

The various forms of knowledge and information which have been outlined and discussed in this study are not necessarily all attempting to offer understanding of the same forms and levels of abstraction. The strengths of some types of theory (for example, modern biology) are that they offer understandings of underlying causal entities. They are outlining laws, relationships, tendencies and potentials which are inherent to the very reproduction of all organic and inorganic life. Their strengths lie in their contribution to the more abstract levels of understanding. Though, as happens with the crudest forms of neo-Darwinism and sociobiology, they run into very considerable difficulties if and when they ignore the mediating and contingent factors, those deeply affecting precisely how, for example, genes affect behaviour. The result is reductionism. This criticism clearly does not rule them out of court in terms of offering useful, even essential, understandings. Rather, it argues that they are nothing like sufficient. Environment, including other organisms, affects and is affected by organisms supposedly driven by their genes. And, in the case of humans and perhaps other species, conceptualising powers also mediate these underlying biological processes.

Realism in the form I am using it here (what Bhaskar calls 'critical realism') stratifies different levels of knowledge. At the most abstract levels are, for example, laws of thermodynamics, those generating the development of organisms within a 'field' and the generative mental structures underlying what is sometimes called 'human culture'. Here, a critical realist epistemology recognises the liabilities, general ways of acting or emergent powers of objects as outlined by theories in these areas. But it would also insist on an understanding of observable phenomena being dependent on knowledge or information of a more contingent, often less abstract, kind. This latter combines with the more abstract understandings to result in observable events or 'conjunctures' – 'the new biology', for example – and provides insights into how organisms and biological life have for countless generations reproduced and changed themselves within fields of other organisms and mechanisms. Social theory's main contribution is to offer other types of understanding which often deeply impinge on but which remain largely contingent to these processes which are the theories of life concerning the biological and physical sciences. But even theories of capitalism can of course be couched in relatively abstract ways. Marx's discussion of the capitalist mode of production, for example, clearly moved between different levels of abstraction.

There are in fact a number of themes in realism. Those outlined here are largely a reflection of Bhaskar's and Sayer's approach.[1] I will shortly be discussing some themes which have developed specifically in relation to the work of Bhaskar. Critical or 'transcendental' realism is a type of epistemology now finding increasing application in the social sciences, largely as a reaction to positivism and empiricism. As a concept it was originally put forward in opposition to idealism, the latter being the notion originally that there is no reality other than that which is perceived. Idealists argued, therefore, that reality is a wholly mental construct. Human understanding is limited to the direct experience of objects. Realism, however, asserts that there are in fact structures and powers which generate phenomena independent of our experience of and access to such objects. In short, an object (and all its causal powers) does not need to be conceived as 'real' for it to actually exist.

Modern, 'critical' realism, as I have said, is a way of stratifying and differentiating theory and information. As such it is potentially valuable as a way of combining insights from a number of disciplinary perspectives. It offers the prospect of integrating knowledge without sinking into a deep and irretrievable eclecticism. Such a fate can, hopefully, be staved off by locating existing knowledge of relations, powers and tendencies of nature within a framework which prioritises and orders knowledge and information and distinguishes between causal powers and contingent factors.

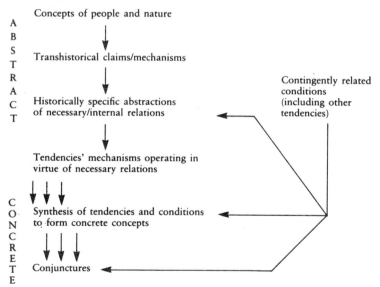

Figure 8.1 A realist aproach to explanation (Source: A. Sayer (1984), *Method in Social Science*, Hutchinson: London)

The distinction between the abstract and the concrete is a crucial one for a realist approach. Figure 8.1 can be usefully referred to at this point. It borrows from Sayer.[2] Abstract theory is associated with the general claims and mechanisms as indicated by the upper levels of the figure. These focus on concepts of people and nature and claims regarding mechanisms which are regarded as transhistorical. Good abstractions isolate what are called 'necessary relationships'. These are theories concerning underlying relations, generative mechanisms and processes. Such relations may possibly change, but they can usually be relied on as constant when attempting explanations. But an understanding of 'conjunctures' again crucially depends, however, on a combination of such necessary relationships with a number of contingencies. There may well be, for example, general laws of nature. But how they work out in practice depends on specific historical and spatial circumstances. As Marx put it: 'It is absolutely impossible to transcend the laws of nature. What *can* change in historically different circumstances is only the *form* in which these laws express themselves.'[3]

Realism therefore starts with a very specific view of causation. This is seen, in Sayer's words, as 'the necessary-ways-of-acting of an object which exists in virtue of its nature. That is, causation is not conceptualised in terms of a relationship between separate events "C" and "E", but in terms of the changes *in* each of "C" and "E".'[4] Again, organisms are seen as having necessary, latent, or potential ways of acting but the actual concrete results of these general relations and ways of acting critically depend on contingent circumstances. In practice, therefore, they are 'historically specific'. Furthermore, detailed empirical research is usually required to understand concrete manifest appearances. Thus, applying this to the life sciences, the underlying mechanisms and tendencies of central concern to physics, chemistry and biology form a necessary part of understanding the relations between organisms, including the relationships between human and other organisms, and their environment. But the precise forms in which they are observed are dependent on the contingent circumstances or the organism's context. Ways of acting are mediated by the latter to produce conjunctures, with contingent factors and relationships possessing their own tendencies.

Two readily appreciable examples can be given here. One is gunpowder. Clearly it has a 'causal power' to explode in virtue of its unstable chemical structure. But whether this causal power is activated or realised depends on contingent circumstances. Is it wet? How is it connected up? Does someone push a button? An example more mundane to our interests concerns nature's own causal powers. A seed has the power to germinate and a plant the power to grow. But whether it does so, and how it does so, depends on other conditions, including forms of human intervention. Similarly, the power of an organism such as a human being to develop depends on the contingent circumstances in which he or she is located. Note, as Sayer himself remarks below, that human interventions here are of a 'contingent' form. The underlying mechanisms of nature stay firm. Human action entails their exploitation towards distinct ends, even though there may be unintended consequences.

On the realist account, as one of nature's own forces, we can only change the contingent relationships between phenomena in accordance with nature's mechanisms, and in fact, this is exactly what we do in *labour*. We exploit the contingency to take advantage of the necessity.[5] [author's emphasis]

As we descend the diagram we encounter information which is less abstract and more concrete. And at the bottom of Figure 8.1 are the 'conjunctures'. These are the observable outcomes of combinations between underlying relations and processes and contingent circumstances. Again, the mechanisms and theories developed in such realms as biology, physics and chemistry have been combined with and mediated by a complex range of factors, many of which are the purview of the social sciences.

Figure 8.2 is intended as a summary of this study's main themes. The key thing to emphasise is its similarity to Marx's conceptual framework as sketched out in Chapter 3. It shows how a stratified understanding of the mechanisms and tendencies can be applied to the study of people–nature relations. It also makes a firm distinction between underlying mechanisms and 'contingent' conditions, a combination of the two being needed to provide an understanding of, say, actual food scares or hurricanes and peoples' interpretations of such events. Observable manifestations or 'conjunctures' are therefore a combination of, on the one hand, the latent capacities and potentials representing the causal powers of organic and inorganic nature. But these capacities are realised, or are indeed stunted, in different ways according to the circumstances in which they are operating. Specifically, under

capitalism and modernity, labour processes alienate people and
separate them from the nature which can realise their full
capacities and potentials as human beings. Fetishised forms of
relationship with nature prevail, including green consumerism and
a number of contemporary forms of environmentalism.

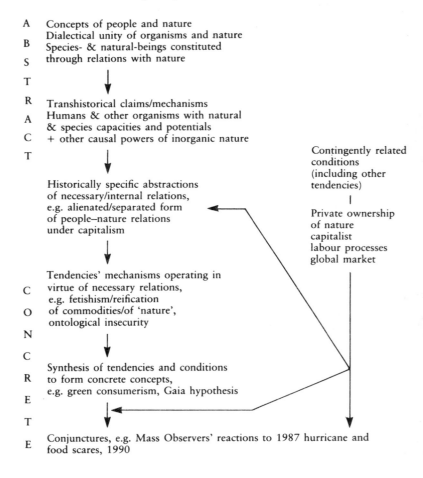

Figure 8.2 Society and nature: a realist approach to understanding
environmentalism

Modern Marxists use realist philosophy in a usually quite

distinct way. 'Necessary' relations are interpreted in a quite different fashion from that being developed here. The core relations involved are usually taken to be those between capital and labour. And the associated tendencies are, for example, the concentration of capital, deskilling the displacement of living labour by capital. 'Contingent' circumstances are represented by, for example, the particular types of social relations constituting areas, regions or states at particular times. 'Conjunctures' or experienced outcomes are typically the product of general tendencies associated with these necessary relations and the contingent circumstances of place and time.

But, bearing in mind the earlier arguments of this book, Figure 8.2 shows realism here being used in a way which more closely reflects the model advanced by the young Marx in 1844. This focuses not just on political economy but on the relations and powers of human beings with distinctive natural and species needs. It reflects too some of the arguments put forward in Chapters 4 and 5, where it was argued that organisms, human and otherwise, should be specified as having powers which are realised in different ways in different contexts.

REALISM: SOME AREAS OF DEBATE

Some recent areas of debate *within* critical realism are very germane to the central issues with which I am concerned. As I have indicated, one of the leading proponents of contemporary critical realism is Roy Bhaskar. His book *The Possibility of Naturalism*, raises the specific issue of how and whether a society can be studied in the same way as nature.[6] His answer is that it can. The natural and the human sciences can be studied in much the same sense; moving, that is, from manifest phenomena towards generative mechanisms. Bhaskar argues, however, that human societies cannot be studied in precisely the same way. By this he means that human societies have distinctive characteristics which indicates that they are not directly amenable to the same type of realist analysis as might be used in the natural sciences.

The reasons for these 'ontological limitations on a possible

naturalism' derive, Bhaskar argues, from societies' distinctive
emergent properties. There are, he suggests, three reasons why a
realist approach based on naturalism cannot be directly applied to
the study of human societies, as follows:[7]

1. Social structures, unlike natural structures, do not exist
   independently of the activities they govern. That is, they exist
   only in virtue of the activities they govern.
2. Social structures, unlike natural structures, do not exist
   independent of people's conceptions of what they are doing in
   their activity.
3. Social structures, unlike natural structures, are usually only
   'relatively enduring'. The tendencies which are incorporated
   within them are not universal or unchanging over time and
   space.

Bhaskar's overall project, therefore, is that of establishing a set of
methods which transcend the sciences. He insists, on the other
hand, that there must be differences in the way these methods are
actually applied to the sciences on the one hand and to the social
sciences on the other. These differences derive from the different
subject matters and relationships involved.

Bhaskar's emphasis on the fundamental differences between the
social and natural sciences has, however, led to a certain amount
of argument. Benton, in particular, has challenged Bhaskar's three
grounds for limiting the application of naturalism to the social
sciences.[8] It is not true, he argues, that social structures do not
exist independent of the activity they govern. A state may, for
example, have powers which in practice it does not use. Bhaskar's
second difference is also, Benton argues, suspect. Social structures
may well exist independent of agents' conceptions of what they
are doing in their activity. Finally, it is true that social structures
are only relatively enduring. But this does not mean that the
realism as used in the natural sciences is not extendable to the
social sciences. In the social sciences universals, albeit those
operating on a relatively short time-scale, can be assumed. The
main thing is to combine these universals with an understanding
of changing contingent circumstances over time and space. The
upshot of Benton's charge is that, in arguing that nature and
society can be examined with the same methods, Bhaskar is
relapsing into the kind of dualism between society and nature

which he says he is rejecting. Method, for 'science' remains one thing but its application to 'social science' must, according to Bhaskar, be strictly limited.

However, in the second edition of *The Possibility of Naturalism* Bhaskar replies to these charges:

Now were I to rewrite *PON* today I would stress the way in which social order is embedded and conditioned by the natural order from which it is emergent and on which it in turn acts back. An ecological interpretation to social life is as important as is recognition of our biological being – both are insufficiently elaborated in the book.[9]

On the other hand, Bhaskar still insists that the working methods of realism as applied in the natural sciences cannot be easily applied to the social world. The categories, concepts and concerns of the two kinds of science leave him doubtful about studying social and natural objects in the same way.

Clearly, this debate can 'run and run'. It is touching on the heart of Western philosophy and its historically ingrained distinction between 'man' and 'nature'. But, in the light of current ecological concerns, it is likely to become an increasingly central focus of debate. The underlying assumption of this book, like the earlier work of Sayer, Bhaskar and Benton and others, is that a set of methods can be developed which allow the natural and social worlds to be constructed and examined in similar ways. As regards the debate between Benton and Bhaskar, this study has been working on assumptions which are, if anything, nearer to those of Benton than Bhaskar. Thus I have tried hard to overrule differences between the sciences; between, for example, biology and culture, mind and body, society and nature and so on. And, in an admittedly selective way, I have identified those features of the sciences and of the social sciences which seem most amenable to one another and to this approach. In general, I have attempted where possible to overcome such dualisms by emphasising different levels of knowledge and their combination with one another.

It remains to be seen, in the light of further empirical and conceptual work, whether it is still possible to assert that similar methods can be used for all the sciences. It may well be, as indeed Benton suggests, that the division between 'science' and 'social science' are too rigid. It seems quite plausible, for example, to state that biology has more in common with the social sciences than other scientific disciplines such as, say, physics and chemistry. At the same time, it is quite possible that some disciplines are not constituted in such a way as to be amenable to a realist approach; they are not organised around establishing knowledge of organisms' ways of acting. Much of contemporary psychology seems to be of this form. On the other hand, as I have shown, Harré's work and that of Vygotsky demonstrate that such an epistemology could be applied to this discipline. But there is of course no necessary reason why the existing disciplinary ways of dividing up knowledge should coincide with the real generative mechanisms of nature.

As regards social theory, I still view Marxist conceptions as offering the best foundations, particularly if the early Marx remains incorporated. Marx's original emphasis on species-being, natural-being, the labour process, the alienation of people from nature and the various forms of fetishism or reification in which people engage, all seem to be the best conceptual framework on which to develop a social theory appropriate to contemporary environmental concerns. Collier usefully sums up some of the key insights of the early Marx:

In the first place, it means that we interact causally with the rest of nature, and are dependent for our existence, and for *what* we are, on that interaction. That we are dependent on nature is obvious enough, but Marx is drawing attention to the special nature of that dependence: on the one hand, that is not dependence on something *external*, in that we are constituted as the beings that we are by the way we live out that dependence; and on the other hand, that we 'live from' nature *actively*, and thereby transform it, so that nature (at least on this planet) is always shot through with human history. . . . Taking these two points together, our transformation of nature is also the transformation of ourselves, and the primary way in which we, as a species, do transform ourselves.[10]

As Collier points out, this amounts to a revised version of Marx's famous aphorism, 'men make history, but in circumstances of their own choosing.'[11] The 'circumstances' are now, however, not just social. They are the ways in which previous societies, generations and forms of accumulation have reconstructed the forces of nature. And, since people are part of nature, this reconstruction of 'man's inorganic body' is how people change themselves.

As regards the sciences, I have discussed studies such as those by Goodwin and Ho in biology, Bowlby in ethology and Harré in psychology which are making important contributions towards a more integrated approach; identifying core mechanisms and latent tendencies. I see these as relatively self-contained academic concerns, but concerns which nevertheless in due course could become linked to other disciplines such as social theory. Such linking could be highly beneficial to the social sciences. They could, for example, greatly improve our understanding of what Marx called 'species being'. More controversially, I also suspect that debates around and within feminism about 'natural differences' could be greatly clarified by more overt discussion of biologically based differences on the one hand and their social construction on the other.

But, as I have been trying to emphasise throughout this study and particularly in this chapter, the most important point is not simply the combining disciplines. It is that of recognising the 'critical realist' picture of stratified and differentiated structures of the natural world, the emergent powers which constitute it and the structures which people and other species simultaneously reproduce and change during their lives. And it is through being part of these structures that they are themselves transformed. It is therefore around critical realism that such a fusion would take place. It is specifically this *kind* of integration which Figure 8.2 is intended to outline.

FROM THEORY TO PRACTICE

Having summarised some of the main themes which would underpin an alternative view of society and nature, I now turn to some of the social and political implications of this approach.

The main arguments outlined here might at first seem broadly in line with those adopted by many contemporary activists who also reject discipline-based understandings, methodological individualism of the kind adopted by sociobiology and analogies suggesting that organisms, nature and the earth itself should be thought of as machines. They also espouse approaches which emphasise organism–environment connectedness, the self-activity of purposive organisms and the self-realisation of human and non-human organisms through interaction with organic and inorganic nature.

These perspectives are built into political programmes. Decentralised, small-scale, community life is often advanced as a way of recovering the separation of people from themselves, from one another and from what they see as nature. Indeed, small-scale communities of the kind still lived in by indigenous peoples are frequently held up as representing an ideal. Not only is this seen as constituted by a broad balance with the natural environment, but the social relations constituted there are seen as in some way preferable to those of the modern world.

Goldsmith, a distinguished environmentalist and editor of *The Ecologist*, has for example recently mounted a sustained attack on the ways in which science has been compartmentalised:

In order to rationalize, and hence legitimize what, in effect, is a totally arbitrary division of the subject matter to suit the requirements of scientific method, *the world must be seen to reflect the same arbitrary divisions*, which in reality it does not. On the contrary, the biosphere – or the world of living things – is a single continuum, and the basic feature of living things and processes is both their similarity and their interdependence.[12] [author's emphasis]

One critical effect of such compartmentalisation, Goldsmith argues, is to create a theory of evolution which makes a rigid distinction between the organism and its environment. Under neo-Darwinism the former is seen as adapting to the latter. But Goldsmith attacks this notion on a number of levels. He rejects, for example, what he calls the 'simplistic' notion whereby

evolution is seen as the outcome of the interaction between two machines – on the one hand, a generator of randomness, and, on the other hand, a sorting machine that arranges them into piles: the 'fit' (that is those that are good at propagating their genes) and the unfit (those that are not).[13]

He also rejects the notion that individuals are passive, that they have no hand in their own behaviour and evolution. Again, Goldsmith emphasises the dialectical relations between individuals on the one hand and the environment on the other. Under neo-Darwinian thinking, he argues:

individuals are made to evolve by gene mutations selected by their environment, and are considered to do so *through no effort of their own*.

The absurdity of that notion becomes apparent when one considers that the environment also consists largely of *other organisms*, and that these are thereby expected to play a dynamic role. . . . Far from dictating evolutionary changes, genes . . . are themselves subject to control and modification from the system of which they are part. And while environments select responses from living organisms, those same environments are themselves subject to modification by such responses.[14] [author's emphases]

Systems thinking therefore allows Goldsmith to emphasise the creativity of organisms and the connectedness of organisms and their environment. He is also rejecting mechanistic metaphors and approaches to evolution and behaviour which concentrate on the individual or the gene.

So far, perhaps, so good. But Goldsmith sees the correct view as one which emphasises nature and the organisms within it as a balanced interacting system. Systems, and subsystems, which he sees as capable of adaptation and adjustment are again active in this process. The biosphere of living things is thus seen by Goldsmith as a self-regulating, creative and improvising hierarchy. He extends the metaphor of an interacting system to include even the relations between people and environment. Indigenous peoples are again seen as part of this self-regulating system. And they have developed hierarchical social structures which allow them to live relatively harmoniously with their environment. This, according to Goldsmith, contrasts badly with modern societies. We have become 'alienated' in a way they have not.

At this point Goldsmith's systems account becomes much more unsatisfactory. This is partly due to the rather shallow notion of 'alienation' incorporated into Goldsmith's account. But this problem is part of a bigger one; that of reifying nature and becoming disconnected in a highly idealistic fashion from the real material world in which real people live. Thus this type of analysis becomes deeply unsatisfactory for most sociologists, especially those trying to understand modern societies. Where in this account are social relations, social institutions, the dynamics of social change and, perhaps most importantly, the labour processes during which people convert nature into commodities?

If one examines those human societies that are capable of self-regulatory and adaptive behaviour (that is tribal societies living within their natural environment), it becomes clear that rather than being geared to perpetual change as in our disintegrated, atomized society, they are, on the contrary, geared to the maintenance of stability, the preservation of their social structure, cultural pattern and natural environment. Such societies survive, not because they produce more offspring than their neighbours but because they are organized in that way that assures the maintenance of the most stable relationship possible with their specific environment. Stability is undoubtedly the goal of living organisms and their ability to maintain their stability in the face of change is perhaps their most impressive achievement.[15]

Such fetishisation of something called the 'natural environment', community and social balance recur, but in an even more forceful way, in the so-called 'deep ecology' movement. At the same time, however, deep ecology does indeed pose a serious corrective to the Marxian paradigm advanced earlier in this study. Let us first examine the themes which combine well with the form of social science being advanced here.

The first use of the term 'deep ecology' is usually credited to the Norwegian writer Arne Naess. 'Shallow ecology', he argues, is associated with relatively modest objectives. These include the fight against pollution and resource-depletion. The central objective is to achieve the health and affluence of populations in the affluent advanced countries.[16] Deep ecology, on the other hand, raises profound questions about people's relationship with the natural world. Very much in parallel with the dialectical view first advanced by Marx and now espoused, as we have seen in earlier chapters of this book, by a minority of biologists and psychologists, deep ecology entails 'rejection of the man-in-environment image' in favour of the 'relational, total field image'.[17]. It envisages:

organisms as knots in the field of intrinsic relations. An intrinsic relation between two things A and B is such that the relation belongs to the definitions or basic constitutions of A and B, so that without the relation, A and B are no longer the same things.[18]

This overview of organisms developing *as* organisms within a 'relational field' is closely related to another key notion in deep ecology, that of self-realisation. This, Naess argues, is a recognition of organisms' potentialities. It is 'used to indicate a kind of perfection'. Naess, using Jungian terminology, is keen to distinguish this kind of realisation from what he calls the 'ego realisation' or 'self-expression' associated with 'the prevalent individualistic and utilitarian political thinking in Western industrial estates'. This latter stresses the incompatibility of individuals and what Devall and Sessions, who are supporters of Naess, call: 'the modern Western *self* which is defined as an isolated ego striving primarily for hedonistic gratification or for a narrow sense of individual salvation in this life or the next'.[19]

The self-development associated with the ecology movement, by contrast, is collective and communal. And this includes communality with the rest of nature. As Deval and Sessions put it:

Spiritual growth, or unfolding, begins when we cease to understand or see ourselves as isolated and narrow competing egos and begin to identify with other humans from our family and friends to, eventually, our species. But the deep ecology sense of self requires a further maturity and growth, an identification which goes beyond humanity to include the nonhuman world.[20]

Such emphasis on self-realisation within a communal setting leads Naess and others, including Bookchin, to argue strongly for the resurgence of a strong local community life.[21] This entails the radical decentralisation of economic, political and cultural power and the establishment of communities where 'numbers are not so numerous that they cannot know each other by acquaintance'. The emphasis in such community life is on local economic and political decision-making and on the promotion of local cultural variation. Perhaps most distinctively, the proposal is for 'bioregional organisation', in which social and political variation is combined with the diversity of local ecological and environmental systems. It comes as no surprise that indigenous peoples are seen as representing models of this new form of society. Interestingly, for some in the deep ecology movement, the preservation of nature entails the preservation of all forms of nature. This seems to be a special recognition of the particular, or especially well-developed, mental capacities of humans. Fox, for example, argues that the preservation of all nature should be insisted on partly because it is a store of genetic diversity which can be used for agricultural and medical purposes. But also, he suggests it has a central role 'for recreation' and 'for aesthetic pleasure/spiritual inspiration'.[22]

In short, the deep green programme as advanced by Naess and others is a view of the world which in many respects, including the realisation of immanent potentials through relationships with other people and with nature, closely parallels the type of theory originally advanced by Marx and Engels. And it links well with the perspective which is now emerging in branches of biology, anthropology and psychology. It is an attempt to overcome the senses of alienation or estrangement as the deep greens understand these concepts. The object is to develop the sense of self and identity through association not only with other human beings but with nature. As Naess puts it:

'To have a home', 'to belong', 'to live' and many other similar expressions suggest fundamental milieu factors involved in the shaping of an individual's sense of self and self-respect. The identity of the individual, 'that I am something', is developed through interaction with a broad manifold, organic and inorganic. . . . To distance oneself from nature and the 'natural' is to distance oneself from a part of that which the 'I' is built up of. Its 'identity', 'what the individual I is', and thereby sense of self and self-respect, are broken down.[23]

Association with nature is therefore one of the key ways in which this self-identity is seen as eventually recovered. And it is at this point that the programme of Naess and others can be seen as raising philosophical issues which are in some respects more profound than anything Marx or Engels considered. The logic of deep ecology is, of course, that nature *as a whole* should be preserved. This includes not simply other species. It includes areas of wilderness or near wilderness which are large enough to allow genetic variations to occur and the growth of animal populations to develop. The question then is, what is so special about people? Why should one species survive and consider the rest of nature to be its 'inorganic body'? Is not, in Marx's terminology 'man' also 'nature's inorganic body'?

Thus an integral part of the deep green political programme is what he calls 'biospherical egalitarianism'; the central notion being that *all* living organisms should have the right to develop in their milieux. All life on Earth non-human and human, is therefore seen as having an intrinsic value. It is worth preserving quite apart from its value for what Naess calls 'narrow human purposes'.[24] In particular, it is the richness and diversity of life forms which Naess sees as possessing intrinsic value. Human beings have no right to interfere with nature and, furthermore, they should contemplate reducing their own numbers: 'The flourishing of non-human life requires such a decrease.'[25] However, the human species will itself benefit from the preservation of nature and other species. It will begin to appreciate 'life quality', dwelling in places of inherent quality rather than adhering in a materialistic fashion to a high material standard of living.

As Sylvan has argued, however, the deep green position regarding the rest of nature is not so straightforward as it at first seems.[26] If, for example, one of the principal reasons for sustaining wilderness and bio-diversity is that it gives the humans a deeper, more spiritual, satisfaction, this can be seen as just as anthropocentric as the positions which it is attacking. There are other related problems. Do literally all organisms (including bacteria and viruses) have an equal right to survive? Finally, why should we assume that all nature is somehow necessarily 'good' and therefore not to be interfered with? The danger in much of this literature is somewhat similar to Marx's critique of earlier forms of 'Utopian' socialism. Intellectuals in Norway or the West Coast of America establish ideal communal relations and relations with nature and leave the rest of society relatively untouched. This is distinctly *not* what Gramsci had in mind when he coined the term 'organic intellectuals'!

But, still more seriously, Sylvan suggests, by burying their heads in the proverbial sand, deep greens are actually in danger of making the situation markedly worse for everyone else:

Biospheric egalitarianism in practice is for people who do not supply their own shelter or sustenance, but pass the business of ecosystem interference and modification on to others (as they typically pass the butchery of their meat and the like on to others).[27]

Furthermore, the uncritical promotion of the lives led by indigenous peoples can also run the deep greens' position into difficulties:

Even if it were desirable, universal hunter–gathering is no longer possible or feasible, with so many mostly unsuited and ill-adapted humans; and even hunter–gatherers terminate the lives of many creatures – a substantial interference with their rights to live and blossom – and, more important, substantially modify their environments, thus interfering directly and indirectly with enormous numbers of living things.[28]

In short, the deep greens are again in real danger of idealising a particular vision of 'nature' and people's relationship to it. The resulting strategies tend to be Utopian, defensive and rejecting modernity as a wholly malevolent influence. Furthermore, their critique of anthropocentrism contains a number of internal contradictions. So, while representing a major critique of the anthropocentric assumptions contained in, for example, Marx and other social theorists, the deep greens can by no means be said to have solved the problem of how humans live alongside other species. But this still leaves the difficult problem of how the Marxist perspective used here might respond to the deep greens' position.

We might first note Sylvan's notion of 'satisizing value'. While certainly learning from the deep greens in terms of becoming 'biocentric' and focusing on how humans 'feed back on' organic and inorganic nature, there is no need to insist on all organisms adopting a Benthamite maximisation of their potential. The emphasis could turn towards sufficient self-realisation and self-direction. As Sylvan puts it, 'the alternative directive to turn out a maximum is to turn out enough'.[29]

But what is 'enough'? How is this judged? Although Marx and Engels clearly gave no sustained critical attention to the major problem of anthropocentrism, Marx's overall programme is compatible with such an approach. As I have outlined earlier, Marx's long-term vision was of a science which dissolved the distinction between 'man' and 'nature'. The construction of a single science would be liberating in that it would enable human beings to see themselves as natural and species beings and as an integral part of nature. But such a science need not necessarily result in anthropocentrism. It could also presumably be a vital first step in the construction of a biocentric theory and one which could seriously address the question of whether, and how, *all* species' potential can or should be realised.

But perhaps the most significant difficulty of the deep green movement is how societies are expected to change from their present form to those in which people and nature live in a more harmonious state. Naess, in common with many others in the environmental movement, looks to a fundamental change in human consciousness as the way forward. It is one which turns its back on Western materialism and acquires a deep identification of individuals with all forms of life. But the kind of perspective represented by the young Marx would surely put a huge question mark over such an assumption. Changing consciousness may be, indeed will be, necessary. But equally important are the relationships and structures which created this consciousness in the first place and which could become the means by which a new consciousness develops.

If the deep green movement has much to teach Marxism and social theory about their tacit anthropocentrism, then critical social theory has much to teach the ecological movement about the social forces and relationships underlying the separation (their notion of 'alienation') with which they are concerned. Furthermore, a combination of social and ecological science suggests that, rather than ignoring social and power relations or hoping that they will dissolve with the rise of ecological consciousness, these aspects of modernity need to be fully recognised. And, perhaps most uncomfortably of all, they need to be seen as part of the solution as well as part of the problem.

It may well be that the principle of private property and market in their present forms pose any number of ecological threats. It may also be, as Marx originally suggested, that capitalist markets result in alienation and a fetishised form of 'nature' and 'the natural'. On the other hand, capitalist forms and social relations of production have brought about benefits and are capable of being modified to produce many more. Similarly, it may also be that states or governments are largely organised around large-scale, potentially disastrous, uses of resources. But again, this does not imply that states or governments should be dispensed with.

The challenge, if environmentalism and deep green thinking are not to be assigned to a political backwater and become a middle-class plaything, is to explore how these dominant economic and political institutions (and the technologies which they have developed) can be transformed in such a way as to be environmentally benign. How can they be adapted towards more emancipatory ends? There are a number of instances (the shop stewards' initiative at Lucas Aerospace being a celebrated example in the British case) where attempts have been made to convert capitalist firms into making environmentally sound products.[30] By no means all of these experiments, it must be admitted, have been very successful. And a number of environmentalists remain deeply

cynical about 'green consumerism'. Environmentalism and capitalism make, in the words of Ellwood, 'some unlikely bed
partners'.[31] But it is just these kinds of alliance which will have to
be attempted.

As regards politics and state intervention, deep greens are right
to assert the importance of locality and of personal experience
between people and between people and nature as a context in
which potential capacities can be developed. As the promoters of
'bioregionalism' insist, for example, localities, with all their vast
variations are clearly an excellent context for people 'to get to
know about the land, its lore and its potential, and live in and not
against it'.[32] The greens are also right to resist 'top-down'
monolithic central or transnational intervention and to assert the
significance of local democratic decision-making. On the other
hand, they would be burying their heads in the sand if they
insisted that decentralisation meant simply or only the establishing
of a number of local Utopias. Rather, and as I have outlined in
some detail elsewhere, a better strategy is to *start* with locality and
everyday experience and to develop strategies at the local level
which are responsive to local social and ecological systems. But,
having developed such strategies, regional, national or transnational governments would be called on, almost as a last resort, to
help local regions implement their own strategies.[33]

But, while accepting the importance of community, face-to-face
interaction and the value of direct experience, there again remains
the danger of excluding all other forms of experience and
interaction as somehow not 'genuine' and not helping in the
realization of human capacities. Modern technologies such as
electronic communications and mass travel allow any number of
additional associations and means by which the human species
can develop itself. The danger of overemphasising locality or
'community' is that of parochialism. As Marx and Engels
continually asserted, for all its faults capitalism continually opens
up new possibilities and potentials; not least that of developing
people's innate capacities. Such capacities will not be developed
only, or even best, in small-scale communities.

In sum, an alternative to the somewhat defensive and
backward-looking attitude to modernity adopted by many
sections of the environmental movement is take a more up-beat
perspective, one which stresses the original Marxian notion that in

interacting with nature, people do not only change nature, they open up new possibilities for changing themselves. In interacting with the external world and changing it, a person 'changes his own nature. He develops his slumbering powers and compels them to act in obedience to his sway.'[34] In ways which could not have conceivably have been envisaged by Marx, people are now beginning to change themselves through growing awareness of their often disastrous interactions with other species and with inorganic nature. The question now is whether human beings can now use their very considerable mental capacities to develop new understandings. These would go beyond the idealisms and arcadian visions adopted by elements of the contemporary environmental movement. They would instead concentrate on revealing the real, material practices involved in contemporary alienated relations with nature. Labour processes, social relations and relations with other species would be the focus of the new understandings.

NOTES

1. A. Sayer (1984), *Method in Social Science*, Hutchinson: London; R. Bhaskar (1989), *The Possibility of Naturalism*, Harvester Wheatsheaf: Hemel Hempstead (2nd edn); R. Bhaskar (1991), *Philosophy and the Idea of Freedom*, Blackwell: Oxford. See also W. Outhwaite (1987), *New Philosophies of Social Science*, Macmillan: London.
2. A. Sayer (1984), *op.cit.*, Fig.10, p. 129.
3. Quoted in A. Schmidt (1971), *The Concept of Nature in Marx*, New Left Books: London, p. 98.
4. A. Sayer (1979), *Theory and Empirical Research in Urban and Regional Political Economy: A sympathetic critique*, Working Paper in Urban and Regional Research No. 14, Centre for Urban and Regional Research, University of Sussex, p. 13.
5. *ibid.*, p. 30.
6. R. Bhaskar (1989) *op.cit.*
7. *ibid.*, p. 38.
8. T. Benton (1985), 'Realism and social science', in R. Edgley, R. Osborne (eds), *Radical Philosophy Reader*, Verso: London, pp. 174–92.
9. R. Bhaskar (1989), *op.cit.*, pp. 173–4.

10. A. Collier (1991), 'The inorganic body and the ambiguity of freedom', *Radical Philosophy* 57, Spring: 3.
11. K. Marx (1969), 'The Eighteenth Brumaire of Louis Bonaparte', in L. Feuer (ed.) *Marx and Engels: Basic Writings on Politics and Philosophy*, p. 360.
12. E. Goldsmith (1990), 'Evolution, neo-Darwinism and the paradigm of science', *The Ecologist* 20, 2, March/April: 67.
13. *ibid.*, p. 69.
14. *ibid.*, p. 70.
15. *ibid.*, p. 72.
16. A. Naess (1989), *Ecology, Community and Lifestyle*, Cambridge University Press: Cambridge, p. 28.
17. *ibid.*, p. 28.
18. *ibid.*, p. 28.
19. B. Devall, G. Sessions (1985), *Deep Ecology*, Gibbs Smith: Salt Lake City, p. 67.
20. *ibid.*, p. 67.
21. M. Bookchin (1982), *The Ecology of Freedom*, Cheshire Books: Palo Alto.
22. A. Dobson (1990), *Green Political Thought*, Unwin Hyman: London, p. 50.
23. A. Naess (1989), *op.cit.*, p. 164.
24. *ibid.*, p. 29.
25. *ibid.*, p. 29.
26. R. Sylvan (1985a), 'A critique of deep ecology', in *Radical Philosophy*, Summer (Pt 1): pp. 2–12; R. Sylvan (1985b), *Radical Philosophy*, Autumn (Pt 2): pp. 10–22.
27. R. Sylvan (1985a), *op.cit.*, pp. 7–8.
28. *ibid.*, p. 8.
29. *ibid.*, p. 11.
30. H. Wainwright, D. Elliott (1982), *The Lucas Plan*, Alison & Busby: London.
31. W. Ellwood (1991), 'Endorsing green capitalism: should environmental groups get into bed with business?', in C. Plant and J. Plant (eds), *Green Business: Hope or Hoax?*, Green Books, Bideford, pp. 38–40.
32. A. Dobson (1990), *op.cit.*, p. 117.
33. P. Dickens (1988), *One Nation? Social Change and the Politics of Locality*, Pluto: London.
34. B. Ollman (1976), *Alienation*, Cambridge University Press: Cambridge, p. 100.

EPILOGUE

In a path-breaking commentary on Marx and Engels' early work, Ted Benton argued that a central part of their enterprise was to create an approach which 'recognises *both* the unity and interconnectedness of the subject-matters of the different sciences, *and* their relative distinctiveness and autonomy'.[1] [author's emphases]

Engels and Marx were working in very particular historical circumstances. Political parties with whom they sympathised, such as the German Social Democratic Party, were adopting a conservative and reactionary form of Social Darwinism. The German workers' movement was being drawn to an understanding of Darwinism whose ritual incantations, including 'the struggle for survival' were being applied in an unthinking way to human societies. The formation of a new science, one which engaged in the difficult but necessary task of making connections between relatively autonomous disciplines, was therefore as much a political as an intellectual project for Marx and Engels. The circumstances now seem right to attempt a similar enterprise; one which recognises and engages in popular concerns but which at the same time rejects simplistic and reductionist explanations and tries to establish an alternative conceptual framework. This book represents a preliminary contribution towards that project.

NOTE

1. T. Benton (1979), 'Natural science and cultural struggle: Engels and
   philosophy and the natural sciences', in J. Mepham, D.-H. Ruben,
   Issues in Marxist Philosophy, Vol.II: Materialism, Harvester Wheatsheaf: Hemel Hempstead, pp. 101–42.

INDEX

Saunders, P.R., 35, 39, 58
Saunders, P.T., 116, 117, 119, 123
Savage, M., 162
Sayer, A., xv, xvii, 2, 176, 177, 178,
179, 183, 195
Sayers, J., 143
Sheldrake, R., 84, 90
Shiva, V., 139–40, 143
Sibatini, A., 123
Simmons, A., 153, 154, 162
Skinner, B., 122
Smith, A., 11, 13
Smith, G., 162
Social Darwinism/social evolution,
20–38 *passim*, 41, 47, 103
social structures/human agency,
145–49 *passim*
society
analogies with nature, 23 *seq*, 28, 34,
38, 43, 45–7, 56, 60
and biology/science, 133, 181–5
and personal insecurity, xvii, 147
and liberal theory, xiii–xiv
and sociology, 6, 20, 97, 100
as an organism, xv, 25, 39
as balanced, 30
compared with community, 36
concepts of, 42, 44, 48, 134–9
developing, 8
gemeinschaft/gesellschaft, 30–1
indigenous, 106–10, 137–9, 147–9
passim
modern/capitalist, 8, 11, 45, 104,
105, 141, 145 *seq.*
relation to nature, 29, 31, 32, 40–2,
51–4, 56, 62, 70–3, 77, 78, 120,
149–61 *passim*, 183, 192, 195
structures of, 3
sociobiology, 54, 99, 100, 103, 106,
111, 128, 129, 185
critiques of, 103, 105, 109–10, 113,
114, 138, 175
see also biology, neo-Darwinism
socioecology, 94, 110–15
sociology, xv, 1, 18–57 *passim*, 60–1,
93, 102, 187
as 'unecological', xi–xii

see also biology, relations to
sociology
Soddy, F., 59
Soper, K., 141, 143
species-narcissism, 85
Spencer, H., 20, 22–8, 34, 35, 39, 57
Stanciu, G., 88
Standen, F., 57, 122
Stevens, A., 142, 143
Strathern, M., 130, 142, 174
'structuration', 145–52 *passim*
Sumner, W., 27–28
Survival International, 109, 122 143
Sydie, R., 143
Sylvan, R., 191, 192, 196

Tansley, A., 111, 122
teleology, 56 *see also* Social Darwinism
territoriality, 103
thermodynamics, laws of, xii, 52, 55,
79, 112
time-space distanciation, xvi, xvii
'Third World', 1, 7–8, 155
Tiger, L., 103–4, 105, 122
time, space and society, 145–9 *passim*,
156 *seq*, 164
Tönnies, F., 19, 29–33, 39, 55, 58, 72

United States of America, 12, 24, 26–8,
35, 57, 190

Vygotsky, L., 134, 185

Ward, L., 28
waste, xvii, 79, 158
Webster, G., 115, 119, 123
Wertsch, 143
Whelan, R., 11–14, 16
Williams, G., 59
Williams, R., 137, 143
Wilson, E., 121, 127, 142
Winch, D., 57
Wolfe, A., 128, 142
Wrangham, R., 122

Yearley, S., 1, 6, 15, 16